Warton Parish
1850 – 1900

Borwick Carnforth
Priest Hutton Silverdale
Warton Yealands

Mourholme Local History Society Book Group

2009

Also published by The Mourholme Local History Society

Warton in the Middle Ages
(by Paul Booth)
How it Was: A North Lancashire Parish in the Seventeenth Century
Warton 1800 – 1850: How a North Lancashire Parish Changed

Published by the Mourholme Local History Society
Printed by 1st Impression,
Nobles Place, Maude Street, Kendal, LA9 4QD

2009

ISBN 978-0-9534298-3-7

To John Marshall
1919 – 2008

Historian, teacher, pioneer thinker and good friend to the
Mourholme Local History Society

John Marshall's contributions to the study of regional history have been outstanding. In the Mourholme Society we have also a particular reason to feel his loss. He was for more than two decades our President and also he made time in his busy life to give us long-lasting help in the task of trying to write a running history of our area, using the valuable research that has been undertaken over the years by members of the Society and others; research that might otherwise have languished unseen in our archives. John was too good a teacher to write the book for us; he preferred the more time-consuming task of helping us to write it for ourselves. That was a fortunate decision, for not only did it enable the Society to write, under his guidance, a book that dealt with our area in the seventeenth century, but, when ill-health gradually reduced his direct support, the Society still felt able to continue its work. It is therefore most fitting that this third volume should be gratefully dedicated to his memory.

Illustrations

The Mourholme Local History Society Book Group would like to thank the following people for their contributions to the illustrations in the book:
Neil Stobbs; Sheila Jones; Pat Jackson; Clive Holden; Phil Grossé; Jenny Ager; Brian Ager.

CONTENTS

Money, Weights and Measures

No attempt has been made in this book to give estimates of the modern equivalents of the nineteenth century prices quoted. It was felt that the changes in prices and wages had been too great, and simple change into modern currency would be misleading.

Money
The coinage was changed in 1971, and for those too young to remember the old values the table below can be used for reference.

12 pence (d)	=	1 shilling (s)
20 shillings (s)	=	1 pound (£)
1 guinea	=	£1-1s

The table below gives modern equivalents of nineteenth century measurements of weight, length and area.

Weight
1 pound (lb)	=	0.45 kilograms
14lbs	=	1 stone (6.35 kilograms)
1 ton	=	1.02 tonnes

Length
1 foot	=	0.30 metres
1 yard	=	0.91 metres
1 mile	=	1.61 kilometres

Area
1 rood (_ acre)	=	40 rods
1 statute acre	=	0.40 hectares
1.4 statute acres	=	1 customary acre

Prologue

Since last we met what changes vast
Have from our labours come;
For Carnforth, with her busy hive,
Increases day by day;
She bears "Excelsior" on her flag,
And works her onward way.
Our village, that was once so small,
Is verging to a town; our staple ware, the iron trade,
Gains more and more renown.
New steelworks, too, have now arisen,
And gasworks, too, as well,
With handsome church to crown the whole,
And cast its holy spell.

*   *   *   *   *   *   *   *   *   *

Since last we met a Templar Lodge,
To which we wish success,
Has started on its cruise of good,
And bravely does progress.
Our Band of Hope is also strong,
Increasing day by day;
Whilst drums and fifes re-echo forth,
As sweetly do they play.

*   *   *   *   *   *   *   *   *   *

Our chapel debt is now paid off,
Thanks to our many friends;
With liberal hands and generous hearts,
Their kindness knows no end.

Written by Mr. Dibb of London specially for the Carnforth Wesleyan
Sunday School tea meeting in January 1872.

(*The Lancaster Guardian*, 6th January 1872).

Introduction

LETTER TO THE READER

This book is an account of late Victorian years in a small area, about sixteen square miles in all, in north Lancashire; an area which contains to-day one small town, Carnforth, and six villages – Borwick, Priest Hutton, Silverdale, Warton, Yealand Conyers and Yealand Redmayne. It is awkward that the area has no name of its own today. Once it was the parish of Warton and was so called in the previous two volumes of this history.[1,2] During Queen Victoria's long reign the large old parish was split into four as some of the growing villages (or townships to use the old northern name for the villages that made up a large parish) built churches and were given status as parishes in their own right. Strictly speaking, Warton parish should now only be used for the smaller parish that centres on the village of Warton. Here was a problem for the writers of this third volume. We really could not write the-area-that-was-once-the-old-parish-of-Warton every time. A compromise was reached, unsatisfactory as compromises usually are. Warton and Warton parish are still used as an incorrect but handy name for the whole area, but where only the village of Warton is meant it is either called Warton township or is referred to by its then formal title of Warton–with–Lindeth. (Fortunately we did not have to face up to the problem that Warton-with-Lindeth ceased to exist in the twentieth century when Lindeth was handed over to the township of Silverdale.[3])

The book has no one author, nor even one editor. The chapters were each written by one or more of a group of people, who live in the area, were all interested in its history, but each had his or her own specialised interest in some part of that history. We met frequently as a co-ordinating editorial group. We hoped, in this way, to harness the enthusiasm and detailed knowledge of non-professional local historians into the production of a book that would be reasonably comprehensive and yet have plenty of the details of people and places that make the interest of a local history. There was an obvious danger in the method. If there was some aspect of the history of the area in which none of the group was particularly interested, then that aspect was likely to receive scant coverage. We hope we have dealt with the themes of major local importance, but we know there are aspects that we have either left out or not covered in the detail they perhaps deserve. All that the members of the group can do is apologise for not tackling subjects about which they had little new to offer. Readers after all, can have the satisfaction of identifying the gaps and the group as a whole would like to apologise for any oversights or errata.

The Mourholme Local History Society Book Group:

Jenny Ager, Joan Clarke, John Findlater, Geoffrey Gregory, Clive Holden, John Jenkinson, Sheila Jones, Jane Parsons, Arthur Penn, Neil Stobbs.

---

[1] Mourholme Local History Society Book Group, *How it Was: A North Lancashire Parish in the Seventeenth Century* (Mourholme Local History Society, 1998).

[2] Mourholme Local History Society Book Group, *Warton 1800 – 1850: How a North Lancashire Parish Changed* (Mourholme Local History Society, 2005).

[3] Mourholme, *Warton 1800 – 1850*, p.2.

Chapter One

AGRICULTURE
IN THE SECOND HALF OF THE CENTURY

The Enduring Foundation

At the start of the second half of the nineteenth century agriculture was still a very important component of the British economy, but it was not the focus of attention that it had been fifty years earlier when there had been worries about feeding an increasing population during hostilities with France. By 1850 the farmers had improved productivity and brought large areas of previously marginal land into cultivation. They had also adjusted to the abolition, in the 1840s, of the Corn Laws which had till then protected them from the competition of imported grain; they had indeed not just survived, but prospered. Yet the growth of Britain's industry was on such an extraordinary scale that it raised the possibility that Britain could make its living by manufacturing goods and exporting them in exchange for food grown abroad, so putting our own agriculture into a subsidiary position.

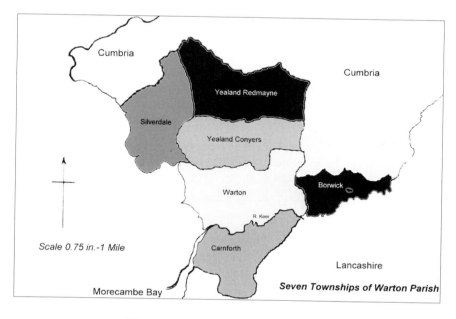

The Seven Townships of Warton Parish

1

In Warton parish the last remaining common land had been enclosed at the beginning of the century allowing further improved efficiency in stock rearing.[1] Over the years some of the peat mosses had been drained and converted to good arable land (as at Leighton Moss) or to reasonable grazing.[2] The parish remained predominantly agricultural, for the growth of the little township of Carnforth into a small town only marginally depleted the parish farmlands. Building in the other townships was not on a large scale. When, later, a free trade policy led to the importation of large quantities of cereals and later of meat, the diversity of the local agriculture gave Warton some resilience in the face of the crisis.

The Land

In 1836 there was a change in the law concerning the payment of tithes to the church; they were still compulsory, but an attempt was made at least to simplify and improve their collection. A rent charge was substituted for the previous complicated system of paying partly in kind. The Tithe Commutation Act is only mentioned here because it involved the measuring and recording of land in every parish to find out who owed what rent. The survey in Warton parish took place in 1846. The recorded result conveniently gives a detailed picture of the parish land, at a date very close to the opening of the second half of the century. A full copy of the return for the township of Warton-with-Lindeth is fortunately available in the archives of the Mourholme Local History Society and from it has been extracted the information that follows. The returns for the other townships are not so easily accessible, but there is little reason to suppose they would show an essentially different pattern.

Size of Holdings in Warton-with-Lindeth 1846

In the Tithe Returns there were records of 110 'occupiers of property' and 99 'landlords', but in various combinations; some were merely occupiers, some owned the property they occupied, some were owners but not occupiers. Altogether there are 158 individual names identified within these groupings. It is noticeable that only 34 landlords held more than 5 acres. The holdings of these 34 ranged between 328.161 and 5.153 acres, with farms of smaller acreage predominating. Only 9 of the holdings were over 100 acres. These 9 holdings range from Edward Dawson's 328.161 acres to John Jenkinson's 100.523 acres. The

Warton Parish: 1850 –1900

Errata

Page 32
Diagram showing the layout of the station
This heading should be:
Diagram showing the layout of Carnforth Station in 1880
The diagram in the book is not very clear, below is a clearer version.

Page 74, line 17
...cutting and filling 7-d p^{er} rood, did not answer so pulled...
should read:
...cutting and filling 7½d p^{er} rood, did not answer so pulled...

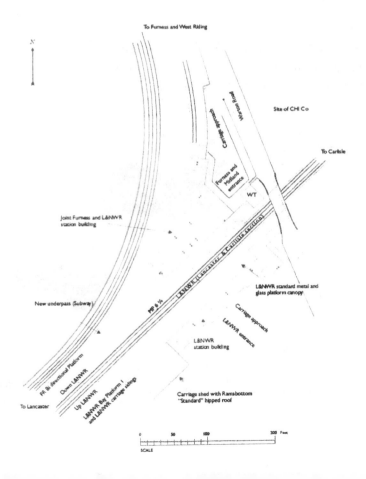

Warton Parish
1850 –1900
Borwick . Carnforth .
Priest Hutton . Silverdale
Warton . Yealands

Errata

Page i
Area
1 rood (-acre) = 40 rods
should read:
1 rood (¼ acre) = 40 rods

Page 1:
The Seven Townships of Warton Parish
The sketch map only shows Priest Hutton very faintly,
below is a clearer version.

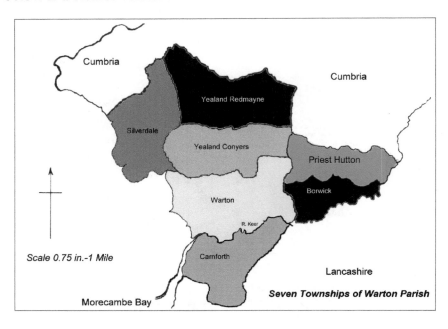

Seven Townships of Warton Parish

pattern of smallholdings was repeated in the other townships. There were no really big landholders in the parish.

Land Usage

A general view of the division of land throughout the parish into various types of management is given in Table 1.1.

Table 1.1

	TOT	AR	PA	ME	PL	COP	BLD	ORC	GN	PB
Acres	2732	1065	1007	448	115	46	29	9	5	8
%age	100	39	36.9	16.4	4.2	1.7	1.1	0.3	0.2	0.3

Distribution of types of Land Use in Warton Parish 1846
(in acres)

Legend: TOT =Total, AR=Arable, PA=Pasture, ME=Meadow, PL=Plantation, COP=Coppice, BLD = Buildings, ORC= Orchard, GN =Gardens, PB = Roadways, Railways, Canal and Waste.

Arable, Meadow and Pasture

In Table 1.1 the 1,065 acres of arable contains a small quantity, about one sixth of the whole of land, described as '*containing some element of arable*'. The same applies in a lesser degree to meadow and pasture – reflecting presumably a tendency of the farmers to use odd bits of land to best purpose. On the other hand a careful distinction is made between meadow and pasture. Meadow was land under grass from which a hay crop may be taken, but is also grazed at various seasons. Pasture, of which there was much more in the parish, was grassland of a permanent nature, i.e. not often subjected to ploughing and mainly used for grazing. Altogether just over half of the parish (52%) was under some sort of grassland and rather over one third (39%) was arable. This is very different from to-day's pattern in which arable forms only a very, very small part of the whole.

Woodland and Coppice

A small amount of land was occupied by orchards, gardens and buildings; 7.61 acres was taken by the railway and the canal, but the other main use of the land was for woodland. The 6% of the land of Warton parish devoted to woodland was unevenly distributed between the townships. Three of these, Carnforth, Borwick and Priest Hutton, were very sparsely wooded in the nineteenth century (0 - 3%). The other four townships were all reasonably well wooded, falling into two distinct pairs.

White areas without information, except Church Property

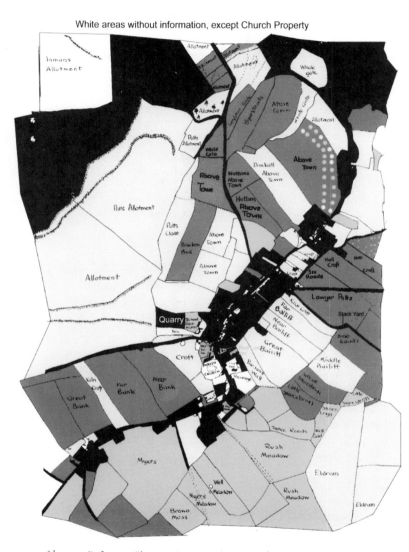

Nineteenth Century Warton: based on the 1846 Tithe Map and Award

Pasture	Meadow	Garden	Public Watering Places	Gardens usually have
Arable	Plantation	Work Places	Roads etc.	one or more houses or
Orchard	Yards	Inns		cottages in the plot.

Distribution of Land Types

4

In Yealand Redmayne and in Warton-with-Lindeth there was a gradual decline, from 1846 to 1895, in woodland cover (from 10% down to 5% in Yealand Redmayne and from 6% down to less than 3% in Warton). In contrast the townships of Silverdale and Yealand Conyers both showed a considerable rise in woodland acreage over the same period, especially in the later years of the century. In Silverdale woodland cover rose from 10% to 15%, and that of Yealand Conyers from 11% to 18%. There is no mystery about these differences. The acreage of plantation and coppice wood is particularly high in Silverdale and Yealand Conyers, mainly because of planting carried out on the woodlands estate in the former township, and by the Gillows on the Leighton Hall estate in the latter township. The planting on the big estates was to a certain extent to beautify the grounds, but woodland and coppice had good commercial value.

The Work Force

Farmhand

Analysis of census data shows that the number of farms in the parish remained more or less unchanged through the second half of the century. Considerable changes had occurred in the first half of the century through buying and selling of land and adjustments needed to absorb enclosed common land and reclaimed peat mosses. In the second half there seems to have been much less change. Farm units were generally convenient to manage, and most had the mix of arable land and pasture that was regarded as best for efficient farming.

Though the number of farms may have remained unchanged the census shows a decline in numbers working on the land. In Silverdale the total number describing themselves as farmers, agricultural labourers or farm servants declined from 51 in 1851 to 31 in 1881. In Borwick the number fell from 39 to 19 over the same period, and in Yealand Conyers from 37 to 32. The

Farmer Sowing

decline can also be shown as a fall in the number of households whose head was occupied in agriculture. In 1851 there were 35 households in Silverdale whose head was working in agriculture, and this declined to 23 in 1881.

Another factor that led to a decline in manpower was a reduction in arable farming. Warton has always lacked top quality arable land, but, historically, had made the best use of what was available. Considerable acreages were ploughed when food shortages were perceived as a possibility during the war with France at the start of the nineteenth century. Plough-land had even extended onto the recently enclosed commons in a few places. Reliable figures for actual acreages of arable land are available from the tithe award schedules of 1846 and from the agricultural statistics collected by the government from 1866 on. These show a considerable decline in arable land. For instance in Warton township arable fell from 42% of all farmed land (arable plus grassland) to 25% of the smaller total of land farmed in 1880. By 1895 arable formed only 21% of the total farmed. The figure for 1901, given in the Victoria County History, suggests a recovery in arable acreage back towards the 1880 figure.[3] The shift is slight however, and the way the figures are recorded makes them not strictly comparable. This was accompanied by a doubling of the total number of households in Silverdale over the same period. The effect was that, whereas in 1851 about two-thirds of the household heads in Silverdale had been involved in agriculture; in 1881 the proportion was down to only about one-fifth. For Borwick (where there were fewer extra households set up) the proportion fell from just over one half to about one quarter. In Yealand

Plough Team

Conyers there was little change - the number of households with heads employed in agriculture declining only slightly from one in three to about one in four, but then Yealand Conyers with its high proportion of gentry households has always had its own character.

Some of the decline in the numbers working on the land can be attributed to the introduction of more machinery. Everything still depended on manpower or horsepower, but newspaper reports of farm sales show that drills, harrows and rollers were improving arable farming, as indeed were mowing machines, reaping machines, threshing machines and winnowing machines. Turnip cutters, pulpers and slicers were in widespread use for preparing animal feed, as were chaff cutters.

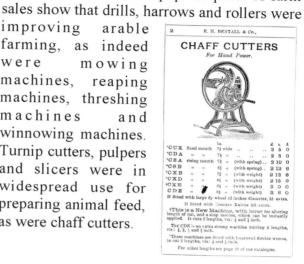

Crops Grown

For information about cereal and vegetable crops in the second half of the century we are dependent on notices of farm sales. When Know Hill Lodge Farm in Silverdale and its contents were sold in 1855 there was 200 stone of oats in the barns, plus a stack of oats. There were also 40 loads of potatoes and two tons of carrots.[4] Probably the potatoes were for human consumption, but root crops for animal fodder were evidently commonly grown by this date, as there were also two tons of mangold wurzels and one and a half acres of swedes and turnips. Turnips and potatoes were to be sold off when Mr G. C. Jennings' farm and its contents were auctioned in 1890.[5] Machinery for cultivating turnips is frequently mentioned in sales.[6]

The Whinnerah diary gives us a useful insight into farming practices in Warton in 1892.[7] The Whinnerahs raised cattle, sheep and horses, and to feed these they grew crops of turnips, mangolds, oats and barley. Turnips were machine-chopped before being given as fodder (though sometimes the sheep were folded on to turnips in the ground). There was also an annual crop of grass seed. The Whinnerahs grew potatoes; possibly some of these were for feeding to stock, but some were supplied to the Carnforth Co-op. for human consumption.

Barley Harvest

in From 1866 detailed statistics of crops and livestock were collected by the Ministry of Agriculture and Fisheries. The predominant cereal crop the parish was oats, as it had been for hundreds of years, with barley occupying only about half as much land. Wheat was still occupying quite a large acreage in 1880, but this fell dramatically by the end of the century, as the impact of North American imports became stronger.

Turnips and swedes were the other large crops. Most of these

Turnips

vegetable crops were probably for consumption locally and until Carnforth's population expanded the market was limited. There was no really large manufacturing town close by to provide a ready market.

Swedes

Night Soil Men

It was different in the areas around the new industrial towns of south Lancashire where intensive farming on market-gardening scale was very profitable for those farmers who had land within carting distance. Not only did these farms carry their produce in abundance into the towns, but they also received from them the wherewithal, that is stable manure and night soil, to grow the heavy crops. The very liberal application of these manures restored the fertility that was depleted by such intensive cropping. The system was once succinctly summarised by one farmer – '*We cart all off and we cart all on*'. In Warton the same system was evidently practised on a small scale, since the Whinnerah diary records the use of night soil from Millhead to fertilize local farmland.

Livestock

"Duke of Northumberland"
Typical Shorthorn of the 1840's

This bull, bred around 1840 by Thomas Bates of Kirkleavington, near Yarm, Yorkshire, (now in Teeside) was one of the foundation animals of all subsequent Shorthorns.

Linksfield Champion

This was the type of Shorthorn bull at the end of the nineteenth Century.

Shorthorn cattle were the mainstay of the Warton livestock farmer in the second half of the century. These sturdy animals were well suited to the local pastures and were suitable for both beef production and for milking. The numbers of cattle in Warton parish rose from 1,950 in 1880 to 2,101 in 1895, a change reflected in the decline in arable land and rise in grassland over the same period. Numbers of milking cattle show a large increase in Silverdale and Carnforth, perhaps the result of the growth in local markets for milk.

Trade in cattle was greatly facilitated by the arrival of the railway in Carnforth, and one of the most significant developments that promoted Carnforth's prosperity (and which tied the town to its hinterland) was the establishment of a cattle market and cattle fair. In 1869 the *Lancaster Guardian* carried an article on Carnforth's proposed cattle market, which was, it was said, to be in the backyard and field behind the Queen's Hotel in Market Street.[8] The first sales were to take place the next week, and the auctioneer would be C. Stephenson (presumably the Christopher Stephenson of Carnforth who appears in the 1891 census as a seventy year old auctioneer). Six weeks after the market opened it was reported that the fortnightly cattle sales had had good attendance. There had been good sales of fat stock and sheep - about 30 head of fat and other stock and over 200 fat sheep as well as two yearling colts.[9] Three months later, in February 1870, the Carnforth cattle market was more popular than ever – '*a real benefit to the rising village*'.[10] At the Carnforth Half-year Fair that year 400-500 cattle from Cumberland and Furness fetched good average prices. By then these cattle from further afield were being transported by rail rather than by droving.[11]

Of course it was in the nature of farming that, shortly after this upbeat report on the cattle fair, herds were hit by disease. At Warton Robert Clark had 16 cattle infected with foot-and-mouth disease; Michael Benson had 5; Thomas Wilcock 15. There were other cases elsewhere, but it was thought that the disease was waning.[12] Then a month later, in July, it was reported that foot-and-mouth disease had reappeared among milch cows belonging to Michael Benson, cows which had formerly been reported as recovered. It was thought to have been brought in from Kendal and Kirkby Lonsdale by a cattle jobber.[13] There was further spread of the disease; lists were reported in the newspapers.[14] This was to be a temporary setback, but a more serious earlier outbreak had been reported in Cumberland in 1866 when 500 cattle had had to be destroyed in one week.[15] This was part of an outbreak that had also swept through the small urban dairies in Manchester and other towns, where cattle were kept, often in very poor conditions, for supplying milk to town dwellers. Serious though this 1866 outbreak was, it brought benefits to unaffected rural areas such as Warton that had satisfactory rail connections and could make good the town supplies lost by the ravages of the disease.[16]

Certainly Carnforth market continued to prosper in the 1880s. Fat and store cattle were being sold on Mondays and Wednesdays by Wm. & Jas. Downham, the proprietors in 1883.[17] In 1886 there was a market every Monday.[18] But though the market in Carnforth was beneficial in so many ways to the growing prosperity of the parish, and to Carnforth in particular, there may have been a negative aspect. Just think for a moment of the squalor of the town centre as these herds of livestock were driven to and fro between the station and the Queens Hotel. The roads would be deep in manure, adding to what was produced by the horse-drawn traffic of the day. The stench must, at times, have been overwhelming. Fortunately it was still a time when such things were part of life and probably someone gathered it up and sold it to a local farmer.

Milk Production

The shorthorn cows kept by Warton farmers produced good milk yields, and the increasing emphasis on dairying is perhaps shown by the reference in the 1861 census to dairymaids - one in Carnforth, two in Yealand Conyers, and three each in Priest Hutton and Warton. In the 1881 census only three were recorded, one each in Carnforth, Borwick and Priest Hutton. However, too much should not be made of the changes in these figures; the recording of women's jobs was always somewhat erratic and arbitrary (see Chapter 10).

New feedstuffs were explored to sustain this round-the-year production of milk. At the end of the century winterfeed could be supplemented by concentrates brought in from outside. There is local mention of pea-meal and oil-dust (a by-product of the nut oil extraction process).[19] Oilcake was well established as another winterfeed. As early as 1854 appropriate machinery to deal with oil cake was available, such as the '*oilcake breakers*' advertised in the *Lancaster Gazette*.[20]

There was a new market for milk in the industrial towns and Carnforth provided an outlet for some sales - an accident to a trap delivering milk in Carnforth confirms that the trade existed by 1894.[21]

11

The larger markets in towns in the south of Lancashire became important when milk could be sent by rail. James Erving, a businessman from Rochdale who had settled at Thwaite Gate in Carnforth in 1850 kept a notebook in which he recorded local matters which chanced to catch his attention. In 1864 he mentioned that milk was being sent from Carnforth to Liverpool and that dealers were offering 7d a gallon for milk.[22]

Fletcher quotes milk prices for various towns in Lancashire, quoting a variety of sources and covering the period 1870-1897.[23] The prices range from 6d a gallon during the summers of 1871, 1872 to 10d a gallon in 1894 in Blackpool. The data, although too sparse for any convincing generalisation, do suggest a consistent pattern of marginal price increases, with a penny or two being added to the price in the winter months.

Fletcher includes figures averaging 8d a gallon for sales *'near Lancaster'* in both 1876 and 1886, somewhat higher than those quoted by Erving in 1864 - though confusingly Erving also quotes a price of 2_d per quart *'at the station'*, which would be 10d per gallon. He was perhaps referring to the difference between what the producer received and what the buyer paid. Erving was writing for his own interest and did not have to explain his meaning to himself.

Towns required milk all year round so, as has been said, farmers had to keep good cattle and feed them well all year round instead of allowing them to go dry in winter in the old way. Town milk came partly from cows kept within the city and partly from the surrounding countryside. Either way milk tended to be of very poor quality, for the city cows were often kept in appalling conditions and country milk inevitably deteriorated on the slow journey to town.[24] In 1864 a London dairyman called George Barham began what he called the Express Country Milk Supply, the forerunner of the Express Dairies, to bring milk into the capital by railway. The use of railway-hauled country milk became common in all British cities and larger towns, but much milk continued, throughout the nineteenth century, to come from stall-fed city cows. Not that milk produced in the country, including the Warton area, was necessarily very satisfactory. In 1898 the Medical Officer of Health for the rural district reported that *'the cattle of this neighbourhood are highly tuberculous ...'* and in 1901 reported that regulations for dairies were a dead letter since *'no attempt* [is] *made to ensure the wholesomeness and cleanliness of the milk or the good health of the cattle'.*[25] Nevertheless Warton parish, like the rest of the countryside, continued to find buyers for its milk.

Sheep and Horses

Sheep continued to form an important part of the Warton Farmer's livestock. The numbers of sheep kept in the parish remained more or less constant at over 3,200 between 1880 and 1895. With lambs added, the numbers approached 6,000. Once Carnforth market had been set up they could be traded there, like the cattle. We have little information concerning sheep breeds, and it is likely that these varied greatly. The local Silverdale and Warton Crag breeds apparently continued to be kept. At the 1891 Burton and Milnthorpe Agricultural Show three ewes of the Horned Crag variety took second prize, as did three gimmer lambs of the same breed for Mrs. Hindson of Carnforth.[26] Leicesters were popular and purebred Leicester flocks were on sale in Carnforth in 1860 and 1862.[27] The annual sheep washing on the shore at Know Hill in Silverdale - evidently an old tradition – was reported. In 1894 six washers were reported to have washed 150 sheep.[28] In 1885 the Rural Sanitary Inspector, Mr. Jowett, reported that sheep washing had polluted a stream at Tewitfield that was used as a water supply for 10 houses.[29] As no action was taken it appears that environmental concerns were not always seriously regarded. The imports of frozen lamb, which began in the last decades of the century, inevitably affected prices, a matter discussed below when the whole question of a depression in farm prices is considered.

Farm horses numbered just over 400 in the period 1880-1895. They were generally not very large, but towards the end of the century larger carthorses appeared in the parish. The sale of Mr. Jennings' stock in Carnforth included *'One Bay Cart Mare 16 hands'*.[30] In the 1890s the Whinnerahs of Warton Hall kept and bred both light and heavy horses.[31] Their shire horses were famous, and the stallions were sent round farms in the area to service mares. The Whinnerahs also kept lighter, thoroughbred horses, and thoroughbred stallions were also sent round the area. Such a stallion could have been used on heavy-horse mares to produce a hunter type foal, or on hunter mares to produce a light, faster hunter. The price of horses was less likely to be affected by increasing imports, so that diversifying into horse-breeding presumably had advantages. There was a huge market for horses. They were the source of nearly all motive power on the farm, whether for hauling machinery and carts or for driving fixed machinery by means of a horse-gin. (An example of such a horse-gin can still be found behind one of the barns at Waterslack in Silverdale.)

Shire Stallion

Farming Methods

Some reports prepared at the mid-century by agricultural experts were critical of Lancashire farming because the writers considered that the Norfolk system of crop rotation was too often not being correctly followed. The Norfolk system, with its four-course crop rotation, was designed to set up a closed system of arable and pastoral farming, each part supplying essentials to the other. Grazing livestock would produce manure, which was used to fertilise the arable land, so producing better crops. The higher crop yield allowed some to be fed back to the livestock, and some to be taken off the farm to be sold for profit. Any surplus animals could be sold off for further profit. The whole system was designed to put production onto a higher level. Achievement of high farming was to be the aim of all progressive farmers. Other experts thought high farming was not necessarily well suited to all areas and that local conditions dictated that there should be major differences.

Haymaker

In Lancashire, and especially in the area in which Warton lay, high rainfall and suitable soil meant that grass grew extremely well, and could provide most of the fodder needed for the livestock, in the form of grass or hay, so that only a relatively small supplement of cereals was needed. The arable land in Warton was not of the best, and the high yields envisaged by the Norfolk system were always going to be difficult to achieve. The only mention of high farming in Warton appears to be in an advertisement for the sale of Brackenthwaite Farm in Yealand Redmayne, after the owner, Mr. Waithman, a prominent local industrialist, was declared bankrupt in 1853. Brackenthwaite was described in the advertisement as a 300-acre estate with farm buildings of modern and improved construction. There was a steam engine for threshing and other purposes and it was all said to be adapted for the system of high farming. While the grazing land at Brackenthwaite could have been described as good, the arable, as everywhere in the parish, would not have been of high quality; and the whole farm was probably far removed from anything envisaged by the full Norfolk system.

How far crop rotations were followed in Warton in the second half of the century is difficult to determine. There are a few notes made for one of the Dawson farms.[32] The notes refer to an 1854 rotation, which was quite elaborate - seven different crops were grown, including barley, clover, wheat and beans. An 1881 directory, under the general heading of Warton Parish, said '*There are many skilful farmers in this part of the county*' and added that '*improved agricultural implements and thrashing machines are in general use in all large farms*'. The entry goes on to list expected yields of corn, oats, beans and swede turnips, implying that all these would have been

Horse Drawn Binder

15

grown.[33] It is likely that most farmers followed habit and custom even though still more complicated crop rotations were sometimes being used elsewhere - rotations which included oats, barley, wheat, turnips, clover and under-sowing with a mixture of white clover, trefoil, cow-grass, rib-grass, rough cocksfoot and timothy grass.

Good farming practice was encouraged by agricultural shows and ploughing matches, the latter sometimes between teams invited by the new owner or tenant, which made the work lighter. It was reported, for example, that 17 ploughing teams competed for James Shaw of Thwaite Farm in Carnforth from cockcrow to four in the afternoon.

What a Ploughing Match May Have Looked Like

The Warton Ploughing Association remained important at the end of the century and local worthies – sometimes respected farmers like Mr. E. Whinnerah, but also men outstanding in other fields like Mr. Barton, the manager of the Iron Works - seem to have been pleased to associate themselves with agriculture.[34] Mr. Barton, although his background was purely in engineering, seems to have liked to take the part of a country gentleman. In 1890 he offered a prize of 10 guineas for the best mare at the Lancaster Agricultural Society show[35] and his obituary notice added, after recounting his achievements in engineering and public life, that he was 'an excellent judge of all kinds of stock'.[36]

The same seems to have been true of a good many of the business people who made their homes in the parish. Mr. Gillow of Leighton Hall, the largest landowner in the parish, though his money had come from the manufacture of high quality furniture, was President of the Burton in Kendal Agricultural Society in 1854.[37]

Fairs and shows were an important part of the agricultural year. Lancaster had its fairs and its cheese fairs. They were so popular that they seriously reduced school attendance while they lasted as the headmaster of Yealand Friends' School resignedly noted.[38] Warton farmers were strongly represented at these shows and well-known local names turn up among the prizewinners. The newspapers, knowing their readers, devoted considerable space to every detail of these shows. More specialist shows also took place - such as the Silverdale poultry and pigeon show, and these are dealt with in more detail later in the book (Chapter 11). Machinery and implements were also featured at the main agricultural shows.

Feeding the Land

The introduction of quantities of manure and fertilizer from outside the farm changed the farming systems. It was no longer necessary to have a closed cycle of manure, crops and livestock production. It was now possible to bring in fertilizers from outside, even from far overseas. The scattered references to fertilizer in press reports indicate that there was a steadily rising consumption of various products. Even before the mid-century there had been large imports into Lancaster of guano, and the larger slaughterhouses had been advertising the waste sweepings and droppings of their sheds as 'abattoir guano'.[39]

The obituary of John Frederick Watson of Craglands, Warton, who died in 1903, noted that he carried on a successful business as wool-merchant and manufacturer of sheep dips and bone manures.[40] In 1887 the *Lancaster Guardian* reported that G. Hadfield & Co., Liverpool manure manufacturers, gave a dinner in Carnforth to 50 farmer customers from the area.[41] The farming diary of the Whinnerahs of Warton Hall Farm for 1892 tells us a good deal about manuring at the end of the century. The Whinnerahs were not only livestock farmers, but also grew fodder crops such as turnips. Naturally their main supply of manure came from the cattle, sheep and horses that they kept. Manure was spread mainly in the months November to January, and meadow and pastureland were treated with manure and fertilizer as well as the arable. A diary entry in May refers to '*tank*' being put on mangolds. This is presumed to be liquid manure and urine collected from the cattle standings and then transferred to a mobile tank to be carted out to the fields. References to '*sowing manure*' suggest that some artificial fertilizer in granular or powder form may have been used. Chemical fertilizers began to be produced in the 1840s, but were not widely used in the nineteenth century.[42] A local directory carries the comment in 1881 that crops of turnips yielding 26-30 tons per acre were usually manured with 15 tons of farmyard manure and 2 cwt. of guano and that old pasturelands were limed.[43]

Market Prices

Local markets played an important part in the lives of the population generally. Meat products, grain and vegetables could be purchased at markets held weekly in the neighbouring villages and towns. The prices offered at nearby Kendal were reported regularly in *The Westmorland Gazette* and *The Kendal Advertiser* and are used here as an indicator of the cost of basic foodstuffs at that time. In the chart below (figure 1.1) plots are shown of the annual market prices of oatmeal (pence per stone) and mutton (pence per lb.). These are averages taken over the calendar year of weekly prices; where a range of weekly prices was quoted, the mid-point of the range was used.

The price of oatmeal showed no evidence of seasonal effects – where increases occurred, they generally persisted for several months. Mutton also was very stable in price; it was not unusual for the price to remain the same throughout the year. Other commodities such as eggs, potatoes, butter and lamb (not illustrated here) showed marked seasonal effects, being significantly more expensive in the winter months. Mutton and beef were consistently at the same price, with veal – when available – generally cheaper than either. On the other hand lamb, also when available, tended to be more expensive than beef, mutton or veal.

To modern eyes the remarkable feature of the chart is the low level of inflation in these prices. Over the 50 years, the price of oatmeal increased by 6.2%, and that of mutton by 21.3%. Moreover both commodities were considerably more expensive in the middle of the half-century than they were at its end, perhaps a reflection of the agricultural depression and the poor growing seasons at that time. To compare prices with local wages and with the economic position nationally, plots have been shown of half-yearly hiring rates for best men at the Whitsuntide Hirings[44] and of the Consumer Price Index published by   O'Donoghue, Goulding and Allen.[45] This index is based on an index of 100 in 1974 (the index value quoted for 2003 is 715.2). It should be treated as a rough guide, since purchasing patterns have changed considerably since the latter half of the nineteenth century.

Figure 1.1

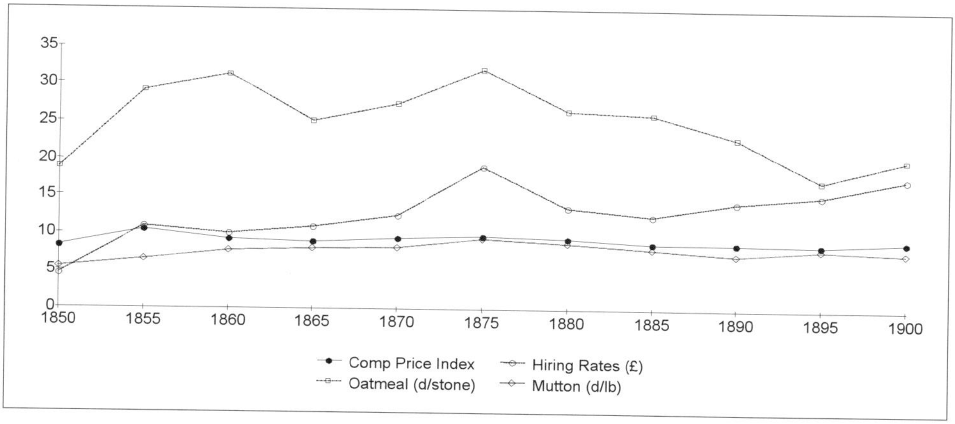

Prices, Wages and the Cost of Living 1850 – 1900

(Note that the units on the vertical scale refer to pounds sterling, (old) pence or index percentages as appropriate to the measure plotted.)

Was There an Agricultural Depression in Warton?

The phrase the Great Depression fairly describes the usual view taken of the condition of agriculture during the last quarter of the nineteenth century. The ruin of her farmers, it was held, was the price paid by Britain for the benefits she obtained, and conferred on the rest of the world, as the great free trading nation.[46] One historian, describing the 1870s, used the dramatic phrase *'British agriculture ... was thrown overboard in the storm like an unwanted* cargo'.[47] Yet it is more and more believed that depression did not press equally heavily on all farmers everywhere. According to one historian, '... *north of the Humber there was not so much wreckage as further south'* and went on to describe

19

Lancashire as in the '*half-light*', nearly as fortunate as Cheshire, long famous for its dairies, which '*suffered less than any county*'.[48] Yet the view remains that depression was universal even if some areas were slightly luckier and suffered less than the majority; areas for example, like the area north of Lancaster described by one recent writer as '*... a narrow coastal strip, partly of limestone, where oats, roots, and seeds were grown for consumption on the farm by sheep and cattle ... mainly of the dairy type*'.[49] In this area lies Warton parish.

In 1866 a decision was taken to collect agricultural statistics. Comparisons are made between data collected from the original parish summaries in the possession of the Ministry of Agriculture quoted by Fletcher in his 1961 paper.[50] Fletcher used the years 1870, 1874 and 1875 arguing that the earlier unreliable years were to be avoided, and that the intervening years (1871, 1872 and 1873) were unavailable. He compared these with averages of the years 1894-98 inclusive. Extractions from his tables are shown in tables 1.2 and 1.3. North Lancashire in these tables is believed to refer to the county (as it was in the late nineteenth century) north of the River Ribble. Also over this period the area of agricultural land in the county had increased from approximately 748 to 823 thousand acres, the former figure being in some doubt owing to changes in the unit of measurement of acreage.

Some of the differences in farming practices between North Lancashire and England generally are shown statistically in the following tables.

Table 1.2

Years	Total Arable		Corn (Oats)		Potatoes	
	North Lancs.	England	North Lancs.	England	North Lancs.	England
1870 - 1875	27	57	13 (7)	32 (6)	2	1
1894 - 1898	23	47	10 (7)	23 (8)	3	1

Crops per 100 Acres of Crops and Grass

20

Table 1.3

Years	Cattle (milk cows)		Sheep		Pigs	
	North Lancs.	England	North Lancs.	England	North Lancs.	England
1870 - 1875	32 (15)	17 (7)	61	81	5	8
1894 - 1898	37 (19)	18 (8)	70	64	8	9

Stock per 100 Acres of Crops and Grass

From these it can be seen that in the 1870s, the decade usually seen as the beginning of a period of depression, North Lancashire had considerably less of its farm land as arable than the average for England and also a smaller area growing corn. It can also be seen that it had a slightly greater acreage of both oats and potatoes. By the 1890s, the end of the period under question, the short fall of arable and corn growing in North Lancashire was less. The excess of the potato acreage in North Lancashire had doubled (and, surprisingly the oat acreage had fallen slightly below that in the rest of England).

Conclusion

Over the 1870s and 1880s, when England as a whole was going through an agricultural depression, the North Lancashire farming regime had swung towards livestock, and though its arable acreages had fallen in true terms, the fall was not as great as in England as a whole. When the scattered evidence from newspapers and other sources is also collected together it appears reasonable to say that Warton's agriculture did experience a difficult time in the 1870s when the ploughing of huge areas of North American prairie led to the production of very large volumes of wheat for export (though it is naturally very difficult to separate this from any accompanying industrial depression). A similar growth in production of beef and lamb in the Americas and in New Zealand started rather later, but that too was to have an effect on prices of meat in Britain. On the livestock side, Warton farmers may have been able to cushion their loss by concentrating on improving dairying, with meat production as an ancillary, so called cow beef.

Nothing could cushion them against the other problem that hit all British farmers in these years. The weather deteriorated in the 1870s.

Most of the summers were wet from 1875 onwards, and in 1879 there was a cold spring followed by an exceptionally wet and cold summer and autumn. *'In some places the corn had still not ripened enough for harvesting even by Christmas 1879.'*[51] Warton suffered along with the rest of the country. Direct comments on the situation in Warton are rare, but there are indications. In 1876 it was reported in the *Lancaster Guardian* that Thomas Stephenson of Hagg Farm in Carnforth was selling cattle, horses and implements because of the decline in farming.[52] The next month Nicholas Marsden of Beech House in Priest Hutton was selling his cattle, horses and sheep, all said to be *'well bred'*.[53] The reason is not given, but in 1879 the Beech House estate itself was for sale. The 1870s saw many farms sold, though no reasons are usually given. The sales include Red Bridge farm with 38 acres in 1873, Challon Hall estate with 139 acres also in 1873, the Row with 16 acres in 1874, and Bradshaw Gate estate together with Hawthorn Bank in 1878, all four in Silverdale. In addition the large Silverdale Hill House estate was for sale in 1872, but this was a consequence of the death of the owner, Christopher Wood. In Carnforth Thomas Jackson, who had inherited Hall Gowan farm from his father, announced that he would be giving up farming, and duly sold off stock, implements and the farm itself.[54]

There is also evidence that times were hard in the 1880s. In 1886 the *Lancaster Gazette* noted that, in an attempt to prevent the decline in prosperity in Furness and Cumbria, landowners were giving remission of rent in the form of lime to improve the fertility of the soil. More significant, perhaps, was the report that Cumberland farmers were migrating to Warwickshire where good land could be rented at one pound per acre. Many moved, lock, stock and barrel, by special train from Penrith.[55] Some folk emigrated to North America, New Zealand or Australia - a trend that had been developing for some time. In 1878 the *Lancaster Guardian* carried an advertisement for emigrant farm labourers wanted in New Zealand.[56]

---

[1] Mourholme Local History Society Book Group, *Warton 1800-1850: How a North Lancashire Parish Changed* (Mourholme Local History Society, 2005), pp.31-32.
[2] Mourholme, *Warton 1800-1850*, pp.21-22

[3] William Farrer, & J. Brownbill, eds., *Victoria History of the County of Lancaster*, vol.8 (Constable, 1914), p.152.

[4] *Lancaster Gazette*, February 3rd, 1855.

[5] *Lancaster Gazette*, February 8th, 1890

[6] *Lancaster Gazette*, February 3rd, 1855; February 4th, 1860; January 18th, 1862; February 8th, 1862; February 8th, 1890.

[7] Neil Stobbs, "The Whinnerahs of Warton Hall Farm," *The Mourholme Magazine of Local History*, no.3 (2000/01); "Further Notes From the Whinnerah's Diary," *The Mourholme Magazine of Local History*, no.1 (2001/02); "Further Information about the Whinnerahs of Warton Hall Farm," *The Mourholme Magazine of Local History*, no.1 (2002/03).

[8] *Lancaster Guardian*, October 9th, 1869.

[9] *Lancaster Guardian*, November 27th, 1869

[10] *Lancaster Guardian*, February 19th, 1870.

[11] *Lancaster Guardian*, May 4th, 1870.

[12] *Lancaster Guardian*, June 18th, 1870.

[13] *Lancaster Guardian*, July 8th, 1870.

[14] *Lancaster Guardian*, August 13th, 1870.

[15] *Lancaster Gazette*, March 2nd, 1866.

[16] P.S. Barnwell & C. Giles *English Farmsteads* (Royal Commission on the Historical Monuments of England, xiv, 1997), p.6.

[17] *Lancaster Gazette*, January 20th, 1883.

[18] *Lancaster Gazette*, February 27th, 1886.

[19] Neil Stobbs, "Further Notes from the Winnerah's Diary," *The Mourholme Magazine of Local History*, no.1 (2001/02).

[20] *Lancaster Gazette*, October 6th, 1854.

[21] *Lancaster Guardian*, June 2nd, 1894.

[22] James Erving of Carnforth: notebook with memoranda on international news and local and family events in Carnforth and Rochdale 1838-73. p.221. Lancashire Record Office, DP494/1 acc 9158.

[23] T.W. Fletcher, "Lancashire Livestock Farming during the Great Depression", *British Agricultural History Society*, vol.9: no.1 (1961).

[24] Anthony S. Wohl, *Endangered Lives; Public Health in Victorian Britain* (Methuen, 1983), p.21.

[25] Lancaster Rural District Council, *Reports of the Medical Officer of Health for* (1898; 1901).

[26] *Lancaster Gazette*, January 1st, 1892.

[27] *Lancaster Gazette*, December 29th, 1860; February 8th, 1862.

[28] *Lancaster Guardian,* June 9th, 1894.

[29] *Lancaster Gazette,* June 13th, 1885.

[30] *Lancaster Gazette,* February 8th, 1890.

[31] Neil Stobbs, "The Whinnerahs of Warton Hall Farm" *The Mourholme Magazine of Local History,* no.3 (2000/01); "Further Notes from the Whinnerah's Diary," *The Mourholme Magazine of Local History,* no.1 (2001/02); "Further Information about the Whinnerahs of Warton Hall Farm," *The Mourholme Magazine of Local History,* no.1 (2002/03).

[32] Note book referring to Leo. Willan and E.B. Dawson with notes and figures relating to estate management, 1846 – 1858. Lancaster Public Reference Library, MS 2905.

[33] Mannex et al, *Topography and Directory of Lancaster and sixteen miles round* (1881), p.244.

[34] *Lancaster Gazette,* January 16th, 1892.

[35] *Lancaster Gazette,* May 13th, 1890.

[36] *Lancaster Gazette,* October 25th, 1913.

[37] *Lancaster Gazette,* September 16th, 1854.

[38] Yealand Preparative Meeting, *Log Book of Yealand British School,* (Yealand Friends' Society, 1868), October 12th.

[39] Mourholme, *Warton: 1800 – 1850,* p.51.

[40] Death of Mr. J.F. Watson of Craglands, Warton, November 18th, 1903, p.48. Newspaper cuttings, Obituaries 1882 – 1905. Lancaster Reference Library, G191 NEW.

[41] *Lancaster Guardian,* October 2nd, 1887.

[42] Barnwell & Giles, *English Farmsteads,* p.6.

[43] Mannex et al, *Topography and Directory of Lancaster and six miles round* (1881).

[44] F.W. Garnett, *Westmorland Agriculture 1800 – 1900* (Kendal: Titus Wilson, 1912).

[45] J. O'Donoghue, L. Goulding & G. Allen, *Economic Trends* 604 "Consumer price inflation since 1750" (House of Commons Library: Office for National Statistics, March 2004).

[46] R.E. Prothero (Lord Ernle), *English Farming Past and Present* (Longman, Green & Co. 1912; 4th edition, 1927), ch. xviii.

[47] R.C.K. Ensor, *England 1870-1914* (Clarendon Press, 1936), p.115.

[48] J.H. Clapham, *An Economic History of Modern Britain 1873-1946,* 3 vols. (Cambridge University Press, 1930-1938).

[49] T.W. Fletcher, "Lancashire Livestock Farming during the Great Depression", *British Agricultural History Society*, vol.9: no1 (1961).

[50] Fletcher, "Lancashire Livestock Farming during the Great Depression".

[51] H.H. Lamb, *Climate, History and the Modern World* (Routledge, 1995), p.245.

[52] *Lancaster Guardian*, September 30th, 1876.

[53] *Lancaster Guardian*, October 14th, 1876.

[54] *Lancaster Guardian*, January 30th, 1892; February 6th, 1892.

[55] *Lancaster Gazette*, February 20th, 1886.

[56] *Lancaster Guardian*, August 31st, 1878.

Chapter Two

TRANSPORT
THE RAILWAYS, THE CANAL AND THE ROADS

The Railways
Carnforth Becomes a Junction: The Lancaster & Carlisle Line

The series of maps that appears at various points in this chapter shows the increasing complexity of the railway lines converging on Carnforth station from its first beginning as a wayside station on the new Lancaster & Carlisle line that was opened in 1846. Carnforth was not planned as a junction; indeed the other northward line from Lancaster, the North Western, that ran across the Pennines to Yorkshire took no heed of it, but was routed to the east of the then unimportant township of Carnforth.[1]

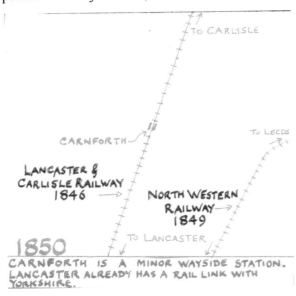

Meanwhile a railway system was being developed in Furness, and it was by connecting with this system that Carnforth first became a junction. The Furness Railway had begun operating in 1846 between Barrow and Dalton-in-Furness mainly for the carriage of minerals and by 1854 it had been extended to Ulverston. A separate company, the Ulverstone & Lancaster Railway completed the link with Carnforth as a single-track line in 1857 (small, hopeful companies were starting up everywhere in this expanding railway age). The first consignments on the line when it was opened for goods on August 10th 1857 were 70 tons of iron ore southbound and, on the evening return journey, coal from Lord Balcarres' colliery near Wigan to Cark for use at Holker Hall. Carriage of coal from Wigan was expected to be an important function of the new railway as it avoided '*the loss and breakage of loading and unloading vessels*' previously experienced through journeys by sea or canal.[2]

Growth of Carnforth as a Junction

On September 1st, 1857 the Ulverstone & Lancaster Railway was opened for passengers also. It was not long before the Furness Railway was seeking authority to purchase the line, which it did in 1862 and then doubled the track in 1863.

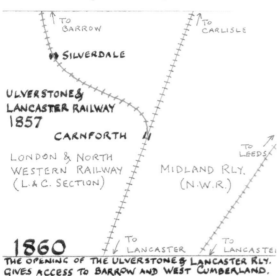

THE OPENING OF THE ULVERSTONE & LANCASTER RLY. GIVES ACCESS TO BARROW AND WEST CUMBERLAND.

The railway was able to promise connection with the arrivals and departures of trains from and to all parts of England. Carnforth, from being a simple wayside halt, had become a junction with rail links to Carlisle in the north, to Furness and the west and through Lancaster to the south. In 1859 The Lancaster & Carlisle was leased to the London & North Western Railway Line and was absorbed by it in 1879.

The Furness & Midland Joint Railway

THE FURNESS & MIDLAND JOINT RAILWAY PROVIDES A LINK TO YORKSHIRE. THE IRON WORKS IS IN FULL BLAST.

In 1867 a short line was opened from Carnforth east toWennington, which meant that Carnforth acquired a direct link with the Midland system to Leeds. It might be mentioned here that the through line from Leeds to Barrow meant another change. Until it opened, boats to Belfast had sailed from Morecambe, but the same vessels, the Roe, Talbot and Shelburne, now flying the flag of the Barrow Steam Navigation Company,

27

started to sail from Barrow.[3] The Midland and the Furness Railways continued as separate concerns, the Furness operating in the Furness peninsula and the Cumberland coast, while the Midland Railway operated (eventually) from London through the midlands to Leeds and Carlisle (with various branches). The link line through Carnforth, the Furness & Midland Joint Railway, was owned (jointly) by the two companies; the Furness Railway maintained the buildings and track, but the line was worked by the Midland Railway, so that engine drivers, firemen etc. would be Midland Railway employees, as also was the station master.

The Growth of Railway Traffic: Goods, Passengers and Trippers

The rail system thus built up must have helped make Carnforth attractive to the entrepreneurs who had opened the Iron Works there in the 1860s (a major industrial venture described in more detail in the next chapter) and the Iron Works in turn meant profit to the railways. Carnforth was able to enter on its period of maximum expansion.

Traffic on all the railway lines grew rapidly. When the Lancaster & Carlisle Railway was opened in 1846 there were only three passenger trains in each direction on weekdays, and one on Sundays; by the 1880s there were no fewer than twelve down and eight up trains calling at Carnforth on the main Lancaster & Carlisle section of the London & North Western Railway. In addition there were five local trains to and from Morecambe.

The Furness & Midland Joint Railway expanded its services equally rapidly. There were in 1875 only four trains arriving at Carnforth, balanced by four departures, (and on Sundays only two in each direction), but the number of trains had risen to ten in each direction by the end of the century. The success of the Ulverstone & Lancaster Railway is shown by its rising revenues. During the week ending May 27th, 1859 the total revenue from the line had been £502. In the same week in 1860 passengers had paid £211, and merchandise brought in another £502 making £713 in all, a 42% rise in a year.

As well as the regular passenger services the railways were increasingly offering special services and cheap fares. Some were offered on a regular basis. By 1859 the Lancaster & Carlisle was issuing sea-bathing tickets for visitors to Silverdale, and in 1861 there was a special train (stopping at Carlisle) for the Whitsun farm hiring fair.[4] Other offers were for special excursions. As early as 1851 the *Lancaster Guardian* has reported what it called '*A Pleasure Trip*,' when some 140 '*votaries of pleasure*' from Preston came to Carnforth and climbed up Warton Crag (despite the rain).[5]

Catering for trippers (a word that was just coming into common usage) was big business and the railways competed with each other to catch the trade. The Lancaster & Carlisle Railway anticipated the opening of the new Ulverstone & Lancaster Railway on September 1st, 1857, by advertising the day before, a special from Preston to Ulverston for a visit to Furness Abbey. The Lancaster & Carlisle Railway continued to take advantage of the new outlet, one of the Whit excursions of 1858 being a 19 carriage train from Preston to Silverdale.[6] Day trips to Windermere were advertised and special cheap excursions soon rose to more than a 100 a year. The majority of these were over London & North Western metals, and were usually for a day, though some tickets were valid for several days, and could be for destinations as varied as the south coast or London (for Paris) with no particular object in view other than travel, or to Liverpool and Manchester for the express purpose of going to the pantomime,[7] or to Birmingham especially for the Onion Fair.[8]

Carnforth Station
In 1846 a newspaper reporter had related how his train stopped at: '*the delightful little village of Carnforth ... for the purpose of getting a fresh supply of water ... All the party alighted to view the new station house* [with] *the greatest approbation*'.[9] The visit was being paid before even this first of all the station buildings at Carnforth was opened to the public.

As new lines were opened this small station was no longer adequate, the first major enlargement coinciding with the arrival of the Ulverstone and Lancaster Railway. The new Furness & Midland Joint Railway built its own station, staffed by Midland Railway men, some distance from the Lancaster & Carlisle station. It opened on June 6th, 1867 (even though work on it was said to be still only nearly finished at the beginning of 1868.) By July 1868 this first station had been closed and replaced by a second Furness & Midland Joint Railway station,

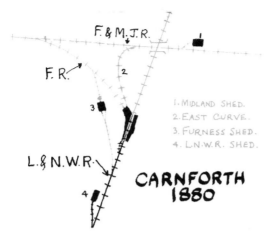

F. & M.J.R.

F.R.

1. MIDLAND SHED.
2. EAST CURVE.
3. FURNESS SHED.
4. L.N.W.R. SHED.

L. & N.W.R.

CARNFORTH
1880

housed in a wooden building sited to the west of the point at which the Furness and the Furness & Midland Joint Railways had their junction. A problem for the Furness & Midland Joint Railway was how to deliver passengers to the London & North Western station. This could only be done by means of reversal, a practice that was frowned upon by the Board of Trade. Nevertheless this problem was not resolved until 1880, when the construction of the east curve allowed the closure of the Furness & Midland Joint Railway's station and direct access to the L.N.W.R. station. The Furness & Midland Joint Railway station building was then removed to a position near East Junction, where it was used at various times as a guards' mess room and by the Signal & Telegraph Department before eventual demolition in the early 1960's.[10]

There could now be a single station complex for all the lines serving Carnforth and modernisation of the L.N.W.R./F.R. station was already under way. Work had begun on the foundations in April 1878, but was slowed down by frost the following winter. Then in February 1879 an iron support collapsed, injuring two workmen.[11] More accidents followed, including one fatal to Joseph Wren, a labourer, who was buried under an earth-fall.[12] Nevertheless the new station was opened on August 2nd, 1880, though before the approach to the L.N.W.R. up side entrance was quite finished. In the enlarged station the Furness side had a handsome overall roof, but was handicapped by having only one bi-directional platform. Not until 1939 was a second platform built for trains to Barrow.

On the L.N.W.R. side the up platform (for south-bound trains), which until then had been described as having very little shelter, was provided with new offices and waiting rooms, and the down platform buildings were further extended. A subway connected it with both the down L.N.W.R. platform and the Furness platform.

30

Furness Platform (Rathbone Collection)

Before the subway was constructed communication had been by a foot crossing at the south end, and in 1877 a horse belonging to Mr. Edward Barton had been killed there. On the down platform, along with offices, waiting rooms and the refreshment room, was W.H. Smith's book stall, a fixture since 1872. Passenger trains ceased to stop at Carnforth in May 1970, and now only the Furness and 1939 L.M.S. platforms are in use.

The Midland Railway, only a tenant at the L.N.W.R./F.R. station, was represented by an agent and two porters. A bay (i.e. dead-end) platform was provided between the Furness platform and Warton Road for its trains arriving via the new east curve. Attractive features of the 1880 station were the platform canopies, those on the platform shared by the London & North Western and the Furness Railway having the companies' initials in the decorative spandrels.

Diagram showing the layout of the station

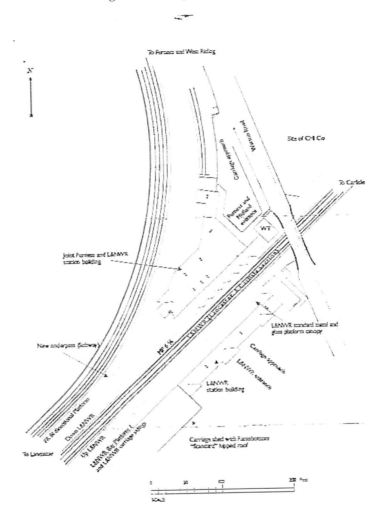

To Furness and West Riding

N

Ste of CH Co

To Carlisle

Joint Furness and L&NWR station building

Furness and Midland entrance

Carriage siding

Watering point

WT

New underpass (Subway)

L&NWR standard steel and glass platform canopy

No 646

L&NWR TELEGRAPH CLASSIFICATION

Carriage approach

L&NWR carriage approach

L&NWR station building

Ex North Western Platform

Down L&NWR

Up L&NWR

L&NWR Bay Platform & L&NWR carriage siding

Carriage shed with Furness Standard hipped roof

To Lancaster

To Leeds

SCALE

Looking for the 1880 Station

In 1939 alterations were made to the 1880 station which left it less aesthetically pleasing, but more functionally efficient. Much of the 1880 station can still be seen to-day, including the stone signal-box, built at the north end of the Furness platform and bearing the Furness Railway crest. It still presents a notable sight today, though it ceased functioning as a signal-box when it was replaced by the present Carnforth Station Junction box in 1903. Other survivals are the abbreviated remains of one of the 1880 stone roof-supporting columns, which still forms part of the

32

station wall next to Warton Road. Unfortunately none of the canopies or the support columns with their initialled spandrels remains in position; nor has the clock tower with its stone London & North Western crest that stood at the south end of the station survived. That tower clock had replaced an earlier one of 1862, but neither could be seen easily from the platform and must have been for the benefit of railway servants rather than the public. Not until December 1895 was the now famous clock placed near the subway on the island platform from which today the trains leave for Lancaster.

The Infrastructure

It goes without saying that such an increasingly important station had to have sheds, wagon-repair shops, locomotive coaling stages, sidings, a signalling system etc, etc. Little is known of the first Furness Railway shed, but the second shed of the late 1860s was one of the principal depôts (though with limited facilities for locomotive repairs).[13] It was closed in 1927 and its stock shared between the other two sheds. The first Midland shed, a small wooden four-road one (four sets of Railway lines), was built in 1867 at the junction of the Furness and Furness & Midland Joint railways. It was soon converted for use as a wagon repair shop when it was superseded in 1874 by the much larger red brick shed built some distance away to the east of the present A6 road. This was of standard Midland Railway square roundhouse design, which meant that the locomotives were housed in a rectangular building inside which was a 42ft. diameter central turntable with 24 stabling roads radiating from it. The first London & North Western shed was a two-road shed of obsolescent design with an allocation, in 1890, of only nine engines. It lasted for 20 years from 1873. It was then converted into a coaling stage when a successor, with a considerably greater capacity, was built nearby. The 1893 Ordnance Survey map shows what a very large area was occupied by the railway complex with its station, sheds, sidings and marshalling yards. Strategically placed in the centre of it all were the Iron Works.

The Station Hotel

The building of the new Station Hotel, though not undertaken by any of the companies themselves was all part of the optimism of the times about the future of railways. There had been an earlier building, usually referred to as the Station Inn, almost opposite to the Iron Works offices; it was demolished to make way for the 1880 extension of the Furness Railway side of the station.

The directors of the Carnforth Haematite Iron Company backed the new development, feeling it would 'supply a great want by businessmen who arrive at the junction too late for conveyance forwards'.[14] The Iron Works management seem to have had a direct financial interest in the project; applications for the lease of the new hotel had to be made to Mr. Edward Barton, the manager.[15]

Station Masters and Shed Gaffers

Another sign of the importance of its station to Carnforth was the standing of its senior staff. There were at least eight station masters employed in the nineteenth century, first by the Lancaster & Carlisle and then by the London & North Western when it took over. Sometimes only the dates of their appointments or removal elsewhere is known, but about others more can be gathered.

Thomas Sproat was station master at Carnforth from at least 1850 to 1855 and may have been the first appointment made. He seems to have been succeeded by Joseph Monk who was promoted to Whitehaven in 1862, an unhappy move as he and his son died there of fever a year later.[16]

The next incumbent, John Farrington Halliwell, is perhaps better known for his wife's career than for his own. In 1865 he married the widowed Elizabeth Carruthers who had been in charge of the refreshment room at the station ever since it was let by the London & North Western Railway in 1862. She was a shrewd businesswoman. In 1878 (by which time John Halliwell must have been dead, for she is again described as a widow) she bought land near the station and presumably made a handsome profit when it was developed as the Station Buildings, which included the Post Office and the Conservative Club. When she died aged 74 in 1896, she is believed to have been still the proprietrix of the station refreshment room.

Halliwell was succeeded by Isaac Birkett, the Oxenholme station master who moved to Carnforth in 1866. By 1873 he had left to take a position with the Carnforth Iron Works Company.[17] He was prominent in local affairs – churchwarden, leading light in the Loyal Unity Lodge and in the Carnforth Floral and Horticultural Society, and one of those responsible for the formation of the Carnforth Water Company.

Mr. Mashiter, who had been his successor at Oxenholme, held brief tenure at Carnforth, being supplanted by George Steele, a man who won high praise for his work and received a considerable sum in gold sovereigns on his retirement in 1880.[18] Of William Hunter who followed nothing is known, but William Haythornthwaite, at Carnforth from 1885 until 1895, is known to have moved on to hold the prestigious post of station superintendent at Carlisle Citadel from 1897 until 1910. The station master was appointed by the London & North Western, but the agent for the Midland was often referred to as station master.

Other important figures in the railway hierarchy were the locomotive superintendents or shed gaffers. Among these, on the Furness Railway, was Samuel Affleck who was the Furness railway shed gaffer for 21 years. He was appointed around 1866 and was still in service when he died, aged 46, at Keer Villa in 1887.[19] He was prominent in Carnforth & Warton Oddfellows Lodge and the Floral & Horticultural Society.

The first Midland gaffer was Francis Henshall Stalvies, son of an engineer from Bromsgrove; he was also a member of the Oddfellows.[20] He became a player for the first Carnforth Cricket Club and then its president; he was also treasurer of the Carnforth & Railway Cricket Club. In 1873 he married a local girl, Anne Richard of Priest Hutton, and left the district shortly after.

The Village Stations
There were two other railway stations in Warton parish besides Carnforth: one at Silverdale and the other at Borwick. Silverdale's was one of the original stations on the Ulverstone & Lancaster Railway and was opened on September 1st, 1857. Though inconveniently distant from the village the railway, as well as effecting improvement in the mail service, quickly attracted many excursionists. The villagers did not consider themselves well catered for, however, either in accommodation or train services. In 1890 requests were made for a waiting room on the up platform (the main buildings being on the down side). They also

wanted a footbridge at the level crossing on the coast road between Silverdale and Carnforth.[21] The first of these requests was granted when in 1892 a building containing a general waiting room and a ladies' waiting room (both with fireplaces) was built on the up platform, but the footbridge over the level crossing did not materialise. The level crossing remains to this day, though the crossing-keeper's house has long vanished. In the same year, 1890, a request was also made for an improved winter train service for Silverdale.[22] The situation was seemingly still unresolved in 1897 when, so far from providing more trains, the Furness Railway must have reduced services, for it was being asked to restore the 2.05 p.m. train from Carnforth. Freight traffic was provided by the nearby Trowbarrow quarry and there was a small goods yard behind the up side of the station.

Borwick station was one of three intermediate stations on the link line between Carnforth and Wennington. It was situated about three-quarters of a mile east of the village and was opened to passengers in

June 1867, and to goods in February 1868. The station buildings were on the up side and some railway cottages in a matching style were built just below the station. By 1880 there were three more Furness Railway houses in Borwick (though unfortunately at one stage they were deemed to be not in proper sanitary condition as the water supply was inadequate in the summer months). There was a goods shed near the Carnforth end of the up line. The passenger service was never frequent. In 1875 there were just two up and two down trains per day (including Sundays), with an extra up train (by request only) on weekdays for passengers wishing to go to London, though the service did improve a little towards the end of the century. Much of Borwick's freight traffic would be in agricultural produce and in stone from the nearby Wegber quarries.

Working Conditions and Accidents
In December 1898 Lux, who commented on Carnforth affairs for the *Lancaster Guardian* wrote that:

'... at Carnforth shunting yards the men will soon have a superstitious dread of performing their required tasks. It is a most unlucky yard – that is the testimony one constantly hears'[23]

If he had penned these words 30 years earlier they would have been equally true. It was an age when accidents were commonplace. Men were expected to work long shifts. It was the opinion of one local historian that *'it was common practice for men to work up to 10 hours beyond the original 12 and without pay.'*[24] The stress of responsibility was great and the physical conditions testing. New safety precautions were indeed constantly being introduced, though many of them were for the benefit of the public rather than the company servants. Yet still accidents continued. The selection from the all too frequent reports of accidents given below throws some light on the fatal combination of dangerous conditions and human error.

The first accident at Carnforth that has come to notice was in 1847 when Thomas Turner, a Lancaster & Carlisle Railway stoker, struck his head against a bridge. He had been returning over the carriage tops to his engine after speaking to the guard (a practice which, though fraught with danger, was apparently common at the time.).[25]

In 1863 an inquest was held into the death of Mr. Thompson, a brakesman, in an accident, which occurred near Silverdale. While he was uncoupling wagons he was run over by a tender and wagons and decapitated.[26]

In 1867 Robert Hayton, a labourer, while tipping earth at the junction of the Furness & Midland Joint Railway with the Furness railway, unhitched his horse and took it onto the main Furness line where both man and horse were struck by a passing train and killed. His brother was a witness of the accident.[27] In the same year Mr. Jackson, a platelayer, was run over at Carnforth by a ballast engine; both his legs were crushed. He was taken to the Lancaster Dispensary, but died from blood loss. He left a wife and seven children.[28]

In 1871 William Stephenson, a ten year-old Post Office messenger, while off duty, was in the station where a mineral train was being shunted. He was warned by the driver of the dangers, but some minutes later was found to have been run over.[29] He died soon after.

In 1872 Thomas Cooper, signal porter (sic) at the Furness & Midland Joint Railway station was making an unauthorised visit to his nearby home for breakfast. He had jumped onto a brake van to get a lift, and on nearing home jumped off again. When he heard a warning whistle he appeared to be confused, stepped the wrong way, and was run down and killed by a train from the Wennington direction. His wife witnessed the accident.[30]

In 1875 Mary West of Borwick, aged seven, was on her way to school at Yealand when she was struck by a goods train at Yealand crossing and died of her injuries.[31] The coroner recommended that a footbridge should replace the crossing, but no action was taken by the railway company.

In 1877 Joseph Gunson, a Furness Railway shunter, got his foot trapped in the points, and was run over before he could release it.[32] He left a widow and five children, and such sympathy was felt that £50 had been subscribed within a week.

In 1878 an accident occurred which highlighted the inadequacy of arrangements for getting medical help for the injured. Isaac Thomas Hinde, a London & North Western watchman, failed to hear the warning whistle of an engine going to the shed and it ran over him causing severe injuries to his leg. Medical assistance was called and Mr. Yorke, the assistant at a local medical practice, applied a tourniquet and advised that Hinde should be taken to the Lancaster Infirmary. Mr. Beatty, the Furness & Midland station master, used the services of his own line and arranged for Hinde to be taken in a brake van, via Wennington where it would be possible to transfer to the Midland Railway to go on to Lancaster. The journey covered 20 miles and took nearly an hour. On arrival at the infirmary Hinde was in a state of collapse and died shortly afterward. At the coroner's inquest Mr. Beatty stated that he was unaware that he could have sent Hinde by the London & North Western line, a much shorter distance. The coroner was extremely critical of what had been done, and further commented on the lack of a cottage hospital at Carnforth to which injured employees of any railway company could be taken.[33]

Only five days after Hinde's fatal accident Joseph Richardson, a fireman on the Midland Railway, taking a goods train from Carnforth to Sheffield, was stopped by signals. Richardson, taking the opportunity to leave the engine to examine the lamps, stepped into the other track and was struck by a passenger train. His skull was smashed in. He was sent to Lancaster Infirmary, one hopes by the shortest route, but on arrival was described as in a precarious condition.[34] It is not known whether he survived.

In 1882 John Lancaster, a London & North Western breaksman or shunter was uncoupling wagons during fly-shunting when his head was crushed between the buffers.[35] Until the shunting pole came into use in 1886 shunters had to go between the wagons to couple or uncouple them. Fly-shunting meant that the driver would set off at some speed, then ease up to facilitate uncoupling. It was strictly against the rules, though another driver testified at the inquest that he had done it for eight or ten years without ever being instructed not to do so. Shunters, it was found by a Royal Commission on accidents in 1900, had a higher rate of fatalities than even miners, and were second only to merchant seamen.[36]

As if accidents were not bad enough there was always the danger of deliberate attacks by drunken or violent passengers. Chris Dodd, a porter, was assaulted by a cattle dealer in 1875; the following year George Steele, the stationmaster, was attacked; James Thompson, a Furness Railway porter, was assaulted in 1880; John Owen, night inspector, suffered the same indignity in 1892, and a London & North Western porter, William Dodd, was the victim in 1893.

Housing the Railway Workers

There would be little need for extra housing for railwaymen in the early days, but by the time that the Furness & Midland Joint Railway was being built in the 1860s the situation had changed. The 1861 census had shown only 26 Carnforth men employed on the railway. In 1871 there were some 110 men (it is not always possible to tell from the census description whether some of those dealing with engines were working on the railway or in the Iron Works). Over the next few years the numbers were set to rise dramatically and the need for new housing was becoming urgent.

Midland Terrace

Some building for railway staff took place in the late 1860s and early 1870s mainly in Carnforth (though there were a few houses in the other villages). Midland Terrace (modern photograph above), a row of 12 houses, and the two semi-detached Keer Villas were built for Midland employees. The account of other housing given below was largely gleaned from advertisements and items in local newspapers and cannot claim to be full. Moreover street names have changed so that it is not always possible to pinpoint the exact locations of some houses. In addition to any new building, already existing housing was leased for the use of railway men. For example, six cottages in Mount Pleasant (thought to have been near Bolton-le-Sands) were leased to the Furness Railway for four years before they were sold on in 1873. In 1876 the Furness Railway took the lease for 21 years of six cottages in High Bank Close (exact site unknown). In 1880, ten houses in Bank Terrace on the Over Kellet road were leased to the Midland Railway. Houses known as Stelfox cottages, the location of which is uncertain, are known to have been leased to the Furness Railway, as in 1888 that company was instructed to remove pig-styes from there. In 1896 the London & North Western Railway acquired land on which to build 41 houses, which were duly completed in 1898 as two terraces forming Grosvenor Place. Only after remedial work was done to the approach road and the sewage system did they meet the requirements of Carnforth U.D.C.

There have been claims that houses in Market Street, New Street and Carlisle Terrace were built for the railway companies, but little evidence supports this, though the 1891 census shows that in the 46 houses in New Street there were 34 men working on the railway, whereas in Market Street there were only three, all lodgers in the Temperance Hotel. The two or three in Carlisle Terrace in Millhead were heavily outnumbered by ironworkers. Canal Cottages may have been built for canal workers and so passed into railway ownership when the London & North Western took over ownership of the canal. Certainly it had a high proportion of railway employees in 1891. The census for that year also shows that by that time there were few streets that did not house railway workers, though on the whole they tended to crowd together in certain streets. So also did the ironworkers, though it is probable that houses built for ironworkers might be made available to others in times of depression in that trade. A certain hierarchy was preserved in railway housing, though it was not rigid; thus New Street railway men were on the whole inspectors and railway clerks while Stanley Street housed drivers and stokers.

Welfare and the Unions

In the face of the accidents and the hard working conditions, the railway companies showed such benevolence to the staff as was customary at the period; reports of the annual suppers, dinners and tea parties and so on which were laid on by the employers are common in the local papers. They were probably also seen as a way of encouraging company loyalty. Fellow workmen and the local community often showed their support for accident victims and their families by such methods as organising benefit concerts which might raise what were, for the period, considerable sums. Not till 1897 did a Workmen's Compensation Act come into force, which made employers explicitly liable to pay compensation for injuries occurring in the normal course of duty, including compensation to dependents in the case of fatality or incapacity. The act did not apply universally, but railway men were among the groups given protection. It is possible that the opening of the Carnforth branch of the United Kingdom Railway Temperance Union in 1883 may have done something to reduce the frequency of accidents by increasing sobriety, but direct attacks on dangerous working practices and the long working hours, which caused accidents, came from elsewhere.

From early years there had been various bodies, such as the Lancaster and Carlisle Railway Sick & Burial Society and the Railway Servants' Widows and Orphans Benevolent Society, which aimed to support railwaymen and their families, but such trade unions as had existed had failed to make an impact and were short-lived.

In 1872, a year in which L.N.W.R. pointsmen working a 78-hour week had asked for a 56-hour week and more pay, the Amalgamated Society of Railway Servants (later to become the National Union of Railwaymen) was formed. One of its main objects was to reduce hours of work in order, among other things, to reduce the number of accidents to railway workers, but until the late 1880s it was a friendly society-type union, which deplored strikes as an evil both to masters and men.[37] A growing membership eventually encouraged the Union to face the problems with a degree more militancy. In 1891 a Carnforth branch of the Amalgamated Society of Railway Servants was formed. Each year its members would march, to the accompaniment of the Carnforth Brass Band, to one of the local churches, there to listen to a sermon whose theme we can only guess.

In 1896 there had been threats of a strike on the London & North Western Railway, which led to the dismissal of local men, among whom were signalman Mattocks (with more than 20 years service) and shunter Sharpe of Carnforth, both of whom were members of the Amalgamated Society of Railway Servants.[38] At a meeting of the Carnforth branch, called to discuss the dismissals, Councillors Vant and Stephenson pledged their support to the railwaymen. Even more important was the intervention in the dispute of Mr. Ritchie, the President of the Board of Trade, who persuaded the London & North Western to relent.[39] The sacked men were speedily reinstated. An indignation meeting was held in the Palatine Hall in Lancaster, attended by signalman Mattocks and two others from Carnforth, but by that time their reinstatement had already been effected. An indirect result of the pressure put on the London & North Western Railway by the Amalgamated Society of Railway Servants was that the Midland Railway decided that shunters at busy stations were to have their hours of work reduced from 60 to 48 a week in winter, while goods guards had theirs reduced from 76 to 60 all year round.[40]

The Associated Society of Locomotive Engineers and Firemen also had a branch in Carnforth. The Society had been founded in 1880 in Leeds, and Carnforth was its eighth branch though apparently the union had little influence there. Despite progress the unions were by no means yet secure. At a meeting of the Amalgamated Society of Railway Servants held in the Co-operative Hall in December 1898 the chief topics of debate were continuing victimisation of members and the consequent need to enrol new members.

The Canal

The railways were a new and most important phenomenon in nineteenth century Warton parish, but the value of the Lancaster Canal should not be forgotten. It had been opened in 1797 and still kept its importance; not as in earlier years for the carriage of passengers it is true, but for the carriage of heavy goods, in particular lime and limestone out of the parish and coal in. The canal company saw itself as the equal of the railway companies and there was a prolonged battle between the two for control of the still lucrative canal. The railways proved the stronger in the end. In 1861 the Lancaster & Carlisle Railway took over the lease of the canal and then, in 1885, the London & North Western which had absorbed the Lancaster & Carlisle took full possession. Thus, although heavy goods were still carried by the canal, control had been obtained by the railways.

The Roads

The turnpike roads, the very latest thing in speedy travel in the late eighteenth and early nineteenth century, were not so fortunate. Passengers were finding it quicker, cheaper and more comfortable to travel by rail. Reports of meetings of the Turnpike Companies all give some indication of their plight. Although the Ulverston, Milnthorpe and Lancaster Turnpike tolls were still being offered to let in 1879, roads were being everywhere disturnpiked (a new word to cover a new situation). That did not mean that roads were becoming less important. They were still needed for local travel and for local carting of goods. Moreover they were needed for the servicing of the railways. The railways had meant an ever increasing movement of goods, and so an ever increasing traffic on the roads to bring the goods to the railhead. There were reports of deterioration in the condition of the roads: in 1875 the *Lancaster Guardian* was reporting neglect in keeping the highway in proper repair at Borwick and Over Kellet. Six months later the highways at Borwick had improved, but the sides needed to be cleaned out, which was said to be the case in most townships. The roads in Warton township were worn through in several places. Maintenance of these minor roads remained the duty of the local parishes, and it was increasingly realized that the task was beyond them. The Highways Act of 1862 had provided for the grouping of parishes into districts, as had been done for Poor Law and sanitary work. A further Highways Amendment Act in 1878 introduced a distinction between local roads and main roads (which included all roads dis-turnpiked since 1870). The Districts retained all responsibility for the former, but the County was to repay them half the cost of maintaining the latter. The actual decision as to who did what was less clear. The County Surveyor became a very important figure, but there remained much that was ad hoc and tentative in the division between the responsibilities of the County and the local authorities.

Vehicles on the road were almost without exception horse drawn. In 1896 the first British car factory was opened in Coventry, but motorcars really made only a negligible contribution to traffic in the nineteenth century. The first London to Brighton car race on November 14[th,] 1896 involved 30 cars (of which only 17 arrived safely at Brighton, the first of them a steam car). From then on motor traffic grew fast, though the indications are that at this date it was private cars not goods vehicles that were coming in. By 1899 Lux, a regular contributor to the *Lancaster Guardian*, was writing of the '*motor car invasion which has captured our whole district of late*' and was astonished by speeds of 15 to 20 miles per hour.[41] He also wrote that at Whitsun that year:

> '... *the* [Carnforth] *station had been very busy; wagonettes and motor cars have thronged the highway, and cyclists have been numbered by the hundreds*'.[42]

An entry in the logbook of Archbishop Hutton's School reports that, on April 30th, 1900, there were only 24 children in school, the others having '*gone to see a Motor car procession on its way to Edinburgh*'.

Steam powered machines were in use, though as a means of powering farm machinery rather than as a general means of transport. Though not really making much difference to the volume of road traffic their presence does seem to have necessitated special regulations. In 1893 Richard Chaplow, farmer, was charged with driving a locomotive which did not consume its own smoke. He said that the engine had got low and he was making up steam. He was fined 5s plus 12s costs and told not to work near the road.[43] Horse-drawn vehicles were not without their own problems. George Thistleton of Borwick, farmer and vet, was drunk in charge of a horse on several occasions. On the third time Superintendent Moss had locked him up overnight. He pleaded guilty and was given a 20s fine with 9s costs.[44] Cases of furious riding (what a splendid offence!) were brought before the County Police Court: Samuel Emmett was accused of furious riding in Carnforth by P.C. Exton. Emmett had been abusive when cautioned. He was fined 10s and costs.

[1] Mourholme Local History Society Book Group, *Warton 1800-1850: How a North Lancashire Parish Changed*, (Mourholme Local History Society, 2005), p.102.

[2] *Lancaster Guardian*, August 15th 1857.

[3] *Lancaster Guardian*, August 31st, 1867.

[4] *Lancaster Guardian*, May 4th, 1861.

[5] *Lancaster Guardian*, June 14th, 1851.

[6] *Lancaster Guardian*, May 29th, 1858.

[7] *Lancaster Guardian*, January 29th, 1887.

[8] *Lancaster Guardian*, September 24th, 1881.

[9] *Lancaster Guardian*, August 29th, 1846.

[10] Michael Andrews, "The Origins of the Furness Railway," part 1, *Railway and Canal Historical Society Journal* (October 1965) and "The Origins of the Furness Railway," part 2, *Railway and Canal Historical Society Journal* (January 1966).

[11] *Lancaster Guardian*, February 15th, 1879.

[12] *Lancaster Guardian*, March 22nd, 1879.

[13] Chris Hawkins & George Reeve, *LMS Engine Sheds, Vol.4, The Smaller English Constituents* (Oxford: Wild Swan Publications, 1984).

[14] *Lancaster Guardian*, June 28th, 1879.

[15] *Lancaster Guardian*, June 28th, 1879.

[16] *Lancaster Guardian*, August 22nd 1863.

[17] *Lancaster Guardian*, February 15th, 1873.

[18] *Lancaster Guardian*, November 20th, 1880.

[19] *Lancaster Guardian*, September 17th, 1887.

[20] *Lancaster Guardian*, October 16th, 1869.

[21] *Lancaster Guardian*, April 25th, 1896.

[22] *Lancaster Guardian*, November 22nd, 1890.

[23] *Lancaster Guardian*, December 24th, 1898.

[24] John Easter Roberts, *The Changing Face of Carnforth* (Carnforth: J.E. Roberts, Mayoh Press, 1974).

[25] *Lancaster Guardian*, December 25th, 1847.

[26] *Lancaster Guardian*, June 27th, 1863.

[27] *Lancaster Guardian*, May 25th, 1867.

[28] *Lancaster Guardian*, June 15th, 1867.

[29] *Lancaster Guardian*, November 25th, 1871.

[30] *Lancaster Guardian*, May 4th, 1872.

[31] *Lancaster Guardian*, May 15th, 1875.

[32] *Lancaster Guardian*, November 10th, 1877.

[33] *Lancaster Guardian*, September 14th, 1878.

[34] *Lancaster Guardian*, September 14th, 1878.

[35] *Lancaster Guardian*, September 30th, 1882.

[36] Jack Simmons & Gordon Biddle eds., *The Oxford Companion to British Railway History* (Oxford University Press, 1997).

[37] Simmons & Biddle, *The Oxford Companion to British Railway History*.

[38] *Lancaster Guardian*, December 12th, 1896.

[39] *Lancaster Guardian*, December 19th, 1896.

[40] *Lancaster Guardian*, January 23rd, 1897.

[41] *Lancaster Guardian*, May 13th, 1899.

[42] *Lancaster Guardian*, May 13th, 1899.

[43] *Lancaster Guardian*, February 18th, 1893.

[44] *Lancaster Guardian*, July 31st, 1886.

Chapter Three

THE COMING OF THE IRON WORKS

The Carnforth Haematite (Iron) Company Ltd. was formed by a group of Manchester businessmen, notable among them H.J Walduck, an entrepreneur with a finger in many local pies. These men saw the opportunity offered in Carnforth by the rail network centred there. The railways meant that iron ore, coal and coke could be brought to an ironworks there, limestone for flux was available locally and could be transported by local lines easily created for the purpose, and the iron end-product could be whisked north, south, east and west by rail. In addition there was water available from the River Keer. The waste slag could be dumped on the shore. The fact that the works could be registered as a Limited Company may also have been of significance in attracting investors. Since the Limited Liability Act of 1855 investors could only be liable for what they themselves had invested; until that time each investor was responsible for the debts of the whole company in the event of failure – a considerable deterrent to the cautious.

The scheme for an ironworks was first heard of in 1861 when the *Lancaster Guardian* carried a report saying that '*There is some prospect that iron works on an extensive scale may be established in this locality*'.[1] It is characteristic of nineteenth century entrepreneurs that, having formed the Carnforth Haematite Iron Company in 1864, they lost no time before acting. In March 1865 the *Lancaster Guardian* reported that the Carnforth site beside the Keer was a chaotic scene. '*Here a number of huge stones thrown anyhow in a heap ... here a steam engine pounding away ... masons at work in one quarter, bricklayers in another*'.[2] In May 1865 Mrs. Barton, wife of Edward Barton who had been appointed to oversee the work, laid the foundation stone of the engine house chimney which was to be 210ft. high and 19ft. in diameter at the base.

Carnforth Iron Works

Initially the construction work must have provided employment for many builders and labourers, and it was anticipated that the ironworks, when completed, would give employment to 200-500 men.[3] The first two furnaces were blown in in 1866, followed by a third shortly after and pig iron was being produced by 1866.[4] A trade directory for 1866 said that '*ere long Carnforth may become a second Barrow*.[5] By 1870 a fourth furnace was in use, the company employing 300 men and producing 300-400 tons of pig iron a week.[6] From 1864 Mr. Edward Barton had been Chief Engineer in charge of the construction work. By 1866 he was general manager. He came from Carlisle and had received his education at Croft House School in Brampton, a private school with a reputation for including technical and scientific instruction in its curriculum. Barton went on to gain experience as an engineer in ironworks in Middlesbrough and Workington. When he was appointed at Carnforth he was still only in his early thirties. When he died in 1913 he was chairman of the company, chairman of the water company, chairman of the gas works, on the Police Court Bench, a Quarter Sessions magistrate and first chairman of Carnforth Urban District Council. He had undoubtedly been one of the most influential men in Carnforth's development.

Carnforth Iron Works Blast Furnaces in Background

Housing the Work Force

Housing development for the Carnforth ironworkers took place, as the 1871 census shows, not so much in Carnforth as just across the River Keer in the township of Warton-with-Lindeth, in an area where once Warton's corn mill had stood and which was still known as Millhead.[7] There were no houses on the site, though on the other side of the Warton Road there stood an older house, Hazel Mount, where John Jennings, formerly publican of the Black Bull in Warton, lived.

It seems probable that in the late sixties, before Millhead was developed, workers would have taken lodgings in Carnforth or in Warton, but that would have been after the 1861 census but before the 1871 census, and so there is no easily available record. Some houses were built for the ironworkers along the road between Carnforth and Warton. The row, known as Bessemer Terrace, was soon demolished and re-erected under the same name, later to be re-named Hall Street, on a stretch of Lancaster Road towards the south end of the village. Other properties built in Carnforth for the ironworkers were named Pond Street, Pond Terrace and Ramsden Street. The 1871 census shows that the houses were being occupied, largely though not exclusively, by employees of the Iron Works. Of the thirty-five families recorded (presumably sometimes two families to one cottage), in fourteen of them the head of the household was an ironworker, and a further twenty ironworkers were recorded as sons or lodgers.

The main housing development however was in Millhead, at first as two rows of terrace houses, fifty-two in all, which were given the names of Albert Street and William Street. They stood back a little from Warton Road, running north to south on a slope towards the River Keer.

There was also a small housing development nearby on a site on the Warton road itself known as West View. Joseph Whiles, a builder and bricklayer, lived there in a household of eight people among whom were two bricklayers and a bricklayer's apprentice. Next-door was the house of John Lithgow, a plasterer.

Also in West View lived Joseph Jackson, a quarrymaster, and a man of some substance since he was recorded as employing twenty-nine men. In addition there was a beer house, the West View Hotel, built and owned by Robert Clarkson. A beer house must have been convenient for the Iron Works, a hot and thirsty trade, but it was apparently viewed with doubt by the magistrates. A full licence allowing the West View to serve spirit was refused in 1873 and it was soon after put up for sale by Clarkson.[8] In 1874 the West View licence was again refused. This did not mean that beer could not be served since no licence was required for that. In 1875 Isaac Robinson of the West View Hotel was fined for serving drink after hours. As far as is known it settled down after that. In 1894 it seems the proprietrix was also making money as a small farmer; at any rate an advertisement appeared saying that Mrs. Wilson of the West View Hotel had two sow pigs for sale as well as other animals, implements and potatoes.[9]

The building of the Iron Works and of the houses in Millhead would plainly have provided much subsidiary employment. There was, however, a downside to this boost to the area. Such large-scale work in a previously rural area led to difficulties.

In 1866, William Redhead, surveyor of roads, had been called up before the magistrates on account of the bad state of the roads. Between Jackson's quarry and the Iron Works, the traffic was so heavy that repairs had cost £50 already; in previous years the cost had been in the region of £4 - £5. Accidents were occurring daily. The surveyor was short of labour to carry out the repairs. Jackson offered to supply materials for road repair and Redhead to carry them out as soon as possible.[10] All the same, in mid-November, the paper reported that '... *William Redhead had again been summoned to the court at the Judges' Lodgings; roads had not been repaired as promised'*. The need for a report with the facts of the weight of transport between Jackson's quarry and the Iron Works was considered and a new agreement seems to have been reached.[11]

Population Change

This expansion in the population of the township of Warton-with-Lindeth occurred very suddenly in the second half of the 1860s. The population rose from 581 in 1861 to 1,035 in 1871. The rise was almost entirely due to the incomers at Millhead; the population of the rest of the township – that is of Warton-with-Lindeth without Millhead – had risen only very slightly. The two figures below show that between 1861 and 1871 there had also been a very clear change in the distribution of age groups over the decade. However for 1871 (figure 3.2) the age distribution is shown separately for Millhead and for the rest of Warton. It can then be seen that it was the incoming population in Millhead that had caused the change. The age pattern in the rest of Warton was much as it had been in 1861. In Millhead 40% of the total were nine years old or under. This, taken together with the wide band of those 20 to 29 years old, certainly seems to indicate (as might have been expected) that those who had left their homes to seek new work in Carnforth were largely the young and their children.

Figure 3.1

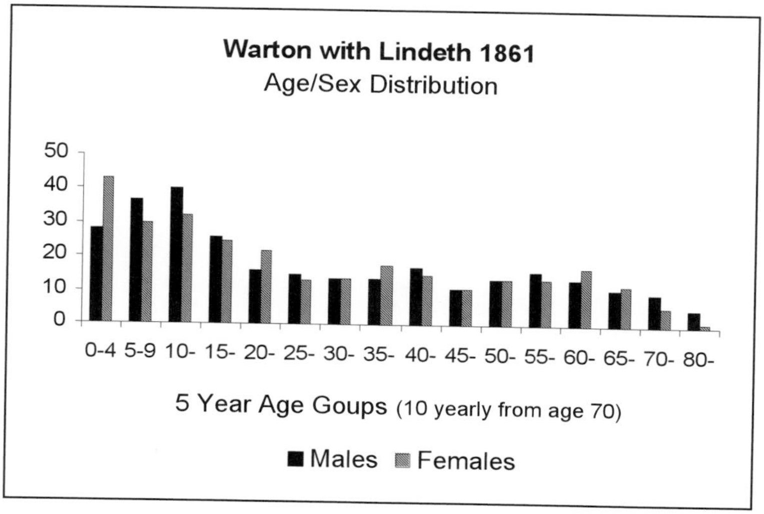

Warton with Lindeth 1861
Age/Sex Distribution

5 Year Age Goups (10 yearly from age 70)

■ Males ■ Females

Figure 3.2

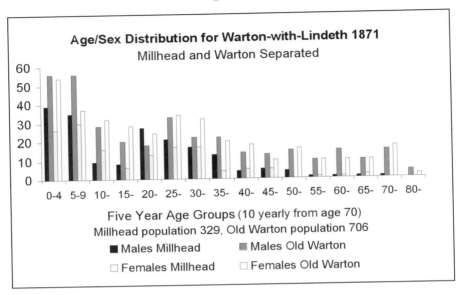

Where the Workforce Came From

The birthplace of all individuals was entered in the census returns, so that it is possible to know where household heads of the Millhead incomers came from, notwithstanding the fact some of the new workers seemed ignorant of where they were born. Some knew their birth town, but not the county. For example Willenhall appears as belonging to both Staffordshire and Shropshire (not unreasonably perhaps since it is very near the border). Some of the places are not traceable, probably because they are the names of houses or farms. In those days when a good many could not read or write it was the job of an appointed census enumerator to visit every house in his district and himself fill in the record.[12] The fact that the enumerator would write down what he thought he had heard and that he would be quite likely to misunderstand unknown names given in strange dialects must have added to the confusion. Only three ironworkers on William Street and Albert Street were from nearby – Bolton-le-Sands, Skerton, and Hornby – the others came from far and wide. Two came from the Isle of Man, three from Ireland, five from Wales, and seventeen from the West Midlands, that is to say from around the Dudley-Bilston-Wednesbury area. These are the figures for householders, but in the 52 houses built in Millhead there were also twenty-three lodgers. If these are taken into account ten more men are recorded as coming from this same West Midlands area. More exactly, they had all been born there which is all the census shows. It does not reveal if they had lived elsewhere before coming to Millhead. When the birthplace of the wives is examined the situation is not a great deal different.

Figure 3.3

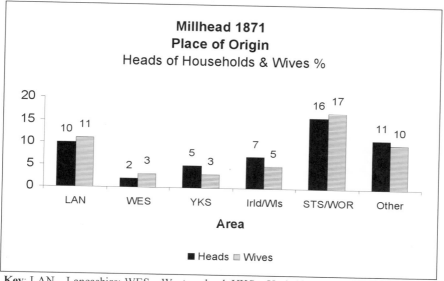

Key: LAN – Lancashire; WES – Westmorland, YKS – Yorkshire; Irld – Ireland; Wls – Wales; STS – Staffordshire; WOR – Worcestershire.

Perhaps more about how families reached Warton township and their new homes in Millhead can be told from the birthplaces of the children. The 1871 census shows that in 19 of the 52 households, at least one child had been born in the West Midlands and only children aged three or under were born in Warton, indicating that these families had come into the area in 1868 or later. It is known that people usually migrated in a step-like fashion, in this case usually from one ironworks/coalfield area to another. By studying the birthplaces of the older children of these families it is possible to trace, in a fair way, the various routes taken by the parents.

Some, like William Ainsworth, Abraham Bettany, and Benjamin Evans, had been born in the West Midlands themselves, their older children were also born there, but the youngest were born in Warton. Thomas Paterson, a 36 year old iron furnace labourer, was born in

County Down and had two children born in the Potteries before coming to Millhead.

William Iniff, a 36-year-old iron furnace labourer, was born in Rochdale, and had a child born in Workington before he came here. Samuel Lunn, also 31, a steelmaker, was born in Bradford and had children born in Oldham and Manchester before his last two were born in Warton. Joseph Wacke, an iron works labourer of 32, was born in Hastings, Northamptonshire, and had come to Millhead via Goldgreen in Staffordshire. Some of the lodgers were married men, sometimes relatives of the householder, but their children, if any, were not present. The lodgers were probably waiting for more housing to be built before moving their own families to the area.

It is remarkable that so few young men born in Warton parish were given employment at the Iron Works. Joseph Bridget, the 17-year-old son of a quarrymaster, and John Newby, a 31-year-old farmer's son, were both taken on, but as clerks. John Atkinson, the 19-year-old son of a carter, was the only man born in Warton taken on as a labourer.

Obviously the managers preferred men with ironworks experience. Undoubtedly much of this migration of ironworkers was of experienced men moving from a declining iron works, belonging to the Earl of Derby at Dudley in Staffordshire, to a promising new works at Carnforth. There were so many from that area that Millhead was often called Dudley (and is actually so named on the 1893 Ordnance Survey map). Tradition has it that many of the labourers walked from Dudley. Although they were skilled workers, railway fares for themselves and their families would have been a heavy item. It is possible that their new employers were anxious to recruit experienced workmen and made special arrangements for them and then for their wives and children.

This picture of migrating workers, with their families following, presents an interesting point. The so-called Act of Settlement, passed at the end of the seventeenth century, was still enforceable even though it had been modified a little. Its original aim had been to exonerate parishes from responsibility for relief of incomers who fell on hard times, empowering them to return such people forcibly to the parish they came from. They might even demand from an outsider some proof of likely ability to support himself before allowing him to settle at all. It seems that either the incomers had somehow obtained sponsorship from their new employers, or that the local Poor Law Guardians were confident that there was enough work available to make it unlikely a young, healthy ironworker would be a drain on the rates. The same must have been happening in other areas where new industries were attracting incomers.

Jon Raven, who has done many years of research into the lives of industrial workers in the West Midlands, and who founded a museum in the Dudley area, was contacted to ascertain whether any recruitment drive was known to have taken place to account for the large number of workers from the Dudley area who came to Millhead. He replied:

> *'at the time ... 1868-71, the Dudley iron mines would have been very much in decline, I believe, as were some of the coal mines. The district was investing its labour and skills in the up and coming engineering industry and many workers were re-training to this end. No doubt the failure of industry in this area was known to those opening the Carnforth Iron Works, and I imagine an agent was sent down to attract people ...'*

Millhead in 1871

The Millhead houses were in some ways state of the art. They had a cold water tap inside the house, a primitive sink in the kitchen, a bricked-in set boiler for washing and an iron fireplace in the living room with an oven on one side and a boiler to heat the water on the other. With a bright fender and fire irons and the application of black leading they must often have looked very pleasing. Those who could afford it could still further liven up the place with brass hanging or table lamps. The houses were however neither spacious nor well ventilated; both William Street and Albert Street consisted of a continuous row of terrace houses, each house with a living room, two bedrooms, a small box room and a cupboard under the stairs. The front doors opened straight onto the street; the back door out into an alley.

Later reports from the sanitary authorities show that the overused privies were often in a foul state of dirt and neglect. What with the size of family and the number of lodgers the majority must have lived in very

55

close proximity. The average household size was 6.3 people (which was large even for the period), the average for the whole parish being 5 per household in 1871. The resulting pressures probably help account for many of the outbursts of violence, which were reported in the newspapers. The population was also a very young one, which may have made violence more likely. The average age of the household head in Millhead was 33.3 years (and of the working population as a whole 29.8 years). The percentage of the Albert Street and William Street population under the age of 20 was 54%. By comparison in the 1991 census 22% of the population of Warton Ward were 20 or under, and in Carnforth Ward 27%.[13]

A sample study of just one street in 1871, William Street, illustrates many aspects of life in Millhead. There were 37 houses occupied on the day of the census, and in these lived 210 people. Of these, 105 were children under 15, and 21 were registered as boarders or lodgers.

At No. 30 lived Benjamin and Catherine Evans, an iron furnace labourer and his wife, both in their twenties, with three daughters aged five, three and one, all from Wednesfield in Staffordshire. In the same house there were five male lodgers, two of whom might have been Benjamin's brothers or cousins as they were also called Evans, only one of whom was not from the Wednesfield area.

No 53 was shared by two families: David and Elizabeth Child, a couple in their early fifties, living with the Slaters, with a young family of two. Perhaps the older couple were the younger couple's in-laws for Elizabeth Child was from the West Midlands, as were the Slaters. Some families in William Street had a house to themselves. Joseph Simpson, a stonemason, and his wife and two infant daughters lived by themselves, as did James Sayle, another stonemason, with his wife and two baby sons.

The Ironworkers after 1871

Those living in the houses were almost all ironworkers in the sense that they worked at the Carnforth Iron Works, but the census shows that there were considerable status differences between the ironworkers according to exactly what they did at work. The different jobs were carefully distinguished in the census returns; pig lifters, blast furnace keepers, steel blowers and boiler-smiths were not to be confused with iron works' labourers who formed the largest single occupational division.

The Iron Works and railways, and the need for new housing had stimulated much secondary employment. Amongst the newly arrived men in Millhead, not directly employed at the Iron Works, were brick makers, plasterers, joiners, key and lock makers, wallers, plumbers and painters.

The only young people for whom there was apparently no work were the unmarried young women. In the census for William Street we find not one girl between 15 and 20. Where were they - out to service elsewhere - back in the West Midlands? Older teenage boys however could find employment as labourers at the Iron Works; there are many examples in the census; the youngest, from William Street, was 14.

Working conditions were hard at the Iron Works. There were also frequent accidents and these, unfortunately, were not confined to the early days, but continued throughout the life of the Iron Works. One of the most horrific occurred in 1891 when John Hodgson lost control of his barrow which dragged him into the furnace. In the absence of any recognisable remains to be buried the Rev. J.A. Fidler held the funeral service beside the furnace.[14]

As happened in other places, the sudden arrival of these numerous newcomers to a rural parish, concentrating together in Millhead in an industrial colony, almost inevitably produced friction. There were incidents coming to court indicating that alcohol was something of a problem amongst the ironworkers. The West View hotel was handy.

In 1870 a newspaper reported that William Darby, charger at the Iron Works, was accused of beating his wife because he wanted money for drink. She had saved him by her testimony from imminent imprisonment and he was only reprimanded and cautioned.[15] This was not an isolated case. Among other incidents there was, in 1881, a general fracas between the English and Irish pig-lifters.[16] However, other reports cast the workers in a better light.

Despite all this drunkenness the Temperance movement took hold. A Carnforth Iron Works Temperance Lifeboat Crew had its first annual general meeting in 1868[17] (the organisation had been founded in 1861 and its colourful name had been chosen to express its aim of rescuing those in danger of ship-wrecking their lives through drink).

In 1869 there was a newspaper account of the laying of three foundation stones for the new Carnforth Methodist Chapel. Mr. Barton gave £5, and the workmen a £7 gift, showing, as one speaker at the ceremony put it, that instead of workers being *'rabble'* as *'natives'* had imagined, many were *'warm-hearted Christians'* who had been some of the first to suggest the project.[18] The founding of their own Primitive Methodist Chapel in Millhead in 1873 was pretty solid evidence of sincere Methodism among the ironworkers.

The Growth and Decline of the Iron Works

In 1870 a newspaper article commented on Carnforth's increasing prosperity. It reported the town was very busy and all the furnaces at the Iron Works were in full blast. The foundations of a steel works on the site had already been laid. There were high hopes of responding to world demand for steel plates and rails. It was thought that this should provide employment for 200-300 additional men. There seemed every reason for optimism.[19] An advertisement in 1871 showed the trend of growth in Carnforth continuing and said that cottages there *'were in great demand, producing large rents'*.[20]

Yet at this time, Britain was entering into an era of tougher competition; there was some lowering of prices for products and talk of capital flowing abroad. Pig iron prices dropped in 1876-7. This would be bad news for Carnforth Iron Works. To judge from contemporary newspaper reports, the iron-making in the Carnforth area was subject to short-term ups and downs.[21] In the seventies iron ore was having to be imported in increasing amounts from Spain to augment Furness supplies. The *Lancaster Guardian* reported that the Thornborough had landed at Morecambe 800 tons of iron ore from Bilbao as the first of eight consignments over the next few years.[22] There were reports also of ships landing ore from Spain at Glasson Dock.

The Steelworks

In 1876 despite, or perhaps because of these troubles, the Haematite Iron Company embarked on the building of a steelworks.[23] By June 1878 the steelworks were thought to be within three or four months of completion.[24] This was over optimistic. In September 1881 the steel plant was still not in operation.[25] Even the ever optimistic Mr. H.J. Walduck admitted, in a letter to the *Lancaster Gazette,* that £330,000 had been spent on erecting the Bessemer steelworks, which had never been put into operation so that pig iron had been sent to Sheffield to be made into steel. Nevertheless he claimed to find the position *'encouraging'.*[26] At any rate the first half of 1884 was full of plans for reviving the steelworks, but it was not until February 1885 that the steelworks were reported to have begun work though *'not on a very extensive scale'.* However the same newspaper article went on to say that that in a few days the steelworks would be *'going on day and night, necessitating the employment of an augmented number of hands'.*[27]

Only eighteen months later, in the summer of 1886 the Carnforth steelworks was in *'regression',* and the men said to be working irregularly.[28] The steel making was on a sufficient scale to be bedevilled by complaints to the Rural Sanitary Authority about smoke pollution.

Mr. W.S. Bolden, a gentleman of means who lived near-by in the Hynings in Warton, complained of the dark brown smoke from the steelworks. A farmer, Mr. Thwaites, agreed, saying that *'corn stacks on a field two miles away were black'.* In October 1885 formal notice was issued to the company to abate the nuisance within 21 days.[29] When the steelworks were visited by the surveyor in November he found that attempts had been made to comply; two *'Green's economizers and smoke preventers'* had been fixed in the flue leading to the chimney and an air bridge in the boilers.[30] Despite these measures complaints continued to be made about this nuisance while the works lasted.

Then, in October 1886, there were rumours that the steelworks would close shortly[31], which proved true and in January 1887 it was reported that there was no immediate prospect of the steelworks re-opening. Any later hope of reviving the steelworks had to be abandoned. In 1889 the permanent closure of the steel works was confirmed. It had, said a newspaper report, employed 300 men and because of its closure forty houses now stood empty.[32] In 1898 the whole of the Carnforth Bessemer plant was sold off.[33] It may be relevant that Carnforth works had originally had the advantage that the local iron ore was low in phosphorus that allowed easier conversion to steel. New technology made it possible to use contaminated ore and Carnforth lost its advantage.

The Iron Works at the End of the Century

Despite the failure of the steelworks the Carnforth Haematite Iron Company continued in profitable business, though not without a struggle. In 1879 it was reported that a quantity of iron had been produced, but *'remunerative prices cannot be obtained'*.[34] Presumably the general depression was keeping demand low. A month later the company felt called upon to contradict a report of total closure; one iron furnace, it announced, remained in blast.[35] Later in the year there was a revival and another furnace was to be put in blast.[36]

It is difficult to keep track of what was happening (after all one does not expect a firm to give an always accurate report on trading conditions). Certainly work carried on and at times four or even occasionally six furnaces were reported to be in blast. In 1881 there were hopeful reports; Messrs. Galloway of Manchester were producing blowing engines for Carnforth blast furnaces; the Iron Works was showing a very satisfactory profit producing a dividend return of 10%, though apparently at a cost since fifteen months earlier the men's wages had been cut by 7.75%. The work force it seems came and went as boom and slump followed hard on each other's heels. One response of the Carnforth Iron Works in times of depression was to allow non-iron workers to occupy Iron Works housing, only to evict them when more iron workers needed to be taken on.

The ups and downs continued through the eighties not only in Carnforth but also throughout the industry. The evidence of a general depression led the government to the appointment in 1886 of a Royal Commission on the depression of trade, an investigation, which included the iron industry.[37]

Locally the Furness Railway was having bad years because of the depression in the Iron and Steel industry,[38] but as if to underline the intention of the company to forge ahead despite the difficulties, the Iron Works management decided in February 1886 to install electric light (presumably from their own generator) in the works in place of gas. It does seem as though from then on the Iron Works revived. In March 1887, as the steel works closed, another furnace was put in blast in the Iron Works, which would, it was hoped, reduce unemployment.[39] There was a particularly bad period from the end of March 1892 when the Durham miners went on strike for a period of two months. Carnforth Iron Works felt the knock-on effect and it went on slack blast and finally all three active furnaces had to be put out of blast, with many men losing their employment. Not until the end of May, when the Durham strike ended, were two furnaces put back into blast after eight weeks rest. After that things apparently settled. In 1899 Lux, a *Lancaster Guardian* correspondent wrote that the Iron Works was very prosperous, three furnaces were in full blast and it was being freely stated that never in the past had the outlook been so great. The Iron Works outlasted the century, only closing finally in 1929.

Unions and Management

The earliest account of an industrial dispute comes in 1867 and throws a good deal of light on the worker/manager divide as well as the legal system that allowed what seems unfair bias against the workers. According to the account in the *Lancaster Guardian*:

> *'Fifteen employees of the company were up before the magistrates for alleged breach of contract by leaving their employment without notice ... some of them were employed as ore fillers others as coke fillers, and the remainder as labourers. A dispute had arisen over a new method of filling a furnace. The men were told by Mr. Williams, the foreman, that they could do the work or take their money and go. The men had taken this to mean they were dismissed'.*[40]

61

All the arguments were heard, it seems, before the men came into court, since the magistrate felt the men might be tempted to alter their story to fit the arguments if they were present throughout the proceedings. When the men were brought into court four of them pleaded guilty and the others were then judged guilty too. Those who had pleaded guilty were sentenced to seven days hard labour, the others to 21 days.

There was one further case in 1875 of Smallwood v CHIC re payment on leaving employment. He claimed £3 1s 8d and won his case.[41] Nothing more has been found until the 1890s. During this time independent action by the men would not, one feels, have been welcomed. Mr. Barton, the general manager, was not a conciliatory man, though possibly a reasonably just one. After a long slump when one furnace was re-lighted and men were taken on again he is said to have *'distributed the work as fairly as possible'*.[42] He also seems to have had on occasions a rough good humour that may have helped. There is a recorded reminiscence that Barton once found a mason who was working on his house looking at a sack of potatoes in a barn. The man promptly asked what they would cost to buy. *'Take them'* was the reply, *'if you don't want them some other b --- will.*[43]

In the early 1890s there was much industrial unrest everywhere. A Carnforth branch of the Blast Furnace Men's Trades Union was formed. It does not appear that there was any active industrial action, but twenty-five men were sacked, followed by another five including the secretary and treasurer of the new local branch.[44] No reason seems to have been given, and when Mr. Barton was interviewed by a newspaper reporter he said he had no objection to men joining as many unions as they liked, but he was not going to allow union men to intimidate their fellows into joining. How far his tolerance of unions really went is another matter. The *Lancaster Guardian* implied, but did not say, that Barton knew of posters on display in the town, which bore the words *'Can Working Men form a Union?'* Legally at that date they could; their right to join unions and go on strike having been established in the early 1870s, but it remained a sore and contentious point. Joseph Kellet, the sacked secretary of the Blast Furnace Men's Union, wrote to the *Lancaster Guardian* complaining that Mr. Barton had repeatedly refused so much as to meet union representatives for any discussion at all.[45]

Millhead after 1871

What of Millhead? It continued to grow. In 1872 it was proposed that thirty-six *'concrete'* houses of *'a peculiar cement construction brought to Carnforth in piece form'* should be erected for the Carnforth Haematite Company. They were to be built by Mr. Hooper, the contractor for the Morecambe sea wall, and were to be followed by fifty more.[46] This development was proposed regardless of the poor sanitary conditions in Millhead.

A newspaper report in 1872 said that in Millhead:

'the houses are crowded together most improperly: the privies and ash pits in some cases actually join the houses, and others face the back doors at a distance of a few feet. There has not been the slightest provision for surface drainage and the impurities thrown from houses are allowed to decompose in the streets.'[47]

Between 1871 and 1881 the population of Millhead increased from 284 to 544. Four new streets of houses were created: Mary Street, Stainton Street, Jackson Terrace and Carlisle Terrace. The last two were mainly for railway personnel and were a little more salubrious, with small gardens. Millhead also acquired a model-lodging house. It is shown on the 1881 Ordnance Survey map. Model had no particular legal meaning in this context. It had come into use in the 1840s when there had been a fashion among philanthropists for building good lodging houses for the working classes, but soon the name was being applied by proprietors of any large lodging houses to their own establishments even those which were far from model.

When Millhead's lodging house was finally registered with the Sanitary Authority in 1889 it was called simply a common lodging house, that is a public lodging-house passed by the local authority as conforming to such standards as they had chosen to lay down. When the application was made the Inspector of Nuisances noted that the house *'had no drains.'*[48] In 1891 it was kept by Richard Knight, aged 51, from

Carlisle, assisted by his wife, who had been born in Yorkshire. There was one domestic servant, Amelia Wilson, born at Whitehaven, aged 15, and 22 lodgers, mostly labourers, but there was also a shoemaker, a 19-year-old engine driver, and a 37-year-old commercial agent. A number were married and two had brought their wives with them. The pattern of lodging was changing. Whereas previously, workers coming into Dudley lodged with private householders, fewer households now had lodgers and instead there was this lodging house available, such as it was.

There was also a more general change in the population of Millhead. A smaller proportion of household heads were ironworkers than in the early days; more were general labourers and a few were railwaymen. Despite the faltering state of the Iron Works Millhead had continued to be seen, for a while at any rate, as an area for profitable property development.

Between 1878 and 1890 plans for 61 buildings were passed for Warton, and building at Millhead accounted for a good deal of this increase. In 1882, there was an advertisement of *valuable building land* on Archer Hill for sale.[49] In 1887, on the contrary, it was reported that four dwelling houses at Archer Hill had been withdrawn from auction at £455, below the £550 reserve. This was possibly one of the first indications that the population explosion was at an end.

Millhead continued to provide very poor environmental conditions (but then so did many of the other townships including Carnforth); conditions which must have posed a growing threat to public health. The Inspector of Nuisances continued to make damning reports. In 1890, speaking of Jackson Terrace and Archer Hill, his report said that *'the existing privies or earth closets are very offensive and should be made into W.C.s ... The drains should also be connected into the main sewer, they now empty into a cesspool'*. Five months later the owners had still not complied with the order to construct water closets.[50]

In 1892 premises at West View were noted to be *'... without proper drains, W.C.s or Ash pits and are a nuisance.'*[51] It is certain, too, in view of the complaints about air pollution from the steel works mentioned earlier, that no-one in Millhead would have escaped the bad effects of this, probably on their health, certainly in the grime and dirt the housewife would have to contend with.

Hartley's Grocery

There was one business sited in Millhead that was undoubtedly thriving. By 1881 there had been a development along the main road to Warton in front of Albert Street, namely, Hartley's Grocery and Provision business. John Hartley had started business in Kendal and then in 1863 he had taken premises in Carnforth on an empty site previously used by the Midland Railway.

The business expanded; stores and a bakery were built at Millhead; later Hartley's opened a new shop at the crossroads in central Carnforth, though still keeping the bakery at Millhead. Hartley's was to have the first telephone in Carnforth, installed to keep the two premises in touch. The Hartley family played a prominent part in the religious and social life of the area, but their bakery seems to have been merely sited in Millhead rather than forming part of the community there. At any rate the 1891 census shows only two young men from Millhead who might have been working there, though it is not so stated – a baker and a grocer's assistant. The five apprentices living on the premises came from outside the parish.

Conclusion

The growth of the Iron Works in Carnforth and the small industrial colony in Millhead, with its own characteristics such as its own pub, own chapel, and its community of jobs, have been described in some detail because they serve to mark the moment when industrial development came to Warton parish, strongly influencing, but not overwhelming its hitherto agricultural economy. How these two sides of Warton parish came together, each influencing the other is discussed in the next chapter.

---

[1] *Lancaster Guardian*, August 24th, 1861.
[2] *Lancaster Guardian*, March 18th, 1865.
[3] *Lancaster Gazette*, May 19th, 1866.
[4] *Lancaster Gazette*, July 21st, 1866.

[5] Mannex and Company, *Topography and Directory of North and South Lonsdale, Amounderness, Leyland...* (1866), p.565

[6] *Lancaster Guardian*, February 18th, 1871.

[7] Mourholme Local History Society Book Group, *How it Was: a North Lancashire Parish in the Seventeenth Century* (Mourholme Local History Society, 1998), p.66.

[8] *Lancaster Gazette*, August 30th, 1873.

[9] *Lancaster Gazette*, January 27th, 1894.

[10] *Lancaster Gazette*, October 13th, 1866.

[11] *Lancaster Gazette*, November 14th, 1866.

[12] Edward Higgs, *Making Sense of the Census* (HMSO, 1989), p.5.

[13] Lancaster City Council, *Census of Population, 1991* (1993).

[14] *Lancaster Guardian*, October 24th, 1891.

[15] *Lancaster Guardian*, September 10th, 1870.

[16] *Lancaster Guardian*, November 19th, 1881.

[17] *Lancaster Guardian*, April 18th, 1868.

[18] *Lancaster Gazette*, July 10th, 1869.

[19] *Lancaster Gazette Supplement*, May 4th, 1870.

[20] *Lancaster Gazette*, April 1st, 1871.

[21] *Lancaster Guardian*, May 8th, 1875.

[22] *Lancaster Guardian*, July 21st, 1877.

[23] *Lancaster Guardian*, December 9th, 1876.

[24] *Lancaster Guardian*, June 1st, 1878.

[25] *Lancaster Gazette*, September 3rd, 1881.

[26] *Lancaster Gazette*, September 17th, 1881.

[27] *Lancaster Guardian*, February 14th, 1885.

[28] *Lancaster Guardian*, August 28th, 1886.

[29] *Lancaster Guardian*, October 3rd, 1885.

[30] *Lancaster Guardian*, November 28th, 1885.

[31] *Lancaster Guardian*, October 30th, 1886.

[32] *Lancaster Guardian*, September 7th, 1889.

[33] *Lancaster Guardian*, April 2nd, 1898.

[34] *Lancaster Guardian*, February 15th, 1879.

[35] *Lancaster Guardian*, March 8th, 1879.

[36] *Lancaster Gazette*, September 3rd, 1879

[37] *Lancaster Guardian*, May 1st, 1886.

[38] *Lancaster Guardian*, February 21st, 1885; February 20th, 1886.

[39] *Lancaster Guardian*, March 12th, 1887.

[40] *Lancaster Guardian,* March 9th, 1867

[41] *Lancaster Guardian,* May 8th, 1875.

[42] Jean Chatterley, "Millhead, Mr. Edward D. Barton", part 6a; *The Mourholme Magazine of Local History,* no.1 (1995), p.27.

[43] *Lancaster Guardian,* November 29th, 1890.

[44] *Lancaster Guardian,* December 20th, 1890.

[45] *Lancaster Guardian,* December 20th, 1890

[46] *Lancaster Guardian,* March 2nd, 1872.

[47] *Lancaster Guardian,* December 14th, 1872.

[48] Reports of Inspector of Nuisances, 1889-1894, Lancashire Record Office, RDLa/12/2, 6.7.89.

[49] *Lancaster Gazette,* November 15th, 1882.

[50] Reports of Inspector of Nuisances, 1889-1894, Lancashire Record Office, RDLa/12/2, 27.9.90; 14.2.91

[51] Reports of Inspector of Nuisances, 1889-1894, Lancashire Record Office, RDLa/12/2, 13.2.92.

Chapter Four

TOWN AND COUNTRY

It is sometimes said that from 1870 to 1914 Britain went through a second industrial revolution, the beginnings of which could be traced back to the opening of the first railway in the 1830s and their rapid spread from then on. By the 1840s the railway had reached this hitherto rural parish. The effect of its coming in transforming one of its villages, Carnforth, into a town was recounted in the chapter two.

Inevitably the rest of the parish was affected also. Until then it had been almost entirely agricultural with only a few traditional industries, and it had centred on the township of Warton, itself no more than the largest of the seven townships in the parish. In Warton township there had been the parish church, the grammar school, four inns, a few small shops and a handful of craftsmen. For any more complicated financial or commercial matters the parishioners were dependent on Lancaster and Kendal. The development of Carnforth changed this pattern even though the other townships appeared to remain unchanged and agricultural.

Population Changes

The decennial census returns from 1841 to 1901 are shown overleaf first in tabular form and then, to bring out more clearly the differential growth of the villages, in chart form.

The main lesson from the data is that whilst the parish population increased by a factor of just over 2.7, much of this occurred after the 1861 census and in the townships of Warton-with-Lindeth and of Carnforth. A similar proportional increase occurred in Silverdale, although the actual populations were much smaller. Warton township slipped from its place as the largest in the parish. Prior to the 1861 census its population had been roughly twice that of Carnforth, a feature that had been more than reversed. The switch in the relative size of the two townships took place even though the majority of the workers at the Carnforth Iron Works, whose coming had such a profound influence on the growth of Carnforth, happened to be housed in the township of Warton, in the new little settlement called Millhead.

Table 4.1

	1841	1851	1861	1871	1881	1891	1901
Borwick	214	199	194	209	246	281	174
Carnforth	306	294	393	1091	1879	2680	3040
Priest Hutton	254	234	218	185	213	242	172
Silverdale	252	240	294	343	489	589	582
Warton with Lindeth	633	600	581	1035	1471	1384	1492
Yealands combined	550	532	481	527	519	526	458
Totals	2209	2099	2161	3390	4817	5702	5918

Population of townships of Warton Parish 1841-1901
(from the published census figures)

Figure 4.1

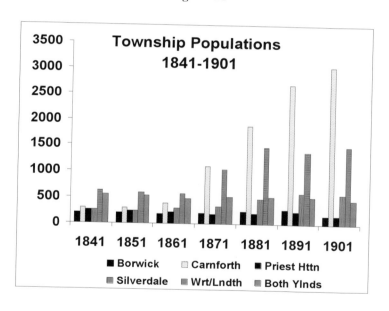

Note: The populations of Yealand Conyers and Yealand Redmayne have been combined as the population of these townships remained, though for different reasons, nearly static throughout the period.

Moving In and Moving Out

It is clear from the previous section that although the parish population more than doubled over the period 1841-1901, the rural townships – Borwick, Priest Hutton, Yealand Conyers and Yealand Redmayne – showed overall a marginal decrease in their populations. The large increases occurred in the townships of Carnforth and Warton-with- Lindeth, with a similar proportional increase to a much smaller population in Silverdale. Warton and Carnforth prior to 1870 had been mainly agricultural communities with a few traditional industries, but the development of the railways in the 1840s and the establishment of the Iron Works in the 1860s transformed the parish into one where industrial and commercial activities moved the population centre towards Carnforth. Minor local perturbations in migration into the townships were caused by one-off occurrences, such as the routing through the parish in 1881 of the pipeline bringing water from Thirlmere to Manchester.

The census returns in the nineteenth century record the place of birth for each individual. Using the term incomer to denote any resident who was not born in the township of residence, it can be seen that in 1871 in Carnforth incomers outnumbered the native born by more that three to one, clearly an indication of the new work available in the township.

Furthermore although incomers generally outnumbered the native born throughout the parish (albeit not to the same extent as in Carnforth in 1871), a clearer picture emerges if a distinction is made between local migrants – i.e. those born in the neighbouring counties of Westmorland, Cumberland and Yorkshire, as well as in other parts and townships of Lancashire – and migrants from wider afield. For example in 1851 over 90% of all incomers were local, one explanation for which may be the practice of taking in farm workers at the annual Whitsun and Michaelmas Hiring Fairs. At the next hiring the farm worker may find employment in a different village and have to move himself and perhaps his family. In May 1867 at the time of the Whitsun Hiring Fair, the Headmaster of Yealand Friends' School noted changing their residence as an accepted reason for a number of absences from school.

Yealand Conyers was a village populated by families requiring domestic servants of all types. It was not the done thing to employ local girls, resulting in an inflated number of non-local migrants in this relatively small township.

Carnforth attracted a considerable number of migrants from towns in Lancashire – Preston, Liverpool, Barrow and Ulverston for example. Others came from further away, with Staffordshire, Scotland and Derbyshire heading the list. Staffordshire in particular lost workers from the Midlands iron industry, whilst Derbyshire contributed mainly railway workers.

Turning now to emigrants, the picture is not so clear, largely because information from the census returns is more difficult to collate, with, at present, only the 1881 census in complete conveniently readable form. Moreover in 1881 there is no clear evidence of movement out of the parish to a particular region of the country or abroad.

It seems therefore that the population of the parish was not only growing, but it was changing as people moved in and out. The picture of an older countryside in which families lived in the same village generation after generation has long been shown to be largely a myth, though family names do persist in Warton parish as they do elsewhere. There were Bainbridges, Bisbrownes, Hodgsons and Nicholsons in Warton in the seventeenth century just as there were in the nineteenth.

The Town

Contemporary local opinion was undoubtedly impressed by Carnforth's growth and increasing prosperity. In 1864 an article in the *Lancaster Guardian*, having spoken of general prosperity in North Lancashire, turned to Carnforth, '*which is just entering upon a similar career of progress and prosperity*'.[1]

In 1870 the paper was still lauding the prosperity of the town.[2] The railway and the Iron Works were primarily responsible for the growth of Carnforth, but the influx of workers to man these industries brought in so many tradesmen, shopkeepers and others to take advantage of the new opportunities that soon they outnumbered the iron and railway workers. This was the sort of process, typical of the Victorian era, being replicated in West Cumbria, South Wales, West Yorkshire and North East England.

Occupations in Carnforth

The census records of occupation of household heads laid out in table 4.2 illustrate what was taking place in what might be called Carnforth/Millhead (for it seems to make the best sense to include Millhead, where the ironworkers lived, with Carnforth where they worked). The different fortunes of the Iron Works and the railway are demonstrated.

At the opening of the second half of the nineteenth century the railwaymen had been few in number, a mere eight in all, and there were no ironworkers yet. In 1871, 23% of the household heads were working on the railway. By 1881 the percentage had risen to 29%. The actual numbers employed on the railway continued to rise, but by 1891 Carnforth had grown so that the percentage remained virtually the same at 28%.

The percentage of ironworkers, on the contrary, which had been slightly larger than that of the railwaymen in 1871, had, by 1881, fallen below that of the railway men (even though the actual number of ironworkers was still increasing). By 1891 the percentage of ironworkers had halved, reflecting the difficulties Carnforth's iron industry had been facing.

Table 4.2

	H'holders	Ironworks	Railway	Agri.	Other
1871	273	69 (25.3%)	63 (23.1%)	36 (13.2%)	105 (38.4%)
1881	469	105 (22.4%)	138 (29.4%)	34 (7.3%)	192 (40.9%)
1891	638	70 (11.0%)	181 (28.4%)	28 (4.4%)	359 (56.2%)

Occupational Groups of Householders in Carnforth/Millhead
1871, 1881, 1891

Carnforth may have become a town, but agriculture was not completely ousted as an occupation there. Up until 1881 the number of household heads working in agriculture remained almost static, but that meant that, since the total population of Carnforth was increasing so rapidly, agricultural work in percentage terms almost halved, falling from 13.2% to 7.3% and then to 4.4% by 1891.

Meanwhile those in other occupations (that is all occupations other than the Iron Works, the railways and agriculture) showed a steady rise both in percentage and in actual number, indicating the growing presence of those attracted to the opportunities offered by a new town. These others included a number living on what was uninformatively called their own means. But most were employed in a wide range of the occupations necessary to support a growing town – people to build it, like joiners, masons, bricklayers, plumbers and labourers; people to service all the new households like gas workers, coal agents, postal workers, shopkeepers, dressmakers, chemists, doctors, hairdressers, innkeepers, teachers, solicitors – the list grew as the town grew.

Carnforth as a Postal Centre

Perhaps the two developments in Carnforth which had the most effect on the rest of the parish, were the cattle market and the expanding postal services. Both were made possible by the coming of the railways. The growth and importance of the cattle market has already been considered in the opening chapter on agriculture.

These same extensive rail connections also meant that Carnforth became the collection and delivery point not only for the rest of the parish but for a very wide area beyond. The postal services seem to have worked very well, though they would never be to everyone's satisfaction. There were inevitably complaints voiced in the newspapers; the Sunday morning collection at the Post Offices in Warton and Yealand were too early; there should be an evening collection instead[3] and other such minor complaints.

Carnforth Central Post Office

The service was enhanced when, in 1887, Carnforth obtained its new Post Office building opposite the station on the Warton Road (the old office which had been down at platform level was converted into the London & North Western Railway's stationmaster's office). A newspaper article described what was planned for the new building. It would be staffed by 20 men and would be three storeys high; the lowest floor would be the sorting area with direct access to the station platform; the next floor was to be on the level of the main road with access for the public for post office transactions. The telegraph department would also be housed on this floor. The postmaster's office was to be on the third floor. The building was to have two mess-rooms. A fire extinguisher and buckets were to be available. There was also to be a resident caretaker.[4]

Carnforth Post Office offered, as far as can be judged, an efficient postal service. Letters, it was said, arrived at 7.22a.m. (one admires the implied precision of train timing) and were dispatched by 6p.m. to 8p.m. The number of house deliveries in the town had risen from two to three a day by 1889.[5]

The Post Office also offered a wide range of ancillary services as can be seen from trade directories. As far back as 1866, before ever it moved into the new building, it was being described as also a Money Order Office and a Post Office Savings Bank. From 1870 all telegraph systems had been taken out of private hands to be managed thenceforward by the General Post Office. In 1881 Carnforth Post Office is recorded as having its own telegraph system,[6] but there seems to have been some sort of system much earlier. In 1854 James Erving of Carnforth wrote in his note book that:

> 'Telegraph wires are being laid in trenches 18 Inch deep
> in wood on the road side for which they pay the men for
> cutting and filling 7_d p^{er} rood, did not answer so pulled
> out the wires'.[7]

Nothing more is said, but at least the Post Office seems to have been more efficient. By 1889 telegrams were so much appreciated that the post office in Carnforth was allowing them to be sent on a Sunday (though only between 8 and 10 a.m.;[8] hours chosen presumably so that no Sabbatarian could complain that the Telegraph service was infringing on Divine service).

The Village Sub-Post Offices

Carnforth was the head office for a number of subsidiary offices in the other townships. Again it is possible to trace this expanding postal service through trade directories of the period, which regularly published considerable detail of their services. Some, but not all, of the other townships in the parish came to possess a post office of their own. They were, as far as one can make out, usually run as a sideline in a village shop or in a corner of someone's house. In 1866 there were post offices at Silverdale (run by Elizabeth Rawlinson, grocer) and at Yealand Conyers (run by Joseph Storey). Not till 1886 was there mention of a post office in Warton township (run by George Tatham, who was also parish clerk, assistant overseer and tax collector). By 1896 there were post offices in Borwick (James Cook) and Priest Hutton (W. Dawson). Only Yealand Redmayne never had its own post office and right to the end of the century the directories simply say of it, letters delivered from Carnforth. The service from these village offices was apparently good; letters arrived at least by eight in the morning, and did not need to be posted in the evening till well after five. The details of how the letters were then sent on from the village post offices for house delivery is not clear.

Telegraph offices were rarer; Silverdale had one by 1885 and Yealand Conyers at least by the next year. Telegraph wires customarily ran along the railway and it might be interesting to know by what route they reached across to these two post offices. The only information so far found is from Carnforth. None of the other townships acquired a telegraph office, not even Warton, the biggest settlement after Carnforth. A 1901 directory said uncompromisingly of Warton '*Carnforth is the nearest Telegraph Office*'.[9]

Tradesmen, Shopkeepers, Insurance Agents etc.

Advertisements in the newspapers and trade directories confirm the rapid growth in Carnforth of small business enterprises – builders, painters, decorators, plumbers and so on. These small businesses were sometimes on a fair scale and were offering services beyond the immediate bounds of Carnforth.

John Rigg & Son, a building firm based in Carnforth, advertised that they were prepared to supply '*limestone heads, sills, steps, kerbing etc. of any size, either dressed or in the rough*'.[10] By 1896 Rigg's had diversified further. An advertisement described the firm as '*Builders, Undertakers, Contractors ... Dealers in Every Description of Building Material*' and offered the services of '*A Public Saw Mill*'.[11]

Around 1890 the barn-like building that is still on North Road opposite the present Church of England school was built. It was a small factory, employing seven or eight men making wooden doorknobs.[12] In 1896 J. Walmsley & Son '*of Carnforth and Arnside*' advertised themselves as '*Plumbers, Glaziers, Painters, House Decorators And*

Paperhangers'. They also had the *'latest sanitary appliances. Pumps and W.C.s'* which they promised to fit neatly.[13]

Retail shops were increasing in number and showing the same tendency to expand beyond what was required for Carnforth alone. In 1851 Mannex's directory only listed one shopkeeper, one tailor and one shoemaker in Carnforth.[14] In 1890 a directory was listing five boot makers, five butchers, a cycle dealer, two chemists and druggists, five coal merchants, two clothiers, five drapers, a glass and china dealer, a fancy goods shop, a fried fish shop, five grocers, two ironmongers, two jewellers, a newsagent's, six shopkeepers (unspecified), also a stationers, a tailor, a tobacconist, a hairdresser and an upholsterer & house furnisher.[15]

It was also noticeable that Carnforth was beginning to acquire shops that were approaching the status of department stores – not on the scale of the London shops such as Whiteley's, Harrod's and Selfridge's, but still definitely multiple stores. By the 1880s Carnforth had Stephenson Bros., at 17 Market Street, calling itself *'linen and woollen drapers, milliners, tailors, hatters, shoe-dealers etc.'*[16] and J. Hartley & Co. *'tea and coffee dealers, family grocers, Italian Warehousemen, provision and feeding stuff merchants, bread and biscuit bakers, confectioners etc.'*.

The Co-operative Society
The major example of this trend was the Carnforth Co-operative Society. In 1876 the Lancaster & Skerton Co-operative Society bought three shops in Carnforth, but in 1881 Carnforth branch members expressed dissatisfaction at the prices imposed on them by the parent Society.[17] However it was not until 1885 that action was taken, and Carnforth set up its own Society independent of Lancaster. By the end of that year it had a membership of over 200 and was able to announce a dividend of 2s 9d in the pound.[18] By 1887 the Society was in a position to build new premises on land acquired in New Street, these were duly opened on 14th July 1888.[19] The architect was Robert Walker of Windermere. The complex consisted of a public hall with a gallery, ante-rooms, offices and a boardroom, stable, a cart-house, a three-storey warehouse and three large shops; one for grocery, provisions and confectionery; one for drapery; and one for boots and shoes. Two

staircases led up to a magnificent hall, which extended over all the shops and was capable of seating 500-600 (the largest in town), which was to be available for hire for such affairs as public meetings, balls, concerts, whist drives and the like. In addition a steep spiral staircase led up to the Co-op. reading room with armchairs and a warm fire.[20]

In 1894 the *Lancaster Guardian* gave an account of the opening (with celebratory tea-party) of further extensions, including a double-fronted draper's shop *'with fitting room, retiring room, lavatories etc.'*. Also a confectioner's shop and a bakery *'with all modern appliances'*, the wall of which was of white glazed brick so that everything could be kept *'clean as a new pin'*.[21] When it was opened the building was described as a very substantial solid pile *'displaying a good deal of artistic treatment in the result'*. Membership had by then risen to 842.

Thus came into being the massive block which can be seen at the top of New Street. It still has the wide arched doorway that led to the great hall, but the whole block is now somewhat shorn of its artistic glory by time and grime and changes in fashion. By the end of the century the society felt strong enough to branch out into the villages and built shops in both Silverdale and Warton.

Other Businesses
All this business activity in and around Carnforth inevitably led to a spread of advertising. Carnforth acquired its own newspaper, the *Carnforth Weekly News,* which was printed by Mr. Dugdale at the Excelsior Press in Market St. In 1887 it sold for 1d. Other forms of advertising were used. There was a Carnforth and District Bill-posting Company at 30 Market St. The proprietor, J. Weeks, claimed that he did 2,000 billpostings on hoardings weekly. Advertisements for Carnforth establishments were still moderate, merely setting forth what the business had to offer, but what of the 1895 advertisement for a Lancaster firm?

> *'Important to Householders. In this age of Progress you cannot afford to lag behind ... you will find that the Lancaster Furnishing Co. keep pace with the times ....'*[22]

The consumer society looming?

Booming development required financing. Of course some of the money came from the ever-increasing rates to fund the necessary public services, but various private financial institutions were appearing.

A branch of the Lancaster Banking Co. was established in Carnforth before the eighteen eighties.[23] The bank went from strength to strength, finally deciding to erect new premises (complete with a branch manager's house) on a site on New Scotland Road.[24] By the end of the century there was also a branch of the Bank of Liverpool.[25]

Building Societies were being established to finance all the new building needed for homes and commerce; accounts of their meetings crop up repeatedly in the newspapers. The Lancaster and District Mutual Benefit Building Society was established in 1861; it was offering 1000 shares at 1s each in 1866.[26] The Carnforth and District Permanent Benefit Building Society was established in 1866. The Furness & South Cumberland Building Society was holding its annual general meeting in Carnforth in 1872.[27] The big Assurance Societies – Scottish Life Assurance and Prudential Assurance both found it worthwhile to have agents in Carnforth.[28] Presumably these financial facilities would have profited not only those living in Carnforth but also both agriculture and industry in the rest of the parish.

It was unfortunate that increasing business was accompanied by many prosecutions for various trading offences (though whether the increase was more than in proportion to the number of businesses is not known).

People used faulty weights, or peddled knick-knacks without a licence, and innkeepers diluted spirits. But then for centuries tradesmen had done these things. One recorded case was possibly rather different. Robert Taylor, manager of the Co-operative store, was charged '*with selling castor oil pills not up to standard*'.[29] The Victorian age was one notorious for the widespread adulteration of food, drink and medicines. New legislation was brought in, but as has been said, '*The ingenuity of those involved in adulteration outstripped the ability of the authorities to check the process ....*'.[30]

The Public Utilities

The growth of Carnforth inevitably threw a strain on the infra-structures (or lack of them), which had more or less sufficed for a small village. Carnforth responded by creating a more modern system for itself, but the rest of the parish (apart from parts of Warton) did not benefit, but remained in the era of privies and rainwater tanks until well into the twentieth century.

In Carnforth a crisis had arisen in the 1870s. It was not so much water to drink or even for washing that was lacking; that need could probably have been met for a while longer, as in the other villages by more efficient collection of rainwater. Two factors, over and above the rise in population, made change necessary. The first was an increasing preference for water closets in place of privies. Water closets needed not only sewers (which had been provided), but also an adequate water supply to flush the sewers. The other factor was an increased industrial demand for water.

In 1876 the two factors came together. The Rural Sanitary Authority was forced to admit, in the words of one of its members, that there was undoubtedly 'a stench' in Carnforth.[31] Then the formidable Mr. Edward Barton, the manager of the Iron Works, came on to the scene. It was a common belief that Mr. Barton was so active in supplying Carnforth with water simply because he wanted a good supply of water on reasonable terms for his Iron Works.[32] However that may be, he overrode the sanitary authority which was just beginning to take action and saw to it that a private company, the Carnforth Water Company, was set up. With great speed the company built a reservoir at Pedder Potts, just east of Over Kellet (it still exists as a fishing lake, though it no longer supplies water). The Carnforth & District Water Company flourished. At the A.G.M. in 1881, with Mr. Barton in the chair, a 3% dividend was declared.[33] At the A.G.M. in 1883 (Mr. Barton still in the chair) the dividend was 6% and in 1885 it was 5%. The company was able (more or less) to supply Carnforth with the water it needed, until the twentieth century.

Another utility had come earlier, when Carnforth acquired its gasworks. The first portion of the mains for new gasworks at Carnforth was laid in 1871.[35] The gasworks were sited alongside the canal basin.

Mr. Edward Barton (who else?) was director, along with Mr. James Erving, of Thwaitegate (who also had his finger in most pies in Carnforth).

Mr. Henry Orr became secretary. He had been the Carnforth Schoolmaster until he was sacked as insufficiently qualified for the post, when he was given this comfortable berth instead. (Mr. Orr also became clerk of the water company. One cannot help noticing how often the personnel of the gas and water companies were identical.)

By the beginning of March 1872 the Carnforth Gas Company had already made its first coal gas and could announce that it would soon be in a position to supply the public.[34] Unfortunately a week later there was an explosion in the houses built by the Haematite Company near Keer Bridge, one house being almost completely wrecked.[35] There were only minor casualties fortunately. It seems that gas had begun to leak from the new pipes and spread along the space under the floorboards until it reached a house where a fire happened to be alight. Nevertheless work went ahead.

At the fourth general meeting the business of the Carnforth Gas Co. Ltd., was reported to be flourishing.[36] At the tenth A.G.M., a handsome 10%

dividend was declared.[37] In 1882 the dividend still stood at 10% and a price reduction from 5s to 4s 6d per 1,000 cubic foot was declared. In October 1884 the principal streets of Carnforth had gas lamps, which were to be switched on at 6p.m. and off at 10.30p.m., by a lamplighter. On the first evening when he performed this duty, he was followed by a crowd of youngsters shouting as each lamp was lit.[38]

Presumably the coal used in the gasworks was brought by the canal. The coke could have been used locally, but it is unlikely it would have sufficed for the Iron Works; the coke supplies for that had been secured from Durham in bulk and were brought via the railway. As well as the production of coal gas other products could be obtained, such as sulphuric acid and tar, which could be further fractionated and ammonia produced. At Carnforth it seems an ammoniacal manufactory was built nearby in the same year as the gasworks.

The Country
Quarrying, Mining and Gravel Extraction
It was not only Carnforth that underwent some industrial development, though it was much less dramatic in the other townships. It took the form of greater exploitation of already known natural resources, especially the limestone which underlay most of the parish. Limestone quarrying was an old industry in the parish and had been carried on at many sites for centuries, though the high cost and difficulty of transporting so heavy a material meant that it could only be used locally. The coming of the canal had made available a much wider market and the industry began to thrive as never before, supplying the construction industry, iron making, road making, and agriculture. The canal had always been highly dependent for its profits on carrying limestone. At Wegber, on the edge of Priest Hutton, the canal passed through limestone, and the quarry that was developed there supplied the boats with limestone to carry south in return for coal which could be brought back as a return load, and before ever the railways came had offered employment in Borwick and Priest Hutton.[39]

The railways were not specifically designed to tap limestone resources, but it was natural to see whether they passed close enough to limestone to make its carriage profitable enough to allow them to compete with the canal. The Wennington and Skipton line from

Carnforth, opened in 1867, crossed the canal very close to Wegber Quarry. Borwick station seems to have been used to carry limestone, but the story is that it was the Martons of Capernwray Hall who were instrumental in obtaining a station at Borwick. They wanted it to transport their livestock, especially racehorses.

There was a small quarry at Millhead, owned by Joseph Jackson Esq., who entered himself in the 1871 census as an employer of 29 men (to whom, we happen to know, he gave a works dinner in that year).[40] His work must have been enhanced by the opening of the Iron Works, but larger supplies were needed to satisfy the heavy demand for limestone both at the Iron Works and in the area generally. A quarry at Scout Scar, on the road between Warton and Silverdale, was opened up and connected to the Iron Works by its own tramway.

It was along the Furness line that there were most possibilities for quarrying however. The line crossed the Westmorland border, skirting the limestone outcrop of Middlebarrow Hill north of Silverdale. The possibilities from tapping these large sources of limestone were obvious. Limestone had probably been quarried there for local use in lime burning and for building-stone long before the railway arrived, but the railway allowed it to expand enormously. A plan dated 1898 shows sidings from the railway into the quarry area. Even larger scale development took place in the twentieth century.[41] The near-by Trowbarrow Quarry was opened in a craggy ridge that lay 600 metres east of the railway at Redbridge. The distance from the Furness line made it necessary to construct a tramway up the slope to the ridge. Towards the end of the century the quarry was in the ownership of Northern Quarries Ltd. Under the enterprising management of James Ward it processed the lime in kilns at the side of the railway. Limestone could also be tarred to produce tarmacadam for the making of roads, a growing industry at the time. At the Silverdale quarry Ward made his own version, which he called quarrite. He seems to have been ahead of his time in realising the importance of quality control in producing the correct size-range of stone and the correct quality of tar coating.[42]

A quarry for a specialised purpose was opened near Jenny Brown's Point in Silverdale, when work was started in the late 1870s on an embankment to be built out into the sands as part of a huge reclamation scheme. Although the proximity of the limestone to the sands was a positive feature, the inclination of the strata at the quarry face must have made the stone hazardous to work. In fact the reclamation scheme was abandoned, but some of the large blocks extracted to build the embankment have stood the test of time and have survived in the sands.

Gravel Extraction

Quarrying left a mark on the landscape, which can still be seen today, but it is less obvious how important an industry gravel extraction was. According to an 1881 directory, *'Immense quantities of gravel raised from pits in the neighbourhood are sent hence* [from Carnforth] *by rail and canal to various parts of the country'*.[43]

The gravel pits, as it happens, all lay in or near Carnforth where the main south/north railway line from Preston to Carlisle passed through the gravel deposits that lay along the course of the river Keer. The business of extracting gravel thrived. Concrete was being increasingly used and this gravel made good aggregate. Its transport gave opportunities for both the railway and the canal. The Carnforth Gravel and Building Sand Company also seems to have diversified, for in 1877 it was advertising best quality paving stone, road material, and coal, to be supplied by rail to any station, or to any wharf on the Lancaster/Preston canal at the shortest notice and on reasonable terms.[44]

Mining

There had always been those hopeful of finding profitable sources of metal in the parish, but they had always been disappointed.[45] The iron deposits were there, but the ore was both limited in quantity and of very poor quality, mainly an inferior iron oxide only suitable for making ruddle.

All earlier attempts over the centuries to make the mines profitable had failed.[46] In the late nineteenth century there was a brief revival of interest. In 1880 the Warton and Silverdale Mining Co. Ltd. advertised for a clerk to take charge of the books, and for a timekeeper; applications were to be sent to Boddington and Bell of Manchester.[47] However, things appear to have gone wrong since, very shortly after, in February 1881, there appeared an advertisement concerning a sale at

Crag Foot Mine - to satisfy distress imposed for imperial taxes (whatever that meant). There was to be an auction of plant, machinery, bar and hoop iron, weighing machines, tram rails, grindstone, pump, gear-rods, iron pipes and blasting powder.[48] The sale was then cancelled and some small-scale mining continued.[49] The iron ore was of too poor a quality to be worth smelting, but it had a sale as paint (the mine was known locally as the paint mine). The ore was sent to Silverdale station and then, among other destinations, to Williamsons of Lancaster who used it to dye red linoleum.[50] H.J. Walduck, an entrepreneur if there ever was one, was involved in the mine as he was in so many local enterprises. He died in 1892, which may have had something to do with the closure of the paint mine soon after. The Warton Mining and Colour Co. Ltd. went into liquidation in 1894 and there was an auction of the leasehold for producing oxide of iron.[51]

The Work Force

It has proved difficult to find how many men the quarries, gravel pits and the small mines employed, largely because the job descriptions in the census returns are too vague. Such evidence as there is suggests that by the end of the century they were noticeable, but not large scale, employers of labour and that considerably more men continued to be employed in agriculture, though the proportion differed from township to township.

Most of the employers of quarry workers lived in Borwick. The 1861 census shows there was a quarrymaster living there who employed 28 men and 3 boys (presumably at Wegber), though only 10 of these quarrymen have been identified in Borwick. By 1891 the number had risen to 13. Silverdale with its two large quarries is another obvious place to look for quarrymen. In 1861 only 1 man was describing himself as a quarryman, in 1871 there were 5 and in 1881 10 (and 2 limekiln labourers who may have been working at Trowbarrow or Middlebarrow). In 1891 there were 12.

In the whole parish in 1891 46 men are specifically said to be working in the quarries (13 in Borwick, 12 in Silverdale, 11 in Warton, 8 in Yealand Redmayne, 2 in Carnforth). Some men entered as general labourers may have worked in quarries at a less skilled level, but there is no way of knowing. It is even harder, in fact impossible, to tell from the census returns how many men were working in the gravel pits. They are never mentioned by name, though presumably a number of men entered simply as labourers worked there.

Mining made no contribution to employment until the end of the century, but in the 1891 census 21 men were employed in the paint mine (1 in Silverdale, 3 in Carnforth and the rest in Warton-with-Lindeth). There were also 4 men boarding in a house in Silverdale who called themselves diamond rock borers. They are unexplained.

The Rural Townships

None of the other townships grew as Carnforth did, but though they remained small they were not completely overwhelmed by Carnforth, but kept some life of their own. Warton-with-Lindeth more than doubled its population between 1851 and 1901, but almost all the increase, as has been said, arose from the housing of ironworkers from Carnforth, in Millhead. That had been a chance matter and Millhead, though included in the township, never quite seemed part of it, but kept a separate identity.

The older Warton was still a farming area with a score of active farms within its bounds, though it had also begun to house a certain number of urban workers, railway men and employees of the Iron Works. It kept its own small shops, (some of them were very small scale indeed), its own craftsmen, its own scattering of professionals. A directory for 1896 lists four grocers and a grocer & draper, a shopkeeper, a tailor & draper, a butcher, a boot maker, a beer retailer and two coal dealers, but Warton township was no longer the centre of the parish as it had been for so many centuries. It hardly developed an industry of its own. There were the paint mines, but they only operated for a few years. One of the traditional crafts did, right at the end of the century, develop into a fairly large-scale business. A Mr. Graveson had started up business, at the Black Bull, using heavy working horses to haul wood. First would come the snigging out, that is hauling out enough of the smaller trees to allow the heavy wagons to get into the wood. The timber was carted away to saw mills elsewhere until Graveson established his own sawmill at Millhead in 1893. Graveson's story however mainly belongs to the twentieth century.

Hartley, the Carnforth grocer, set up his bakery in Warton, but that seems to have been a matter of chance and not really part of Warton's own development.

Silverdale, the next largest township to Warton (though less than half its size), also had, according to the trade directories, a good number of shops – in 1896 two grocers, a butcher, two boot makers and a newsagent.[52] It had three joiners and a blacksmith but otherwise no evidence of village craftsmen, perhaps because Silverdale's craft was cockling and somehow no one ever admitted, either in a directory or in the census, that that was what they did. Agriculture and

fishing remained the predominant occupations (it was apparently acceptable to call oneself a fisherman and in the 1891 census seven men did so). It is not always possible to see why some men called themselves farmers and some fishermen, since it is known that many families combined the two, doing a little of each as season and profits dictated. It has seemed more reasonable to give a combined figure for the two. In 1851 this stood at 53.7% of all household heads. In 1861 the figure was 51.6% and in 1871 it was 52.7%.

Silverdale had a steep rise in population in the seventies and eighties, after the opening of a railway station there. By 1891 the township was changing and offered a picture of a rather different sort of place with only 22.2% of heads of households recorded as employed in fishing or farming, and quarrying 4.4%.

It is known that cockling remained an important source of income, though it is not mentioned as an occupation. As a matter of passing interest, there was a report in the eighties of what might have been a major development in Silverdale. A Mr. West demonstrated a cockle-gathering machine on Silverdale sands, claiming that 30-40 bags a day could be collected in place of the usual two collected by a cram, or bent rake, in the time-honoured way. It was suggested this could affect the jobs of 300-400 men, women and children working in the Morecambe bay area[53]. This ' *much dreaded* ' improved cockling machine (manufactured by Ransome and Son) made its appearance in 1887,[54] but either it did not make the impact expected, or the cockling community froze it out, for no more was heard of it.

For the rest, no one single occupation seems to have taken the place of farming and fishing. What is clear is that Silverdale was becoming a haven for tourists, the retired and business people who preferred living in a pretty village now that a train service made it possible.

Tourists themselves do not feature in the census returns, as the returns were usually taken too early in the year, and moreover a good many of the visitors seem to have been day trippers taking advantage of the offered excursions described in the earlier chapter on transport. Four women are listed as keeping lodging houses.

An 1899 directory confirms that it was *'a very popular district in the season with excursionists'*. It adds that though the station is one and a half miles from the village *'Busses meet all trains for the convenience of those who wish to ride'*[55] – perhaps run by the Robert Shaw who is listed in the same directory as *'cab proprietor and lodging house keeper'*.

The other townships, Borwick, Priest Hutton and the two Yealands failed to increase their population at all, but they did manage to retain some local life. All of them had a shop where groceries could have been bought and some had a butcher as well. All had a boot maker and all except Yealand Conyers had a blacksmith; any more extensive shopping would have meant a visit to Carnforth – not all that easy in the days before buses and cars, which was presumably why the small grocers and shopkeepers survived.

Borwick, Priest Hutton and Yealand Redmayne remained largely dependent on agriculture despite the work offered by the limestone quarries, and so would be vulnerable to that flight from the countryside which was beginning seriously to exercise people's minds.

Yealand Conyers, as always, was slightly different. Certainly it developed no industry or trade, but its economy, more than in any of the other villages, was dependent on the wealth brought in by those who, having made their money elsewhere, were able to settle in a pleasing country village. They, and the domestic servants, gardeners, grooms etc. needed to maintain their style of living, made up most of the population. They contrived to

MORECAMBE LODGE,

keep the village exclusive. There is an unkind story that even after World War 2, when housing was badly needed, certain inhabitants of Yealand Conyers saw to it that the council estate was sited in Redmayne.

Conclusion, the State of the Parish

In the seventies and eighties, when the nation as a whole was struggling with a lasting depression, was the parish on the up and up economically, or static, or slipping down hill? The possibility of an agricultural depression in the parish was discussed in a previous chapter. The conclusion was that there probably had been some depression, but that it had been less noticeable than in some parts of the kingdom. Because of special features it had in common with other parts of the northwest, agriculture was better able to diversify, turning from arable to pasture.

Is it possible to say whether industrial development did or did not go into recession? The question primarily applies to Carnforth, but since Carnforth had become a new centre for the parish what happened there was bound to affect the rest. Equally Carnforth was going to be influenced by the wider conditions in the northwest. Did Carnforth, as has been said of the country in general, experience '*a spectacular 20 year deflation*',[56] or can the postulated Great Depression of the last quarter of the nineteenth century be dismissed as a '*myth*'?[57] Since the issue is everywhere unresolved it is unlikely to be answered by a study of a small area such as is being dealt with here, but at least some effort can be made to draw a picture of the industrial scene.

The buoyant feeling about Carnforth's future in the early 1870s set out above perhaps began to seem illusory in the next years. Hard figures are difficult to come by. In the nineteenth century unemployment figures were not available and the rate of applicants for poor law aid was about as close as can be got to them. Even these figures tend to be suspect as too inadequately collected to be a reliable basis for judgement.

In February 1870 there was a report in the *Lancaster Gazette* of an increasing number of paupers in the Lancaster Union,[58] but in May the *Lancaster Guardian* was saying this was misleading and did not correspond to a '*revival in trade*'.[59] In 1879 there was a further report showing a continued increase in pauperism and in vagrancy.[60] This chimes in with a small piece of news from Carnforth itself. A tea party was held in the National School, which raised £30 2s 3d for relief of the poor. Twenty-six cases had been relieved and the committee was making enquiries in the village also.[61]

Carnforth's prosperity was inevitably particularly closely linked to the national state of the iron industry, and in 1886 even the local press was reporting that it was, in general, going through a depression.[62] The difficulties and vicissitudes of the Carnforth Iron Works and its subsidiary steel works were described in the preceding chapter.

There were instances of failures in other types of business. In 1877 Edward Crosland of Yealand Conyers, the lime works manager, was made bankrupt under the Bankruptcy Act 1867.[63] In 1886 James George Pye, bill poster and game dealer, of Edward Street, Carnforth, came before the Deputy Registrar of Bankruptcy in Preston, having unsecured debts of £100 13s 4d. He had begun by borrowing £7 10s 0d from the Sheriff's Officer who had charged excessive interest.[64] Extreme usury seems to have been common (though one would hardly expect it from an officer of the law). To find if these failures were becoming more frequent would require further investigation. Even at the best of times individual businesses come to grief.

Yet the Iron Works survived and even flourished, and somehow the general impression is that Carnforth as a whole continued to flourish. The population continued to increase, even though not quite as fast as in previous years; money was being found for new retail stores and public buildings, the gas works and the water company were able to pay their investors a large interest.

In the rest of the parish quarrying was increasing. Above all the railway continued to grow and the cattle market to flourish, supported as it was by the solid backing of the still profitable agriculture in the parish. Perhaps one can say, as with agriculture, that there had been enough diversification in industry to tide Carnforth over some bad times.

---

[1] *Lancaster Guardian*, March 19th, 1864.

[2] *Lancaster Guardian*, May 21st 1870.

[3] *Lancaster Gazette*, April 7th, 1883.

[4] *Lancaster Guardian*, February 12th, 1887.

[5] Wells, *Lancaster District Directory* (Wells & Co., 1889).

[6] Mannex & Co. *Topography and Directory of Lancaster and Six Miles Round* (1881).

[7] James Erving of Thwaite Gate, Carnforth: notebook with memoranda on international news and local and family events in Carnforth and Rochdale 1838-73, Lancashire Record Office, DP494/1 acc 9158.

[8] Wells, *Lancaster & District Directory*.

[9] W.J. Cook, *Lancaster and Morecambe District Directory* (1901).

[10] *Lancaster Gazette*, January 23rd, 1883.

[11] W.J. Cook, *Lancaster, Morecambe and District Directory* (1896), p.248.

[12] Marion Russell, *How Carnforth Grew. A Simple Outline to 1900 AD.* (Carnforth Bookshop, 1997), pp.64-65.

[13] W.J. Cook, *Lancaster, Morecambe and District Directory*, (1896), p.266.

[14] Mannex and Co, *History, Topography and Directory of Westmorland and the Hundreds of Lonsdale and Amounderness in Lancashire* (1851).

[15] Wells, *Lancaster District Directory*.

[16] P. Mannex & Co. *Topography and Directory of Lancaster and Sixteen Miles Round* (1881) p.247.

[17] *Lancaster Guardian*, November 5th, 1881.

[18] *Lancaster Guardian*, January 16th, 1886.

[19] *Lancaster Guardian*, July 21st, 1888.

[20] *Lancaster Guardian*, July 21st, 1888.

[21] *Lancaster Guardian*, March 17th, 1894.

[22] *Lancaster Guardian*, October 12th, 1895.

[23] Mannex & Co. *Topography and Directory of Lancaster and Sixteen Miles Round* (1881).

[24] *Lancaster Guardian*, March 17th, 1888.

[25] W.J. Cook, *Lancaster and Morecambe District Directory* (1901).

[26] *Lancaster Gazette*, January 20th, 1866.

[27] *Lancaster Gazette*, February 17th 1872.

[28] Watson & Co., *History, Topography, General and Commercial Directory Lancaster and Morecambe* (1899), p.252.

[29] *Lancaster Gazette*, March 5th & March 19th, 1879.

[30] Anthony S, Wohl. *Endangered Lives; Public Health in Victorian Britain* (Methuen, 1984), p.52.

[31] *Lancaster Guardian*, April 8th, 1876.

[32] Joan Clarke, "Pedder Potts and Mr. Barton", *The Mourholme Magazine of Local History*, no.2 (1996), pp.16-23.

[33] *Lancaster Gazette*, February 16th, 1881.

[34] *Lancaster Gazette*, March 2nd, 1872.

[35] *Lancaster Guardian*, March 9th, 1872.

[36] *Lancaster Guardian*, July 24th, 1875.

[37] *Lancaster Gazette*, July 30th, 1881.

[38] *Lancaster Gazette*, October 15th, 1884.

[39] Mourholme Local History Society Book Group, *Warton 1800 -1850: How a North Lancashire Parish Changed* (Mourholme Local History Society, 2005), pp.82, 83, 98.

[40] *Lancaster Guardian*, January 28th, 1871.

[41] Kevin Heywood, "End of an Era for Middlebarrow Quarry," *Keer to Kent, Journal of the Arnside/Silverdale AONB Landscape Trust*, no 45, (Summer, 2001), p.9.

[42] Anonymous, "James Ward – Pioneer of Tarmacadam ," *Keer to Kent, Journal of the Arnside/Silverdale AONB Landscape Trust*, no 40, (Autumn/Winter, 1999), p.15.

[43] Mannex & Co. *Topography and Directory of Lancaster and Six Miles Round* (1881), p.245.

[44] *Lancaster Guardian*, March 3rd, 1877.

[45] Mourholme Local History Society Book Group, *How it Was: a North Lancashire Parish in the Seventeenth Century* (Mourholme Local History Society, 1998), p.144; Mourholme Local History Society Book Group, *Warton 1800 – 1850: How a North Lancashire Parish Changed* (Mourholme Local History Society, 2005) pp.81-82.

[46] Robert Ashmead & David Peter, "Warton Crag Mines" *The Mourholme Magazine of Local History*, no.1 (1983), pp.5-9; no.2 (1983), pp.5-8.

[47] *Lancaster Gazette*, March 6th, 1880.

[48] *Lancaster Gazette*, February 19th, 1881.

[49] *Lancaster Gazette*, February 23rd, 1881.

[50] Robert Ashmead & David Peter, "Warton Crag Mines" *The*

Mourholme Magazine of Local History, no.1 (1983), p.8.

[51] *Lancaster Guardian*, January 20th, 1894, p.8.

[52] W.J. Cook, *Lancaster, Morecambe and District Directory* (1896), p.265.

[53] *Lancaster Gazette*, October 20th, 1886.

[54] *Lancaster Guardian*, September 17th, 1887.

[55] Watson & Co. *History. Topography, General and Commercial Directory Lancaster & Morecambe* (1899).

[56] E.J. Hobsbawm, *Industry and Empire* (Penguin, 1968), pp.127-8.

[57] S.B. Saul, *The Myth of the Great Depression 1873-1895, Studies in Economic and Social History* (Macmillan, 1968), pp.54-5.

[58] *Lancaster Gazette*, February 23rd, 1870.

[59] *Lancaster Guardian*, May 7th, 1870.

[60] *Lancaster Gazette*, November 19th, 1879.

[61] *Lancaster Guardian*, January 11th, 1879.

[62] *Lancaster Gazette*, February 17th, 1886.

[63] *Lancaster Guardian*, July 14th, 1877.

[64] *Lancaster Gazette*, April 17th, 1886.

Chapter Five

REFORM AND PARTY POLITICS

Part I
Parliamentary Elections
    The reader may wonder how much politics had to do with life in seven small northern villages, especially as at the opening of the second half of the nineteenth century, the majority of the inhabitants of Warton parish would have had no vote.

    The 1832 Reform Act had only given the parliamentary vote to about 18% of the adult (male) population.[1] Yet in Warton, as in the rest of the country, this restriction had led to a natural interest in further political reform.

    Another political issue of great interest to any rural parish had just been settled, when Sir Robert Peel repealed the Corn Laws, in 1846. Until then British agriculture had been protected by a system of Corn Laws, from competition from foreign imports. Industrialists and their work force complained that the system kept the price of staple foods like bread unnaturally high; those dependent on agriculture said that abolishing the Corn Law system would be their ruin. The controversy had been bitter, and for a while after 1846 farmers were despondent about their future. In fact, as explained in the opening chapter of this book, their fears proved unfounded.

    Then there were, as ever, the troubles in Ireland. The potato famine of 1845-6 had brought crowds of not very welcome starving Irish workers to Lancashire. Ireland, after the terrible devastation of the famine, was beginning to unite again in its demand for freedom from English rule. The Irish Republican Brotherhood (the formal, but less well known name for the Fenian Movement) was founded in the late 1850s. It deliberately advocated the use of violence as a necessary means of achieving its aim of an independent Ireland. The rising trouble exacerbated England's long-standing dislike and fear of Catholics. Almost no overt evidence of anti-Catholic or anti-Irish feeling in Warton parish has been found, probably because Catholicism was known in the unthreatening form of the long established community centred on

Leighton Hall, rather than as something brought in by newcomers. Though people of Irish extraction are found in the census returns there was never a flood of Irish labour into the parish.

Upsurge in Demands for Electoral Reform

The pattern of parliamentary representation that had been created by the great 1832 Reform Act, continued into the second half of the century, but agitation for further reform had been building up from the moment the Act was passed, and continued throughout the fifties and sixties. Such radical advocates of manhood suffrage as the Chartists had seen this first Reform Act as a sell-out, leading to no more than *'repressive policies towards trade unions and the poor, and apparent indifference to working class grievances'.*[2]

There was also a demand for reform from those far less radical than the Chartists. Country areas in the north, like Warton parish, had a special grievance. The distribution of seats and the great inequality of population size between constituencies had not been adequately dealt with by the 1832 Act. It has been reckoned that the counties had only half as many seats as the boroughs despite having a population some 3 million larger.[3] The demand for reform, taken against this background of unrest, meant that both political parties had to consider further parliamentary reform.

It was the Conservatives, under the Earl of Derby (though largely influenced by Disraeli) who brought in the second Reform Act in 1867. It was more extensive than perhaps had been intended, virtually doubling the number of working class votes (which meant that those votes could determine the outcome in many towns).

In these urban boroughs all adult male owners or occupiers of dwellings became eligible, whatever the value of the property (previously the property needed to be worth at least £10 a year). Lodgers were now also given the vote (though a financial limit was kept for them; the lodgings they occupied had to be worth at least £10 a year). Both types of voter had to prove twelve months continuous residence, which did tend to limit the potential number of working class voters because of their less settled life style. The changes were less sweeping in the county seats. A property qualification, fixed at a value of £5 a year, was retained for both owners of property and long-lease holders. Unlike urban voters, county voters did not have to be resident to be eligible for a vote; it was enough if they could show that they owned or leased suitable property; a proviso which led to much difficulty in settling who could vote where.

The electorate rose from about 1.1 million to 2 million; one in three of the adult male population was empowered to vote, in place of the one in five empowered by the 1832 Reform Act. There was, however, a difference between urban dwellers and county dwellers. The borough electorate increased by 134% after 1867, the county electorate by only 46%, with the result that a smaller proportion of the male population had the vote in the country than in the towns. There was, however, some increase in the number of county members, thus going some way towards rectifying the imbalance between urban and rural representation. Lancashire received three extra county seats. North Lonsdale, in which Warton parish voted, remained with two members, both being held to represent the whole constituency, so that voters were allowed to cast two votes.

In 1872 a Ballot Act was passed that established secret voting in both parliamentary and municipal elections. It was a major step forward in freeing voters from intimidation by employers and landlords. No direct evidence has been found of such intimidation in Warton parish, but open tactics had hardly needed to be used; the wisdom of not publicly voting against the wishes of one's landlord would be obvious.

Bribery on a large scale certainly was occurring locally. In the 1865 general election corruption was so flagrant in Lancaster that the borough was actually disenfranchised for a time, that is to say the voters there could no longer vote for a member of their own.[4] The Lancaster Society of Friends felt obliged to set up its own enquiry. Evidence of malpractice in the Society was minimal, but the investigators were shocked to discover what had been happening in the constituency and reported that:

'For a long time past it has been the custom for country freemen to receive small gratuities nominally in compensation for loss of time and expenses incurred.

These payments have gradually increased in amount until their reception ... clearly amounts to bribery.[5]

In 1884 there was further electoral reform, passed, this time, by the Liberals under Gladstone. This Act put an end to the differences between urban and county voters. The male household franchise already allowed in the boroughs in 1867 was now to apply everywhere. A property qualification for lodgers still remained, but otherwise the act established at least a household franchise. It was a long way even from manhood suffrage (and still further from including women), but it did allow a large increase in the number of men able to vote.

One early twentieth century historian wrote of the change it brought to rural areas, saying of its results that *'the new fact in English life was the enfranchisement of the field labourer'*.[6]

North Lonsdale

A year later, in 1885, the Redistribution of Seats Act was passed. It was an attempt at last to deal with the inequalities arising from the great difference in size of parliamentary constituencies. It did not quite create constituencies of equal size, but it did move in that direction. Lancashire's seats rose to 58 from the previous 28.[7]

In North Lonsdale both parties were on the alert to see what the Revision of Seats would entail locally. There was a meeting of the Conservatives at the Station Hotel, Carnforth, to consider the proposals for this North Lancashire division (which in those days included a good deal of what is now in Cumbria, including all the Furness peninsula from Ulverston down to Grange-over-Sands).[8] Some local suspicion seems to have been aroused that the new arrangements would shift the political, and therefore the business, centre of the area from Carnforth to Ulverston. It was agreed that a deputation be sent to the Commissioners deploring this proposed change.[9] Subsequently there was another public meeting on the same subject, presumably sponsored by the Liberals since a resolution was sent to the Prime Minister to say the electors were '*totally satisfied with the policy of the government*'.[10] Nothing has so far been found to suggest that either communication made any difference.

These parliamentary reforms had apparently little effect on people's voting patterns. Lonsdale continued consistently to return Conservative candidates. In 1874 the successful candidates were Frederick Arthur Stanley, second son of the Earl of Derby (who was still being returned in 1880) and John Wilson Patten. The latter was a Conservative of a reforming frame of mind and sat for the constituency from 1868 until he was raised to the peerage as Baron Winmarleigh in 1878. In the subsequent by-election another Conservative candidate, Thomas Henry Clifton, was voted in. He was subsequently made Secretary of State for War in Disraeli's government, and died in 1880 at the early age of 35. There was nothing unusual in North Lonsdale's repeated Conservative vote.

Apart from Liverpool and the towns in the cotton heartland, all Lancashire followed the same pattern for decades; it was everywhere found, as John K. Walton observed in his history of Lancashire, that '*The Liberals occasionally won parliamentary elections, though almost always for local reasons of a temporary nature ...*'.[11] In part this may have been due to improper bribery and intimidation, or as Walton put it, '*... the leading landed families continued to divide the spoils in the county elections*'.[12] Walton's own conclusion is, however, that '*There seems no way of explaining away the Tory victories except in terms of a solid base in working class support*'.[13] He was writing of the urban voters, but a conservative attachment to tradition was probably even more deeply entrenched in the countryside.

Local Political Activity

The immense increase in the numbers of those with power to vote altered the political scene radically. In 1879 Gladstone went on tour and made a series of rousing speeches in his Midlothian constituency. He even addressed the crowds from the window of a railway carriage. The Queen was said to have been shocked. Yet Gladstone was only responding to a general change in attitude. With the new, enlarged electorate, parties could no longer be managed from the old, aristocratic and monied coteries.

> '... *local Associations ... gave to the humbler members of the party up and down the provinces more control over the policy of the chiefs.*'[14]

In North Lonsdale both political parties took part in this trend, showing great and increasing interest in local opinion. Some flavour of it can be picked up from the local newspapers. The *Lancaster Gazette* and the *Lancaster Guardian* both faithfully reported, sometimes at great length, the local activities of the parties. The *Gazette* was the organ of conservatism, while the *Guardian* was in favour of the Liberals.[15] Reporting by both papers could, naturally, be sometimes more taken up with local wrangles than with major issues.

An article in the *Gazette* in 1863 consisted almost entirely of hints of a party ruse (the details of which are very obscure to-day), on the part of the Liberals. On the whole, however, one is impressed by the length and detail of the political articles that readers of the two papers were prepared to accept. There were long accounts of Parliamentary debates and local speeches. For instance, in April, 1880, in the run up to a general election, the speech that Thomas Storey, the Liberal candidate, made in the yard of the Station Hotel, Carnforth,[16] and a meeting of the Conservatives also held in Carnforth,[17] both attracted one to two columns each. In the small dense print of newspapers of the time, without breaks, headlines or illustrations, even one column meant a good deal of concentrated reading.

Revision Courts

Revision Courts, set up to monitor the validity of claims to a vote, were an important feature in local politics. Before universal manhood suffrage simplified matters, the legal entitlement to vote was very complicated and one way to reduce an opponent's chances was to contend that his potential supporters were not legally entitled to vote at all. There is an example of one such court held in 1884 at Carnforth to consider the polling districts of Carnforth and Yealand. Conservatives had made 35 objections, of which 27 were sustained,[18] '*radicals*' (the name the Conservative *Gazette* used for their Liberal opponents) had made 22 objections, of which six were sustained. The courts were still meeting in 1894; one was held at the Station Hotel, Carnforth to consider lists for Lindeth, Silverdale, Yealand, Over Kellet, Borwick, Priest Hutton, Nether Kellet, and Carnforth.[19]

Political Clubs

As local political organisation increased, both parties felt the need for their own premises. In May 1886 a branch of the Primrose League had been established in Carnforth. The Tories had founded the League in 1883, two years after Disraeli died, to honour his memory. Now Carnforth could enjoy all the rather self-conscious rituals of League meetings in what they liked to call a habitation (which in Carnforth's case was a hired room decorated with primroses, trailing ivy and a portrait of Disraeli). The members were dames and knights and associates.[20] All the same, judging by newspaper reports, the League seems to have done solid work in promoting the Conservative cause and supporting its candidates. By 1887 the Conservative party was looking forward to having its own accommodation in Carnforth. In June 1886 the *Gazette* carried an article

Disraeli

about a planned building, which the Conservatives hoped would be a focus for people from '*a wide area*'.[21] By May 1887 '*work in connection with the erection of the new building*' had begun.[22] It was very much a local enterprise; the stonework was by Thomas Pool of Carnforth, the joiner was W. Wilson of Warton, the plumbing by J. Walmsley of Carnforth; only J. Cross of Morecambe who did the slating and plastering came from very slightly further away. The club formed part of the handsome new stretch of building opposite the station, which also housed the new post office. The buildings are still there towering above the station yard (though by error bearing the date 1873), the Post Office is now closed to the public, though operating as a sorting office, and the Conservative Club is still in existence.

In 1887, the Liberals were in the process of opening their club in a building at the top of Stanley Street, an enterprise begun in direct response, it would seem, to the opening of the Conservative Club. At the Annual Meeting of the Working Men's Institute in Carnforth the members heard that patronage and funding had fallen since the Conservative Club had opened (the connection between the two events is merely stated, not explained). The Mechanics' Institute, it was felt, could not continue and it was hoped to strike a deal

... Building and Conservative Club

with the Liberal Association.[23] At the next meeting, two weeks later, it was announced that the Liberal Association was taking over the Institute *'with all its habitations'*. The financial agreement would leave the Institute with £20 in hand. It was agreed that the proceeds were to be distributed *'discreetly'* to persons in reduced circumstances.[24] By August the Liberal Club had been formally opened.[25] In September it was reported that there were already 150 members.[26] At the time of the first A.G.M. the club had a flourishing balance sheet.[27]

Co-operative Hall Carnforth

Politics in the Final Years of the Century

Local political interest continued unabated. In the 1885 election Conservatives had still triumphed in North Lonsdale,[28] but in the 1892 general election there came a change and a Liberal candidate was returned. There was a great celebration held in the Co-operative Hall in Carnforth.[29]

The problem of Home Rule for Ireland was, however, splitting the Liberal party at the time. Many Liberals, faced with the prospect of severing Ireland from the United Kingdom, preferred to vote with the Conservatives as Unionists.

A week after the Liberal party's celebration there was a meeting of Unionists and Conservatives held under the presidency of Mr. Edward Barton, at his home, Warton Grange.[30] Unionists gradually merged with the Conservatives so that the Conservative Party was often spoken of, in the first quarter of the twentieth century, as the Unionist Party.

In 1894 Richard Cavendish, grandson of the Duke of Devonshire, was the Unionist candidate for North Lonsdale. He came to a meeting in Warton and, in the new style of wooing the small voters, is reported to have kicked off for Carnforth's 1st XV in a successful match against Roose.[31] In the 1895 election he won as a Unionist against a Liberal candidate, Baron Halkett,[32] but apparently himself remained a Liberal at heart, reverting to that party in 1904. He had other Liberal attitudes, which would probably not have pleased the more conservative members of the Unionist party. In 1897 he presented a petition to the House of Commons in favour of the Parliamentary Franchise (Extension to Women) Bill.[33]

Despite their repeated failures in elections (apart from the one-off win in 1895), the Liberals continued to be active in the area as can be seen from newspaper reports. A Liberal meeting at the Carnforth Market Hall, chaired by William Dodd of Silverdale, was reported in 1887.[34] In the same week there was also a meeting of the Silverdale Liberal Association, held at Thomas Bolton's, Know Hill Farm, again with William Dodd in the chair. Three weeks later the newspaper reported a meeting of the Carnforth Liberal Association at which the Irish question was to the fore. Photographs of Irish cabins, of evictions at Glenbiogh and of poverty in Kerry were shown. After discussion, a motion was carried supporting Gladstone and Home Rule. In 1894 the *Lancaster Guardian* was reporting on the North Lonsdale Liberals[35] and on the Women's Liberal Association, which had recently been founded.[36]

Part II
Local Government, the Parish

Until well into the nineteenth century local government was still much as it had been for centuries. The parish vestries collected the rates, allocated their use, and appointed such officials as were needed. Vestries had grown up somewhat haphazardly over the centuries, acquiring new powers along the way, so that their nature is difficult to summarise. Perhaps the following dictionary definition will suffice. It says that a Vestry is:

> *'an assembly or meeting of the parishioners, or a certain number of these held usually in the vestry of the parish church, for the purpose of deliberating or legislating upon the affairs of the parish ...'.*[37]

The definition draws attention to three relevant points; the vestry was not primarily an agent of central government; the parish was a geographical as well as an ecclesiastical entity; a vestry was not necessarily a democratic body, for while it was a meeting *'of the parishioners'* it need not be a meeting of all of them. Occasionally it was so (in the so-called open vestries), more usually it was only *'a certain number of these'*, (usually, as in Warton parish, those who were not only parishioners, but ratepayers too).

New Local Authorities

Gradually over the nineteenth century this age old tradition was broken up. The first serious breach had been made with the passing of the Poor Law Amendment Act of 1834. Parishes, which had until then all been independent of each other, were brought together in larger Unions, for the purpose of administering the Poor Law. Warton parish became part of a Lancaster Rural Union, which included some score of townships both north and south of Lancaster.

A central Poor Law Commission in London had also been created, with certain (very limited) powers of control. Then in 1848 a far-reaching Public Health Act had set up a central General Board of Health and enabled the setting up of local boards to control all sanitary matters in the parishes grouped under it. However, it was only where the death rate rose above a certain figure that central government had the power to insist on the creation of a board. Warton parish, lying as it did in a relatively healthy rural area, was able to keep sanitary matters under the control of its own vestry.

The Public Health Act of 1871 was a different matter. It was mandatory and required the setting up of Sanitary Authorities, in such a manner that every part of the country was incorporated into either a Rural or an Urban Sanitary District. These new districts incorporated the old parishes, and provided them with a single authority administering sanitary law.

The Lancaster Rural Sanitary Authority was established in 1872. Since it covered the same area as the Poor Law Union, Warton parish became part of it. Even after this, much of the vestry system remained, in the sense that vestries still appointed their own officials to the Unions and they still collected the rates, though in certain matters new and ever increasing central demands might constrict their freedom of setting and spending these. There was no real gain in democratic representation as a result of the setting up of the new Unions. The members were elected by the parish vestries and could be no more representative of the general body of parishioners than the vestries were.

Vestry and Township

Some idea of the range of work undertaken by vestries can be obtained through the reports of township meetings in the local newspapers. Township meetings were a northern development from vestry meetings. Historically northern parishes had tended to be large, as Warton itself was, and had often become divided, for convenience, into smaller townships (such as the seven townships or villages which made up Warton parish). These townships had taken over many of the functions of the parish vestry. It had come to be accepted that the inhabitants of a township (or at any rate those who paid rates there) had the right to be summoned each year as a township meeting with the power to set rates, impose local taxes, make local by-laws and to act as a convenient means of communicating with the wider authorities. They served also as a local forum in which township inhabitants could express their concerns on both local matters and on those which had to be referred to higher authorities. Representatives appointed to, say, the Board of Guardians would take from these meetings concerns and instructions for consideration at the board meeting. The newspaper reports show well-attended township meetings. An account of some township and vestry meetings in 1887 and 1888 is given below. The selection may serve to illustrate the wide range of tasks, which fell to township and parish. The two years chosen come late in the century, but will serve to illustrate the nineteenth century system at any time before the Local Government Act of 1894.

1887. A Lindeth township meeting was held in Silverdale National School in March. The surveyor's accounts were presented.[38]

At the annual Carnforth township meeting, held in the schoolroom, ratepayers' accounts were presented; the poor rates for the two half years were reported to have been 4d and 6d in the pound. Overseers were appointed; Mr. S. Wrightson was nominated for churchwarden to represent the interests of Carnforth people[39] (the nomination was formally accepted at the annual Vestry Meeting at Warton).[40]

1888. Warton held its township meeting in the vestry, with the vicar of Warton, Rev. T.H. Pain, in the chair. The surveyor's accounts were presented and officers elected.

At the Silverdale township meeting, chaired by the vicar of Silverdale, Rev. J.L. Pain, Mr. Dodd was re-appointed as their representative on the Lancaster Board of Guardians. Mr. Dodd took the opportunity to complain about the unequal share rural districts had to contribute to the poor under the Union Chargeability Act.

At a Carnforth meeting Mr. Barton urged everyone to watch out over the new Local Government Bill (the forerunner of the 1894 Act that set up District Councils). It was a matter close to his heart and at a Board of Guardians meeting that year he was already suggesting that Carnforth might choose to separate itself from the Lancaster Rural District; not yet actually mentioning the possibility of it becoming an Urban District Council, but saying:

'it was not impossible that Carnforth would seek to form itself into a Board of Health District or into a new and separate sanitary centre'.[41]

In Warton there was a large attendance at a Special Vestry Meeting. The Local Government Bill was discussed. It was proposed *'that the parish of Warton, including the township of Carnforth, be constituted as a Local Government District'*. It might be interesting to speculate what the situation would be today if Warton and Carnforth had united. However, Mr. Barton immediately opposed this subordination of Carnforth to Warton, and said that Carnforth had not yet *'taken steps'* to decide its own future and until it did, nothing could be done. In general, inter-township feeling seems to have been running high. According to the newspaper report *'considerable annoyance was evinced by the ratepayers from Lindeth, at the conduct of the meeting'.*[42] This was all preliminary skirmishing before Carnforth finally went its way in 1894 and became an Urban District.[43]

The County Council

It was not until towards the end of the century that the reforming spirit, which had brought a measure of democracy to the political scene, led to a radical alteration of the vestry system.

The Local Government Act of 1888, which set up County Councils, can be seen as a milestone in the evolution of elected local government, though in practice it was surprising how little it affected affairs at the parish level. The Lancashire County Council in effect took over the supervisory functions hitherto exercised by the county magistrates. The members of the council, unlike the magistrates, were elected, though of course at this date by householders only. The personnel, perhaps because of this restricted franchise, changed little. In the optimistic words of the *Lancaster Guardian*, *'throughout the country the best of the magistrates have offered themselves as elected representatives and many have been elected'.*[44]

Lancashire produced a body of councillors fairly evenly balanced politically. It was not that elections were uncontested, for, as Dr. John Marshall has pointed out in his history of Lancashire County Council, *'what is impressive is ... the eagerness with which the elections of county representatives was anticipated'.*[45]

Local contention about seats on the Council could, it seems, sometimes descend into malice. In 1900 a columnist, writing in the

Lancaster Guardian, under the name Lux, suggested that one candidate, Mr. Joseph Barrett, would represent not the interests of Carnforth, but only of the Carnforth Co-operative Society which was, Lux said, rumoured to have threatened to close their connection with the slaughterhouse in Kellet Lane if their candidate was not elected. Trying to think of a telling local comparison that everyone in Carnforth would understand, Lux added that it was as if Mr. Barton had been put forward for Carnforth as an *'Ironworks representative'.*[46]

The Parish Councils

It was the Local Government Act of 1894 which most radically altered the whole parish system. The Act transferred the civil function of vestries to elected Parish Councils (or in populous areas to Urban District Councils). The Act set up a two-tier elected system, the lower being the Urban and Parish Councils, the upper the County Council. Each householder was given one vote in parish council elections and it was specifically laid down that women could not only vote, but could stand for office. It goes without saying that rates still had to be paid, but the old freedom of parishes to control the spending of rates was being eroded, for the amount of the rates collected to be allocated to the parish councils was limited, particularly after 1895 when the rate on agricultural land, a major source of Parish revenue, was reduced.[47]

Parish Councils were to be set up if the population of a parish or township exceeded 300. The census of 1891 had shown the following totals

Township populations 1891

Township	Population
Borwick	281
Carnforth	2680
Priest Hutton	242
Silverdale	589
Warton with Lindeth	1384
Yealand Conyers	304
Yealand Redmayne	222

By December 1894 both Warton-with-Lindeth and Silverdale had held their first elections.[48] Yealand Redmayne was too small for a Parish Council to be mandatory, but the Act allowed such small villages to make application for one, and in November it was decided at a township meeting by eight votes to seven to do so. Yealand Conyers had already set up a Parish Council.[49] It seems that neither Borwick nor Priest Hutton took up the option at that time.

Carnforth, with its population of over 2,000 could, and did, opt for becoming an Urban District and so take into its own hands responsibilities beyond those allowed to a parish. Among the most important of these Mr. Stephenson said, when chairing a preliminary meeting, were the management of roads, drainage, recreation grounds, lighting and burial grounds. All these were now on a scale which must have been becoming increasingly beyond the scope of a township meeting.

At the first meeting of the Urban District Council (at the Temperance Hotel and with Mr. Edward Barton in the chair) on January 7th, 1895, it was pointed out that Carnforth had six miles of streets and sewers to maintain. Hitherto they had been overseen by the Rural Sanitary Authority under whose auspices Mr. Jowett, Inspector of Nuisances to that authority, had been asked to give his opinion on how many were ready to be taken over. These were now the responsibility of the new Council.[50]

There was a financially alarming possibility that Warton, whose burial ground was 'very full', might close it to Carnforth who would then have to find money for their own.[51]

Carnforth already had its own Water Company and a Gas company (though both privately owned). It had its own Fire Brigade, for in 1890 the ratepayers of the township had decided to set up a

brigade of at least 26 men and to purchase their own fire engine, a 26 manual one, presumably meaning that all 26 men could help pump.

Carnforth had also housed the district fever hospital since 1888. It was a lot to take on all at once and there were difficulties. A General Purposes Committee was set up, but when it decided to meet behind closed doors there were complaints that they were trying to keep the public in the dark. There were complaints

Fever Hospital
as may have been built at Carnforth

that the nine members of the Council were allowing their business interests to override the public interest. The finger was pointed especially at the Iron Works, the Gas Works and the Water Company, all very much under the control of Mr. Barton. When Barton made clear his intention of applying for voting rights on matters affecting his companies he came under such heavy criticism that he withdrew the application.[52] There had been complaints, also, that only two out of six furnaces were in blast, consequently Carnforth ratepayers were somehow having to pay for the four which were idle, and that this accounted for £1,900 of Carnforth's rateable value of £18,000.[53]

Difficulties continued. When Mr. Barton declined to continue as chairman (though continuing as vice-chairman), there were complaints that the new chairman, Mr. Lancaster, had not been elected, but had simply taken over. The Liberal opposition party said that minutes had been wrongly signed as a true record, and so on and so forth. When Mr. Vant, the chairman of the Co-operative Society, a long-term opponent of Mr. Barton, lost his seat on the council, the *Lancaster Guardian* lamented that it was a triumph for the Iron Works.

It is impossible now to judge who was in the right or whether the whole thing was routine political party wrangling. All the same, Mr. Barton cannot have been an easy man to deal with. Once, when asked his views on setting up a Board of Health for Carnforth, he had replied that he was against it because '*they would probably make him chairman, and he would not care to have the annoyance of elections or to sit with a number of men who had different opinions from himself* ',[54] hardly the ideal attitude for the chairman of an elected council. Nevertheless, despite the wrangling, the council did get through much useful work in its first few years. Perhaps more important than all was the replacement of the inadequate sewerage system, in many places having to take out inadequate 9 inch pipes and re-lay with more suitable 24 inch ones, though there was difficulty with the London & North Western Railway which objected to having a sewer run under its permanent way.[55]

Retrospect, Whitehall Looms

Before these nineteenth century reforms, the piecemeal development of separate local authorities over time had resulted in a system of extraordinary complexity. For most of the nineteenth century there was, as it has been put '*one authority for every privy and another for every pigsty*'.[56]

This, it has been suggested, was the result of the profound (and very understandable) contemporary conviction that all could and should be done by the immediate local authority, so that public expenditure should be, as far as possible, controlled by those who paid for it; that is by the local rate payers themselves. In opposition to this trend, however, there had developed, at least from the 1870s, a more collectivist trend, that is to say, one that favoured a more centralised approach and the idea that the collection and expenditure of public money was to be '*increasingly undertaken ... by "Whitehall" and Parliament*'.[57]

---

[1] Mourholme Local History Society Book Group, *Warton 1800-1850: How a North Lancashire Parish Changed* (Mourholme Local History Society, 2005), p.112.

[2] John K. Walton, *The Second Reform Act* (Methuen, 1987), p.5.

[3] Charles Seymour, *Electoral Reform in England and Wales*, (David & Charles, 1915; reprinted 1970), p.320.

[4] J.D. Marshall, "Corrupt Electoral Practices at the Lancaster Election of 1868", *Transactions of the Lancashire and Cheshire Antiquarian Society* 63 (1955-6), pp.117-130.

[5] Lancaster Friends Monthly Meeting Minute Book, 13 January 1864 – 13 August 1879. Enquiry into the part played by some members in the Lancaster election of 1865. February 1867, pp.114 – 118. Lancashire Record Office, FRL 2/1/1/20.

[6] George Macauley Trevelyan, *British History in the Nineteenth Century (1782-1901* (Longman, Green and Co, 1922), p.389.

[7] John K. Walton, *Lancashire; a Social History 1558-1939* (Manchester University Press, 1987), p.258.

[8] *Lancaster Gazette*, January 21st, 1885.

[9] *Lancaster Gazette*, January 21st, 1885.

[10] *Lancaster Gazette*, March 14th, 1885.

[11] Walton, *Lancashire; a Social History*, p.257.

[12] Walton, *Lancashire; a Social History*, p.257.

[13] Walton, *Lancashire; a Social History*, p259.

[14] Trevelyan, *British History in the Nineteenth Century*, p.381.

[15] *Lancaster Gazette*, March 21st, 1863.

[16] *Lancaster Gazette*, April 10th, 1880.

[17] *Lancaster Gazette*, April 14th, 1880.

[18] *Lancaster Gazette*, September 27th, 1884.

[19] *Lancaster Guardian*, September 15th, 1894.

[20] *Lancaster Gazette*, May 1st, 1886.

[21] *Lancaster Gazette*, June 17th, 1886.

[22] *Lancaster Guardian*, May 7th, 1887.

[23] *Lancaster Guardian*, May 28th, 1887.

[24] *Lancaster Guardian*, June 11th, 1887.

[25] *Lancaster Guardian*, August 13th, 1887.

[26] *Lancaster Guardian*, September 3rd, 1887.

[27] *Lancaster Guardian*, January 21st, 1888.

[28] *Lancaster Gazette*, September 9th, 1885.

[29] *Lancaster Gazette*, November 12th, 1892.

[30] *Lancaster Gazette*, November 19th, 1892.

[31] *Lancaster Guardian*, October 6th, 1894.

[32] *Lancaster Guardian*, July 27th, 1895.

[33] *Lancaster Guardian*, May 15th, 1897.

[34] *Lancaster Guardian*, April 2nd, 1887.

[35] *Lancaster Guardian*, January 13th, 1894.

[36] *Lancaster Guardian*, March 17th, 1894.

[37] W. Craigie, *The New English Dictionary,* vol. 10 (Oxford University Press, 1926).

[38] *Lancaster Guardian*, March 26th, 1887.

[39] *Lancaster Guardian*, April 2nd, 1887.

[40] *Lancaster Guardian*, April 16th, 1887.

[41] *Lancaster Guardian,* January 28th, 1888.

[42] *Lancaster Guardian,* June 9th, 1888.

[43] *Lancaster Guardian Supplement*, May 26th, 1894.

[44] *Lancaster Guardian,* December 22nd, 1894.

[45] J.D. Marshall, ed., *The History of Lancashire County Council 1889-1974* (Martin Robertson, 1977), p.5.

[46] *Lancaster Guardian*, March 24th, 1900.

[47] Eric Evans, *The Complete A-Z; Nineteenth and Twentieth Century British History* (Hodder & Stoughton, 1998), p.225.

[48] *Lancaster Guardian,* December 8th, 1894.

[49] *Lancaster Guardian,* November 30th, 1895.

[50] *Lancaster Guardian,* November 3rd, 1888.

[51] *Lancaster Guardian,* November 3rd, 1888.

[52] *Lancaster Guardian,* October - November 1895; January 1896.

[53] *Lancaster Guardian,* October 5th, 1895.

[54] *Lancaster Guardian,* November 25th, 1876.

[55] *Lancaster Guardian,* August 29th, 1896.

[56] Geoffrey Best, *Mid-Victorian Britain 1851-1875* (Fontana, 1979), p.56.

[57] Best, *Mid-Victorian Britain,* p.59.

Chapter Six

POVERTY, DRINK AND CRIME

It seemed reasonable to write a chapter embracing the three social evils - poverty, drink, and crime - as being linked to each other in various ways, or at any rate very much so linked in the Victorian mind. Poverty might, perhaps, have been considered in the chapter on health, there has always been a close link between the two. Similarly, excessive consumption of alcohol, considered here mainly as a cause of misbehaviour and the descent into poverty, might just as well have been considered as a health problem, or indeed as a moral problem. All these strategies might have had their advantages, but this one of linking them causally has been chosen.

Poverty

The arrangements and institutions for dealing with the poor in the parish mostly stemmed from the Poor Law Amendment Act of 1834, helped out by charities of various sorts. The system remained basically unchanged for the rest of the nineteenth century. It had really little more to offer than rather uncoordinated, stop-gap doles to the destitute - excluding tramps and beggars, who were seen as pests and were in much danger of being dealt with by the police on a charge of vagrancy.

In this area, vagrants were sometimes found sleeping in the warm cinder-ovens; it seems that '*sleeping in a coke-oven*' was an offence in itself (though one wonders under what law) since that was all John Hindle of Kirkby Lonsdale was charged with when a policeman found him asleep in an oven at Priest Hutton. He was given 14 days hard labour.[1] In one way he was lucky; there were other cases that had resulted in fatalities from the fumes.

The Poor Laws and charity between them probably ensured that no one needed to die of starvation, but it has been well-said that, '*... the terms on which public relief was offered were usually humiliating ... and so were those of private charities.*'[2]

There was a general dread of being reduced to accepting help on such terms. As one historian puts it, '*Independent, thrifty members of*

Co-operative and Friendly Societies ... placing great store by the virtues of self-help and respectability ... regarded both poor relief and private charity with contempt'.[3] Charles Dickens made dramatic use of this attitude in his novel *Our Mutual Friend* in which the washerwoman, Mrs. Betty Higden, preferred to die by the roadside rather than accept aid from the parish.

Unfortunately one of the main causes of poverty and the need for relief was the precariousness of employment. A growing understanding of the realities of the trade cycle in an industrialised world was undermining the previously prevalent idea, that able-bodied people were poor from wilful idleness. During trade depressions there simply was no work even for those most eager to be self-supporting. Public opinion changed slowly, but as time went on it seemed to be *'becoming more worried and compassionate about it'*.[4] As well as acceptance that no-one should be without the necessities of life, there was a developing consensus with Adam Smith who, long before, had made the novel claim that:

> *'by necessities I understand not only the commodities which are indispensably necessary for the support of life, but whatever the custom of the country renders it indecent for creditable people, even of the lowest order, to be without'*.[5]

This view, however enlightened, raises as many problems as it solves, including how one identifies what the custom of the country is.

From the 1830s philanthropists and reformers had been deep in the minefields of social investigation, including investigating workhouses and various other aspects of the giving of assistance. They included work by the various local statistical societies that were such a feature of the nineteenth century.

The same period also saw the founding of many societies concerned with improvement of conditions for the poor; for instance the Workhouse Visiting Society, with which Miss Twining of the tea family was closely involved, was founded in 1858.

The Poor Law Medical Officers' Association of 1855 became in 1869 the Charity Organisation Society, with its new emphasis on the importance of investigating the individual circumstances of those needing help, rather than doling out the standard relief of the Poor Law. Almost certainly this activity resulted in better treatment at least of all those who were paupers because of age and infirmity, but clearly the system of Poor Law Relief as a whole, which had been so hastily put together in 1834, was coming to seem more and more unsuited to changing conditions and changing attitudes. Yet despite this, no radical change in the basic form in which poor relief was given came until the twentieth century.

Poor Relief in Warton Parish

There remains the problem of identifying what was actually happening in Warton parish in the light of all these changes. Even though Warton parish may have shown a different pattern of trade depression from other parts of the country (a matter which was discussed in earlier chapters) it is reasonable to suppose that, there too, poverty fluctuated according to the state of the parish economy. Also, as elsewhere, there would remain, in both good times and bad, those who inevitably gravitate down into poverty and dependence – the sick, the elderly and the widowed with children to support.

In this context it is useful to appreciate that the authorities could expect and require support from the family before giving doles. There were court cases brought against those who neglected their families and so left them chargeable on the local rates.

'Henry Ashton of Carnforth, labourer, left his wife and two children who became so chargeable. He was made to promise to pay eight shillings a week and also had the costs of the case to bear.'[6]

'Thomas Beckett, who described himself as a post messenger earning 18 shillings a week, was summoned to show why an order should not be made on him to contribute to the maintenance of his eighty year old father, John Beckett of Warton. Two other brothers were contributing 2/6d a week each, though one claimed only to earn 13 shillings a week as a labourer. Thomas had been paying his share, but he was now £2 in arrears. His plea that he had been ill was not accepted and he was ordered to continue payment'.[7]

There are indications to be found in the local newspapers of a growing wish to promote the welfare of paupers, more especially perhaps pauper children. In 1883 the Lancaster Board of Guardians was reported to be considering the question of whether to send John, Robert and Agnes Hall, orphans of 12, 11 and 9 years, to the Children's Emigration Home in Birmingham, with a view to their being sent to Canada. The practice of sending unaccompanied children overseas has been condemned as putting them at risk of exploitation, but in this case the Guardians seem to have taken what care they could of the children's subsequent welfare. A decision was deferred while the question was considered of whether the children should be under the charge of someone duly appointed by the authorities of the home.[8] The necessary expenditure was only sanctioned if annual reports on the children were received.[9]

In 1898 the *Lancaster Guardian* reported on a suggestion that fostering of pauper children was preferable to leaving them in the harsher atmosphere of the workhouse.[10]

In 1887 the *Lancaster Guardian* gave an account of a proposed improvement in the meals for the workhouse children. The change certainly showed consideration – the children were to have a tea at half-past four as soon as they came back from school instead of having to wait till supper. Whether, today, we should think what was offered entirely satisfactory is another matter. There was, at any rate, plenty of milk in it. Tea was to be half a pint of *'new milk'* and three ounces of bread and butter or bread and treacle. Supper was to be the same plus a pint of milk porridge.[11]

Not all reporting was positive. In the same year, 1887, there had been a newspaper investigation of imbeciles (accepted terminology in those days) in the workhouse. All one can say is that it did demonstrate that general concern was being felt about such placements. It is true that the authorities had decided that each particular case was correctly placed, but they seem to have meant that the classification was right and, that being so, there was nothing better to offer.

The description the newspaper article gave, of what the workhouse could offer to imbeciles is not encouraging - the accommodation afforded by the day rooms was '*cheerless and scant of comfort*', the beds of straw were clean and '*fairly good*', but the reporter recommended that they should have '*flock pillows instead of the ones filled with chaff now in use*'. However the diet was '*not unsatisfactory*', and the inmates were '*sufficiently clad*'. Several of them, the reporter noted, '*do useful work about the house*'. To do the workhouse justice this report was made just before work began on improvement of the accommodation.[12] There is local evidence, too, of consideration for the health of paupers of all ages. In 1883 Mrs. Ellen Mark, of Yealand Redmayne, was appointed nurse at the workhouse.[13] The employment of a nurse in workhouse infirmaries was very far from standard at that time, for it was often held that other paupers could do all that was needed; it seems that Lancaster was ahead of its time.

All of this, naturally, required greater expenditure, and consequently more from the rates. The burden must have been particularly felt in hard times. The pattern of extra help in times of economic depression can be followed through reports in the local newspapers.

In 1886 the *Lancaster Gazette* reported that pauperism had risen locally by 17.35% over that recorded in 1885. The paper wrote that '*Trade was so bad that it was causing distress and destitution; bad weather had made matters worse*'.[14]

Both the Poor Law guardians, through outdoor relief, and the charitable agencies, through such measures as opening soup-kitchens, were attempting to cope. There were soup-kitchens open in West Cumberland, Carlisle, Penrith and Kendal and more locally too. In a spell of very bad weather in 1895 a soup-kitchen was opened in Silverdale National School and at Mrs. Hebden's home at Woodlands. Another was opened by the Carnforth Co-operative Society in Carnforth. There was not only a soup-kitchen, but *'other help for the needy'* was supplied.[15]

It seems likely that other bad times called forth similar charitable support, though it may often have been given in less formal ways that were not reported in the newspapers. There was an account of *'a meat tea'* given by a *'spinster lady'* in 1891 to 60 old people in Carnforth.[16] It was still an age when the gentry felt it part of their life style to be charitable, and in which there were recipients in such dire need that charity in any form was likely to be most welcome.

Existing poor law measures were seen to be failing. In an attempt to grapple with the plight of the Lancashire cotton workers, a Public Works (Manufacturing Districts) Act of 1863 had given powers to local authorities to apply for cheap loans from the Public Works Commissioners to finance local improvements as a way of creating work.[17] Though the results of this reaction against the previous attitude of laissez-faire were disappointing, their very failure could be said to have symbolised the failure of the nineteenth century Poor Law to cope with large-scale industrial unemployment.[18]

Joseph Chamberlain, the radical president of the Local Government Board in the mid-eighties, issued a circular urging local authorities to undertake public works for the relief of the unemployed. In line with *'new liberal thinking'*, he urged *'that it would prevent the genuinely unemployed from having to submit to the humiliation of applying for poor relief'*.[19]

There were reports in the local papers of road and sewerage works being undertaken in the northwest to give employment.[20] Unemployed men at Barrow, thought to be at risk of starvation, were taken on to construct a new road.[21] Ironically, one of the biggest public works in the north west, that of taking water from Thirlmere in the Lake

District to Manchester, was itself the cause of distress. In 1886 work on it had been held up because of bad weather. In February it was reported that the Thirlmere waterworks' navvies were still unable to work because of the severe weather, and were starving. Monetary relief was eventually given on this occasion and a decision deferred as to whether to continue it or send the men to the workhouse as current law demanded for the able-bodied destitute.[22] Whether Warton parish would have been directly affected at this date is not known. The pipeline ran through the edge of the parish but may not have reached it till later when the 1891 census shows 13 men, all entered as *'general labourers'*, lodging in a building called merely *'outhouse'* at Tewitfield. It has not been found whether this was a private enterprise or something with the backing of the guardians. A farmer called Bowness, who had apparently simply divided his farm, Starricks, into two and packed four pipeline workers in as lodgers, presumably merely preferred more income and less space.

The water scheme continued to be a problem for the Poor Law guardians all along the line of the pipe. In 1889 the *Lancaster Gazette* reported a large influx of paupers from the Manchester Water Scheme applying for medical relief and funeral expenses.[23] It was difficult to send them back to their own Union and they were a notorious burden on Lancaster lodgings. The Lancaster Board of Guardians discussed finding extra accommodation for vagrants at the workhouse.[24] In all, 500 to 600 men of mixed nationalities were employed on the project. They were unfortunately prone to fighting and more constables were wanted to keep the peace.

Inevitably, in so large scale a public organisation as the Poor Law system, officials were at times found to have breached regulations or trust. In 1855, for instance, Thomas Muckalt, Overseer of the Poor, was found to have falsely certified the rent of John Thistlethwaite's house at £8 instead of the true £3, so that the latter would qualify to retail beer. Muckalt was fined 40 shillings and costs. In 1884 James Baines of Washington House, Warton, Relieving Officer for the area and Registrar of Births & Deaths, was dismissed as an uncertificated bankrupt in circumstances *'making him totally untrustworthy and no longer fit to retain the confidence of the Board'.*[25] There seems, however, no evidence of wide-scale corruption.

Drink and Temperance

Throughout the nineteenth century there was general concern about excessive drinking and its effects. An all time peak of alcohol consumption in the United Kingdom was reached in the mid-1870s. In 1875 *'each national individual had consumed 1.30 gallons of spirits'*. That was the high point for spirits. Beer consumption peaked in 1876 when the figure for each individual (all ages, both sexes, and the teetotal included) was 34.4 gallons.

By comparison the consumption of alcohol in the mid-twentieth century (1963) was about a third of this - 0.31 gallons of spirits and 13.1 gallons of beer - though the figures are not strictly comparable; the 1963 figures are for England and Wales, those for the 1870s include Scotland and Ireland.[26]

Much of life and much of business was drink related and alternative beverages were expensive and not readily available, though temperance enthusiasts were doing what they could. Mr. Rawlinson Ford of Yealand Manor paid for the erection of a small hall, locally known as The Wooden Hut, near the Iron Works, as a place where, he hoped, *'the men employed at Carnforth might congregate in inclement weather'*, and also might get *'a cup of tea or coffee at a reasonably small charge.'*[27] By 1899 there were in addition two establishments claiming to be Temperance in Carnforth, *Nelson's* in Market Street and one called *Pedder's* in New Street.

The Drinkers

Unsurprisingly, there does not seem to be much doubt that a great deal of disorderly behaviour, thieving and violence was drink-related. Reports in the local papers give ample confirmation of violence associated with drink, though there is room for only a few examples here. Moreover they hardly reveal anything new, or special to the nineteenth century, except in the punishment meted out.

James Dixon (a Carnforth man) was charged with assaulting Police Sergeant Singleton when drunk, and was given six months hard labour[28]. Richard Knight, keeper of the lodging–house at Millhead, and Robert Richmond, a retired ironmonger, were each accused of being drunk and disorderly and charged with assaulting Police Sergeant

Percival and Police Constable Barnfather who had found them fighting. Knight was acquitted, but Richmond was fined 10s (plus 11s costs) for drunkenness with a further 20s fine and £1 2s 6d costs, presumably for the assault.[29] This would not be the last time Richard Knight was in trouble from drunkenness. In 1894 he was again before the county police court charged with being drunk and disorderly, though was again acquitted.[30]

Michael Sullivan, pipe-track labourer, was charged with using a knife on Robert Collins, ironworker. Both were Irish and had lodged together at Millhead for two days. Both had been drinking at the Carnforth Inn, had quarrelled and fought outside. A knife was found. Sullivan was committed to the assizes[31]. At the assize court he was charged with grievous bodily harm. The jury settled for a verdict of unlawful wounding. The sentence was four months hard labour[32].

The Providers of Drink

In the Tory budget of 1829 the duty on beer had been abolished, though the tax on malt continued. The Duke of Wellington's Beer House Act followed in 1830; by it anyone who paid the poor rate could, on payment of an annual duty of two guineas to the excise, obtain a licence to sell beer (to be drunk on or off the premises) without the need of approval by the licensing magistrates. This sort of free trade was designed to persuade people to drink healthy, wholesome beer rather than spirits.

A Licensing Act in 1872, passed by Gladstone's government, was a major attempt to bring some order into the loose system of control, which had grown up over the generations. It placed all drinking places under the licensing justices (control of off-licenses was added in 1882). Beer-houses had always had some legal limitation of opening hours imposed on them, but pubs had been remarkably free to open at all hours (except that there were restrictions on the Sabbath, especially during the hours of divine service). The measure was not popular. Gladstone's government was defeated in 1874 and Gladstone is supposed to have said *'We were born down on a torrent of gin.'*[33] Nevertheless the Act remained and in a few years, whether because of that or not, the United Kingdom had passed the absolute peak of alcohol consumption. In 1880 Gladstone, now back in power, had repealed the malt tax (making farmers happy) and re-imposed a beer duty to produce equivalent revenue. The 1872 Act also gave the magistrates new power to deal with landlords watering or adulterating beer, allowing drunkenness on their premises, etc. In Carnforth, Eric Sinclair Cambell, of the Carnforth Inn and William Scaife, of the Shovel Inn, were among those fined for adulterating the drink they sold.[34]

In Warton parish, as anywhere else, the licensing laws were frequently ignored. At County Petty Sessions in Lancaster Castle in 1858, Francis Walker of the Station Inn, Carnforth, was charged with having served a traveller from Bolton 'between the hours of three and five' on a Sunday afternoon (a complicated case since it was apparently accepted for the landlord to have served a whole Brass Band on its way from Lancaster to Holker Hall).[35]

The owner and landlord of the Golden Ball public house in Carnforth, John Mashiter, was charged with allowing drunkenness on his premises. Fines of 20s and 17s costs were imposed on Mashiter. The case was tried before Mr. E.B. Dawson of Aldcliffe Hall, a man who felt very strongly on temperance and might have been expected to view the matter seriously.

On the other hand Mr. Tilly, a solicitor, in his tribute to Dawson after his death, said that 'as a magistrate he was just and impartial in every way' and particularly instanced that as a magistrate he never let his temperance principles interfere with his judgment.[36]

The permitted hours of opening varied with the density of population (though why rural pubs had to close earlier than town ones is not obvious).[37] The connection between hours of opening and density of population seems to have left room for manoeuvre.

Application was made in 1885 to the County Licensing Committee for Carnforth to be declared a 'populous place within the meaning of the Licensing Act'.[38] That would have meant that pubs could legally stay open until 11p.m. Carnforth contained a large enough population, but objectors said that in Carnforth this population was contained in 324 houses within a radius of 550 yards, within which there were already five pubs and the railway refreshment room.[39]

In 1889 John Atherton applied for a full licence for the Cross Keys in Over Kellet Road, Carnforth, which was already licensed to sell beer under Wellington's much easier Beer House Act of 1830. It was not the first application for the Cross Keys; there had been one three years before which had not been granted. John Atherton claimed his was the only pub within a radius of a quarter mile, the nearest 360 yards away (something odd about Mr. Atherton's mathematics?). Opposition was expressed by locals who pointed out that there were five pubs and three shops licensed to sell spirits, and three beer-houses already in Carnforth. There was, in fact, also another beer-house very close to Carnforth, though outside the boundary at West View in Millhead (it was even closer to the colony of ironworkers, a thirsty occupation). The licence was refused.[40]

There was no lack of places to drink elsewhere in the parish. An official survey in 1871 listed 11 inns and 3 beerhouses, 14 in all. Since the population of the parish at the time was 3,390 that was one for every 242 inhabitants (man, woman and child). A search through directories and censuses seems to show that the ratio of pubs to inhabitants fell during the second half of the nineteenth century from a high in 1851 of one drinking place to every 191 inhabitants to a low of one for every 455 inhabitants at the end of the century. The area seems to have lost inns rather than gained them since then, but a modern day count would be merely misleading since the pattern of drinking has changed, and there are so many new outlets for purchasing alcohol.

Temperance and Temperance Societies

Lancashire's special contribution to countering alcoholism was centred on Preston and identified with Thomas (later Sir Thomas) Whittaker. The movement advocated moral suasion, which meant persuading people to the taking of a pledge to avoid all alcohol consumption. Very many organisations grew up from this. They were often associated with the nonconformist churches. The Church of England Temperance Society on the other hand advocated moderation rather than abstinence.

The temperance movement underlay, assisted, and strengthened so much activity in Warton parish (as everywhere else at the time) that references to the societies are almost overwhelmingly frequent in the local newspapers. It is the moral suasion outlook, which is reflected in most local reports with Band of Hope meetings particularly well attended. In 1891 the Warton branch had 100 members and was holding weekly meetings.[41]

There were also meetings of the Rechabites, the United Kingdom Railway Temperance Union, the Good Templars, the Druids' Friendly Society and the Temperance Lifeboat Crew at the Iron Works. It is to be presumed that the meetings included exhortations and calls to take the pledge, but the newspaper accounts tend to report on the social and entertainment side. Many of the items in concerts were songs or recitations on the theme of temperance. The societies, indeed, never tried to limit themselves to serious meetings. They sought to make abstinence attractive by supporting all sorts

of sports and recreations; outings and picnics for children, such as the treat for children put on every year by the Railway Temperance Union on Carnforth's Cricket field, and by encouragement of such healthy games as cricket and football, also instructive lectures, penny readings, and such other popular activities as were not based on drinking and the pubs. There is no doubt that the various temperance movements played a big part in promoting recreational activities in Warton parish as elsewhere. It was a time when, in general, support was being given to prudence by the growth of the Friendly Societies; one of these, the Rechabites, was specifically teetotal and took care that the members did not have to go into pubs to pay their contribution as was customary before the societies grew big enough to have their own offices.

There is no way of proving whether the temperance movement can claim success; if total abstinence for all was the goal, then it must be counted as a failure. If the campaign had success at all, it was probably to be found in its influence in encouraging all the many activities outlined above and so helping to obtain the consent of the many at least to the view that excess of alcoholism was reprehensible, even if modest consumption was acceptable.

Crime
The Law Breakers, Crime and Punishment

Crimes related to drink were not the only ones the police and courts were busy with. Infringements of the law of all kinds were many, far too many to give in any detail. However, setting out the different types with a few examples may give some picture of the pattern of law breaking and its punishment at the time, and in what way it differed from today's pattern and in what way it was all too similar. The system could still act, at times, with what now seems unbelievable severity.

In 1849 a fifteen-year-old boy was transported for seven years for stealing some trousers in Warton.[42] This was, however, something of a hangover from the harsh attitudes of the eighteenth century. Things were changing. There was no further transportation after 1868 (though admittedly this was largely because Australia was refusing to receive convicts).

By contrast with the 1849 case one can quote a case from later in the century where the accused was handled with considerable sensitivity. In 1892 George Hall (in the earliest reports called Holt) of Silverdale was accused of attempted suicide. A rather different view was taken of suicide then from that of today. It was legally a felony, and attempted suicide led to a court appearance. Hall was said to have attempted suicide by taking potassium cyanide. Police Sergeant Percival said that when he was called he found him in bed being attended by a Dr. Dinwoody. Hall was taken to the police station at Carnforth. There Dr. Jackson saw him several times in the night. Hall was remanded. When he came before the court Superintendent Moss deposed that, in his opinion, it had not been a genuine attempt and recommended discharge, which was granted.[43] One is left with the impression that, within the legal bounds of the time, doctors, police and the court were compassionate and did what they could.

There were other cases in which magistrates were lenient. Richard Woods, a labourer, accused of stealing coal, was imprisoned until the court rose, and then released.[44] John Shuttleworth, formerly a labourer at the Carnforth Iron Works, was given another chance after being caught poaching at Kellet.[45] Elizabeth Smith, a tailoress from Manchester, was charged with being drunk and disorderly at West View Hotel, but the magistrates discharged her and paid for her train fare back to Manchester.[46]

Capital punishment, which had once been meted out for even trivial crimes, had become more and more restricted in its use, and after 1861 was limited to cases of murder, treason and piracy.

Even so hangings continued to take place in public for anyone to watch who liked, and there was a good deal of disquiet at the macabre interest taken in the hangings. A Commission on Capital Punishment in 1866 came to the conclusion that the public was not ready for the abolition of public hanging. Two years later a private member's bill was brought in and was passed. It laid down that all future executions should be carried out within the prison walls. Of course interest in murder remained. Newspaper reporters were allowed to watch and report. In 1879, when a Barrow man who murdered his wife was hanged in Lancaster Castle the *Lancaster Guardian* offered its readers nearly two columns of the intimate details, including the alarming information that '*the drop*' was only six feet.[47]

The gallows illustrated on this page, were those at York, but were similar to those in Lancaster Castle with the balcony.

Meanwhile lesser offences went on, just as they do today, and cases of family neglect and failure to maintain, vagrancy, trading offences, bankruptcy and other financial matters as well as traffic offences have all found a place in appropriate chapters in this book.

Just to show how some things never change one can also mention that cases of sexual and matrimonial offences, rape and attempted rape were all frequently reported.

There was an attempted rape in Warton reported in 1875. The culprit, who was undefended, pleaded that he was so drunk he knew nothing about it until the arresting constable told him of it. He was found guilty and given two years imprisonment with hard labour. The magistrate regretted that this was the maximum allowed by the law for this *'atrocious'* crime.[48]

In 1887, Thos. Mansley, canal boat discharger, had attempted *'indecent liberties'* with Hannah Kay of Yealand Conyers, wife of the lock keeper at Tewitfield. Mansley apologized to her, her husband and her grandfather, but her husband took it further. He was subsequently sentenced to 18 months hard labour.[49]

Theft cases were fairly common. Wm. Ainsworth, employed at the Iron Works for nine years, robbed the railway at Carnforth of 32 tarpaulins. He was given six weeks hard labour.[50] Thomas Ashton of Carnforth, labourer, was charged with stealing two tame pigeons from Charles Parker at Bolton-le-Sands, but the case was dismissed.[51] In another case Wilkinson, a railway porter, was witness against James Bland, railway pointsman, who was charged with stealing a pair of boots from an LNWR wagon at Carnforth, and also against George Clark, foreman shunter, who stole 4lbs. of tobacco.[52] Then it turned out that Wilkinson, the grass (to use an anachronistic term), had been the prime mover in wholesale pilfering which had been taking place. All three were given 12 months hard labour.[53]

Offences Concerned with Animals

In the later part of the century there appears to have been an increase in cases concerning cruelty to animals. It is only an impression, but likely to have been true, for attitudes were changing. New legislation to protect animals had been introduced at the beginning of the century.[54] The Royal Society for the Protection of Animals was founded in 1824; all hopeful signs that people were more aware of this dreadful behaviour and readier to take action. Charles Stewart of Warton, earthenware hawker, was charged with working his mare in an unfit state. P.C.

Percival had found a raw wound covered with a piece of sheepskin. A fine of 2s 6d with 13s costs was imposed.[55]

Even apart from cruelty there were many ways in which animal owners could offend. Sometimes at the police court whole batches of people were fined for neglecting to license their dogs (a very old offence). On one occasion in 1894 those summonsed included at least five men from Warton parish, among them Rev. W. Sleigh, vicar of Silverdale. Col. Marton of Capernwray Hall had four unlicensed dogs. It seems that none of these gentlemen took licensing very seriously. Marton's lawyer said that, like so many people, after receiving the due form he had simply pushed it aside and forgotten it.[56]

Leaving a dog un-muzzled was potentially a more serious offence, since a main reason for muzzling was undoubtedly the persisting presence of rabies in the country. Towards the end of the century a concerted effort was made to eliminate it by ordering the muzzling of all dogs. In 1891 the muzzling order was withdrawn,[57] but apparently too soon, so that it had to be re-instated. In 1899, at a Carnforth Urban District Council meeting on June 7th, Mr. Miller, the headmaster of the National School, said that he proposed asking the Board of Agriculture to rescind the muzzling order again as there had been no case of rabies for a number of years.

Allowing cattle to stray was another offence, as was leaving a horse unattended. Of a rather different nature was the charge of moving swine without a licence, legislation passed to try to control the swine fever which caused such havoc.[58]

Misuse of Explosives

Naturally in an area with so much quarrying there was a need for explosives, but it seems that otherwise respectable people did not feel it important to obey even such limited safety control measures as were in place under the 1875 Explosives Act. Mr. E. Barton, manager of the Carnforth Haematite Iron Co., was an offender. The inspector of explosives, Lt. Col. Ford, after an inspection of Scout Quarry, brought the charge. Supt. Moss said the licence had not been renewed on the due date and Mr. Barton was fined.[59] The equally respectable Mr. Walduck, of the Warton Mining Co., was charged with four offences relating to explosives at Crag Foot mines. He was fined £2.[60]

Fines for offences were so small that one does not get the impression that the law was taking the matter very seriously. The children certainly did not. One boy casually brought some explosives into school to play with; he was not even very severely punished.

Young Offenders

The offences that brought children and young people to court were very much what they are today. The difference is in the punishment and in the legal procedures. All children, however young, were tried in the same court as adults. They could be sent to adult prisons, though the more usual punishment was a birching, administered by the police (with due formality and in the presence of the parents). The cases involving the really young (including a little criminal of five years who tried out his pocket knife on a shop front) are considered, along with the rest of childhood, in chapter nine.

Young offenders over 14 or so seem to have been dealt with as adults. A seventeen-year-old girl, who stole a pair of boots, was given 1 month hard labour.[61] A youth who stole from his employer was remanded in custody, which would have meant awaiting trial in an adult prison whatever the final outcome (which was that his employer appealed on his behalf, and he was discharged with a caution).[62]

There were, by this time, reformatories to which young offenders could be sent in the hope that they might be helped to a better way of life. The drawback was that, to give the reformatories time to do their work, a reformatory sentence tended to be much longer than a prison sentence.

Some Lancaster boys, aged 12 - 17 were engaged in organised shoplifting. The two oldest were given four months with hard labour, the rest were sent to a reformatory for five years.[63]

The equation of adolescence with full adulthood led sometimes to considerable insensitivity as in the case of James Beck, a young apprentice. Apprenticeship was a way of acquiring profitable skills. The indentures, which opened such a position, were legally binding and the apprentice, as well as the employer, was bound to stick to the terms. Rather naturally, young adolescents did not always take to the job chosen. In 1895 James Beck had been given financial help by the local Mansergh Charity (set up in the seventeenth century for this very purpose) to begin a seven-year apprenticeship with John Gaffney, a plumber. James went absent from work and his employer, who had had to pay a man in his place, took the case to court. James's mother, Mary Gutteridge, testified that he had been unsettled since she re-married and had spoken of joining the navy. The boy was simply ordered to comply with his indentures and had also to pay £1 a week (presumably to indemnify Mr Gaffney).[64]

Just to show that yobs were not unknown (even if not by that name) there is the case of the Carnforth Reading Room. Some 'young fellows', constant frequenters of the Co-op. Reading Room, had been behaving increasingly badly. They had broken a window, upset the fire buckets, wrenched a door off its hinges and destroyed the newspapers provided in the reading room. This was at the time of the Boer War and the loss of the papers was much resented by other users who wished to read the war news from South Africa.[65]

The Misfits

As always the law found itself dealing with the eccentric and the mentally disturbed. In 1894 the *Lancaster Guardian* reported on the case of Henry Hutton of Silverdale. In January he had used threatening language to Elizabeth Bisbrown, his neighbour. In February this strange old man had threatened to murder her. There was a history of previous trouble. He was referred for medical examination, declared insane and sent to the workhouse. The diagnosis may well have been right and the need for other help than the law appreciated, though from this distance the workhouse seems to be a rather unsatisfactory way of dealing with the problem.[66]

At the other end from the case of this sad and confused old man was the case, back in 1858, of Roger Preston, a Yealand Conyers Quaker of good standing, who was charged with non-payment of church rates. Consequently he suffered distraint of his property in lieu. Unlike Henry Hutton he knew exactly what he was doing and was prepared to break the law for conscience sake.[67]

Law Enforcers, the Police Force

A Lancashire Rural Police Force had been inaugurated in 1839. In the early years there were very many who felt the gain in security in no way matched the cost. By 1842 such doubters had managed to get the force so whittled down that there was only one officer, stationed in Carnforth, to police a dozen or so of the surrounding townships.[68] The force built up again gradually, but at the time of the 1851 census there seems still only to have been one policeman resident in the whole of the parish, a police constable, Marmaduke Taylor, aged 39, living with his wife and four small children in Warton township.

Considering the size of the parish and that only very senior officers were allowed the use of a horse, this would have meant many miles of foot slogging, for constables were supposed to do the round of their whole beat each day.[69] There would have been other policemen active in the area though not resident, for a small force of rural police was based in stations in Skerton and Lancaster and these men were expected to go out as needed to the rural areas.[70]

As late as 1857 the Carnforth section of the South Lonsdale Police Division (comprising all the townships of Warton parish plus Over and Nether Kellet and Bolton-le-Sands) still had only one resident policeman.[71] In 1861, P.C. Francis Fell, aged 40 and born in Aughton, is recorded as a lodger with a farm labourer's family at 17b Main Street, Warton, and was still the only constable in the parish.

It is scarcely surprising, then, that in this period, the old and new systems had to be left overlapping. Old style parish constables for the different townships were still being appointed at County Petty Sessions. In 1855 a detailed account of the appointment of these parish constables was reported[72] and again in 1864. [73] The dual system was not abolished until 1872.

By that time there were, according to the 1871 census, four police constables living in the parish, one each for Carnforth, Warton, Yealand Conyers and Priest Hutton. There were still four in 1891, but differently distributed; Carnforth now had two police officers and Priest Hutton none (though a retired policeman lived there). Carnforth acquired its own police station on Lancaster Road in 1880 (the building survives as a private residence today, still with its coat of arms on the front). Police Sergeant Charles Percival, a married man of 43 from Leicestershire, lived there at the time of the 1881 census and police constable John Barnfather, a bachelor of 35 from Alston in Cumbria, lodged with him. A police station was also built in Yealand Conyers. The building, which still survives, is dated 1904, but the 1891 census for Yealand Conyers records a policeman Robert Roberts, a married man of 38 from Southport, as living in the Police Station. That all these serving policemen were born outside the parish was not by chance. Captain John Woodward, the first chief constable of the Lancashire rural force had laid it down as desirable; local men, he thought, might be tempted to show favouritism.[74]

Even routine changes in police personnel were considered worthy of newspaper reporting. In 1896 there was a report of a change of police constable at Carnforth; also that P.C. Cummings had been made a sergeant and was going to Widnes.[75] In 1897 the arrival of new men in the police station at Carnforth was reported,[76] also that the Warton constable had been promoted to merit class for stopping a runaway horse.[77]

---

[1] *Lancaster Gazette*, January 31st, 1852.

[2] Geoffrey Best, *Mid-Victorian Britain 1851-1870* (Fontana/Collins, 1982), p.96.

[3] Michael E. Rose, *The Relief of Poverty 1834-1914* (Prometheus, 1986), pp. 38, 39.

[4] Best, *Mid-Victorian Britain* p.142.

[5] Adam Smith, *An Inquiry into the Nature and Causes of the Wealth of Nations*, book v, (Chapter 2, part ii, 1779).

[6] *Lancaster Gazette*, April 14th, 1883.

[7] *Lancaster Guardian*, November 17th, 1888.

[8] *Lancaster Guardian*, October 13th, 1883.

[9] *Lancaster Guardian*, October 20th, 1883.

[10] *Lancaster Guardian*, November 19th, 1898.

[11] *Lancaster Guardian*, March 23rd, 1887.

[12] *Lancaster Guardian*, February 23rd, 1887.

[13] *Lancaster Guardian*, October 13th, 1883.

[14] *Lancaster Gazette*, February 17th, 1886.

[15] *Lancaster Guardian*, February 23rd; March 2nd 1895.

[16] *Lancaster Guardian*, February 7th, 1891.

[17] Rose, *The Relief of Poverty*, p.38.

[18] Rose, *The Relief of Poverty*, p.39.

[19] Rose, *The Relief of Poverty*, p.39

[20] *Lancaster Gazette*, February 24th, 1886.

[21] *Lancaster Gazette*, March 10th, 1886.

[22] *Lancaster Gazette*, February 24th, 1886.

[23] *Lancaster. Gazette*, April 6th, 1889.

[24] *Lancaster Gazette*, April 27th; May 11th, 1889.

[25] *Lancaster Gazette*, January 26th, 1884.

[26] Best, *Mid-Victorian Britain*, pp. 218-219; n.34.

[27] *Lancaster Guardian*, December 22nd, 1866.

[28] *Lancaster Guardian*, July 9th, 1879.

[29] *Lancaster Gazette*, March 4th, 1891.

[30] *Lancaster Guardian*, Supplement, October 27th, 1894.

[31] *Lancaster Gazette*, December 6th, 1890.

[32] *Lancaster Gazette*, February 21st, 1891.

[33] Eric Evans, *The complete A-Z, 19th Century British History* (Hodder & Stoughton, 1998), p.162.

[34] *Lancaster Guardian*, February 28th, 1885.

[35] *Lancaster Gazette*, January 19th, 1858.

[36] *Lancaster Guardian* May 13th, 1916

[37] Brian Harrison, *Drink and the Victorians* (Faber and Faber, 1971), p.329.

[38] *Lancaster Guardian*, October 10th, 1885.

[39] *Lancaster Guardian*, October 7th, 1885.

[40] *Lancaster Guardian*, September 3rd, 1889.

[41] *Lancaster. Guardian*, February 14th, 1891.

[42] *Lancaster Guardian*, October 20th, 1849.

[43] *Lancaster Gazette*, June 18th; June 22nd, 1892.

[44] *Lancaster Guardian*, April 5th 1884.

[45] *Lancaster Guardian*, February 4th, 1888.

[46] *Lancaster Guardian*, September 25th, 1897.

[47] *Lancaster Guardian*, February 15th, 1879.

[48] *Lancaster Guardian*, October 23rd, 1875.

[49] *Lancaster Guardian*, December 10th, 1887; December 17th, 1887; January 7th, 1888.

[50] *Lancaster Guardian*, November 25th, 1879.

[51] *Lancaster Guardian*, March 17th, 1877.

[52] *Lancaster Guardian*, March 12th, 1887.

[53] *Lancaster Guardian*, April 9th, 1887.

[54] Mourholme Local History Society Book Group, *Warton 1800 – 1850: How a North Lancashire Parish Changed* (Mourholme Local History Society, 2005), p.220.

[55] *Lancaster Gazette*, January 19th, 1890.

[56] *Lancaster Guardian*, Supplement, March 31st, 1894.

[57] *Lancaster Guardian*, June 13th, 1891.

[58] *Lancaster Gazette*, February 18th, 1893.

[59] *Lancaster Gazette*, August 2nd, 1882.

[60] *Lancaster Guardian*, August 5th, 1882.

[61] *Lancaster Guardian*, April 22nd, 1893.

[62] *Lancaster Guardian*, October 3rd, 1891.

[63] *Lancaster Gazette*, April 8th, 1890.

[64] *Lancaster Guardian*, February 17th, 1900.

[65] *Lancaster Guardian*, March 3rd, 1900.

[66] *Lancaster Guardian*, February 17th, 1894.

[67] *Lancaster Guardian*, May 15th; December 11th, 1858.

[68] Mourholme, *Warton: 1800 – 1850*, p.140.

[69] Bob Dobson, *Policing in Lancashire 1839 to 1980*, (Landy Publishing, 1989).

[70] *Lancaster Gazette*, November 5th, 1842.

[71] *Lancaster Guardian*, January 17th, 1857; January 24th, 1857.

[72] *Lancaster Gazette*, April 14th, 1855.

[73] *Lancaster Guardian*, April 2nd, 1864.
[74] Dobson, *Policing in Lancashire*.
[75] *Lancaster Guardian*, June 10th, 1896; July 4th, 1896.
[76] *Lancaster Guardian*, August 28th, 1897.
[77] *Lancaster Guardian*, December 25th, 1897.

Chapter Seven

CHURCH, CHAPEL AND MEETING HOUSE

Church Attendance

In the 1851 census the Registrar General included questions on attendance at places of worship. It was the one and only time such questions were included. The figures collected were, for various reasons, not fully reliable, but they can be used to give a general picture of the provision and use of places of worship at the beginning of the second half of the nineteenth century. In the old parish of Warton four denominations were represented; the Church of England, Roman Catholicism, Methodism and the Religious Society of Friends. Starting with the Church of England, which was standard for the time, three churches were recorded.

The parish church of St. Oswald (sometimes called Holy Trinity) claimed to have seating for 1,200, but the attendance was not entered as the vicar put it on record that he thought it would be *'prophaning God's Holy Sabbath'*. The ancient chapel-of-ease at Silverdale had an average morning attendance of 95 and 30 Sunday scholars. The new parish church at Yealand Conyers had 59 adults and 48 children in attendance. In addition a regular service had recently been started, by the vicar of Warton, in the schoolroom in Carnforth, with an average attendance of 80.

Of the places of worship of the other denominations the oldest was that of the Society of Friends, the Quaker Meeting House in Yealand Conyers, with an attendance of 21. The Roman Catholics had a presbytery and chapel, also in Yealand Conyers, with an average attendance of 170.

Wesleyan Methodists had a chapel in Tewitfield, on the edge of Priest Hutton, with an average evening attendance of 106 and 22 Sunday Scholars. The chapel at Warton had an average attendance of 12 and 6 Sunday scholars. A little group of Wesleyan Methodists was recorded in Yealand Redmayne. They did not have a chapel, but met in a private house where there was said to be an average attendance of 20 adults and 12 Sunday scholars.

It might have been interesting to come up with figures comparing attendance at Church of England and dissenting establishments, but there is too much discrepancy in the way the different returns were made to allow this. Some places, like the Tewitfield chapel, had three services a day, others two, others only one, and one does not know if the same people went to morning and evening service. Then there is the problem of the vicar of Warton who would not count his congregation at all.

Between them the places of worship in Warton parish claimed to be able to offer 2,642 sittings, of which 798, or 30.2%, were non-establishment, a rather higher percentage than that of 28.8% given for all the parishes of the Lancaster Poor Law Union. Of the 1,844 sittings in the established church in the parish, St. Oswald's accounted for 1,200.

The Church of England, the Background

The finance of the ancient parish of Warton came first from tithes and secondly from the church rates, fixed and collected by the parish Vestry. The tithe system in Warton was in two parts. Since the time of Henry VIII the rectory had been impropriated to the Dean and Chapter of Worcester Cathedral, which meant that it was to them that the greater tithes were paid. The Cathedral was now the rector, and the vicar, as its deputy, received the small tithes on the minor crops, which he would collect himself.

The greater tithes were farmed to a layperson who bid for the position of tithe farmer and recovered his costs out of the collection and sale of the tithed goods. In Warton the Lambert family of Kendal had been tithe farmers, and members of the family at one time lived in the Old Rectory (a fine hall, the ruins of which can still be seen) while the vicar lived in the grounds.[1] The present vicarage was erected there in 1826. In return, Worcester was responsible for the maintenance of the chancel of the church (the maintenance of the rest fell on the church rates) and for part of the vicar's stipend. Worcester also had the advowson, or right of appointing the vicar.[2] Tithes were originally collected in kind – hence the need for tithe barns where the produce could be stored pending sale. In the nineteenth century there were two tithe barns surviving in the parish, one in Carnforth and one in Priest Hutton. The Tithe Commutation Act of 1836 had substituted a rent charge for collection in kind, and both tithe barns found a new life as schools. The system of church rates also underwent change when, in 1868, they ceased to be compulsory.

St. Oswald's Church, Warton

An earlier volume of this history, which had brought the story of St. Oswald's up to 1850,[3] described some controversy about moves by Thomas Dean, vicar from 1844 to 1871; moves which some in the parish saw as dangerously Romanising, or so we learn from one of his churchwardens, James Erving, who thought such practices as the vicar displaying *'a scarlet Book mark and device like a Cross also a fancy plate for collecting the offering before sacrament'* had been one of the causes which led to *'a large falling off'* in those attending church from Carnforth.[4]

Among reasons for this falling off, Erving mentioned the installation of stained glass windows. The medieval glass, which had still existed in a fragmentary way up to the late seventeenth century at least, had all been replaced with clear glass by 1850.[5] The first new window was the east one in memory of John and Mary Bolden of Hyning Hall and this was erected in 1856. (Erving was particularly displeased because he felt the window had been installed without consulting the churchwardens).[6] Another leading parishioner, William Sharp of Linden Hall in Borwick, cannot have shared the prejudice for he provided a window in the Lady Chapel in memory of his wife in 1858. Others followed, so that within six years seven windows were installed. Most of these were made by Henry Hughes, of the London firm of Ward and Hughes. Before the end of the century all the visible windows were made of stained glass. In 1895 six still remained without, but in that year another Bolden was commemorated by a window (now in the vestry) made by Shrigley and Hunt of Lancaster; and five, made by Ward and Hughes (by then directed by T.F. Curtis in a different style) were given in memory of members of the Sharp family of Borwick.

The fabric of St. Oswald's is largely medieval and restorative work had been needed at various times, not always, it seems, very sympathetically carried out. Towards the end of the eighteenth century *'… the people in authority in those days … stripped the roof of most of its lead to help defray the cost'*.[7] The lead roof was replaced by a slate one, covering not only the nave but also the aisles and obscuring the medieval clerestories.

In 1848 the new vicar, Thomas Dean, met a crisis when he noticed cracks on the south arcade. A report by the architect Edward Paley, (partner at the time with Edmund Sharpe and later famous as partner with Hubert Austin, in the Lancaster firm of Paley and Austin) was alarming, stating that the whole south arcade was failing, with the wall 12_ inches out of perpendicular. He recommended the propping up of the aisle and nave roof and then the rebuilding of the arcade with new stone, carefully following the proportion and moulding of the existing arches. His estimated cost was £130. The Worcester Chapter was approached and proved most helpful. The work was completed by August 1849 at a cost of £131 5s 0d, of which the Dean and Chapter paid half, the rest being raised by a rate.[8] Other work, plastering, flagging and decoration took place, paid for by a subscription list of £247 16s 6d raised from far and near.

Another interesting improvement was the tiling of the Lady Chapel floor. This was done, as the tiles show, in 1849 with encaustic tiles similar to Minton, but made by Chamberlain of Worcester. A variety of patterns occur in a somewhat haphazard way, and as this was just when Chamberlain gave up making tiles and sold out to J.H. Maw, it would appear that Dean, with his Worcester connection, got these tiles as a job lot.[9]

In 1888, in the time of Dean's successor, Thomas Holland Pain, restoration was in the air everywhere, and a radical one was proposed for St. Oswald's including the renewal of the roof, and the surfacing of the floor, in which for centuries burials had taken place. The tower was in poor

St Oswald's Church
Warton

condition, the south wall was out of perpendicular, and windows were decaying and so on.

A Manchester architect, William Ball, made a report on all these matters and an appeal for £2,000 was made (by this time compulsory church rates had been abolished and the sum had to be raised voluntarily). Mr. Ball also discovered the details of what had happened when the lead roof was replaced at the end of the eighteenth century. In his report he said:

> *'Works carried out from time to time have to a great extent obliterated traces of the ancient building on the south side of the nave, but on the north, concealed in the present roof, are five clerestory windows of simple design and square-headed but much mutilated'.*[10]

Unfortunately all this led to trouble. The 1888 appeal made for the planned repairs was very successful and it was decided that something much more radical was needed, including the replacement of the pews and the 1712 pulpit, the removal of the west gallery and the opening up of the tower arch. In 1889 a faculty was sought from the Manchester Diocesan Chancellor to carry out all this work, but here a difficulty arose.

The Battle of the Pews

Many of the pews, which would be replaced, were held by parishioners. There was nothing special about private ownership of a pew in a church. The 1851 Religious Census had shown that in all the denominations, except the Society of Friends, there was private ownership of up to a half or more of sittings. In St. Oswald's, ownership of a pew seems to have been viewed as an inheritance attached to certain properties (though apparently the tradition had arisen without any formal faculty to support any claim made in a court). The sweeping away of ownership of pews in St. Oswald's was opposed by two large landowners; one was Colonel Marton who lived at Capernwray, outside the parish, but who owned property within it, and the other was Mr R.T. Gillow, of Leighton Hall. Both claimed *'prescriptive rights'* to a number of pews.

Mr R T Gillow

A suggestion was made that an amicable arrangement should be reached by which the two objectors should have similar rights in the replacement pews. This was resisted by the vicar on the grounds that there were others who claimed such rights, but were prepared to waive them so that all the pews could be free, but would not contribute to the scheme if preference was given to just one or two claimants. He and the churchwardens also pointed out that since 1824 the Gillows, being Catholics, had never used their pew and for forty years they had let it to others.

The chancellor considered the question as to whether the rights claimed could be lost by a period of what was called in legal language non-user, but was guided by a dictum of Lord Denman, that '*in the case of Roman Catholic owners they were not to look for the same amount of 'user' that they should in an ordinary case*'.

Colonel Marton finally did withdraw his objection, provided such of his tenants as held land in the parish were allotted other accommodation, but the aged Mr. Gillow refused, on the ground that the pew was an ancient appurtenance of his house and he was defending his rights of property of which he was a tenant for life. The Chancellor said that Gillow's bona fide claim ousted the jurisdiction of his court and would have to be tested in Queen's Bench. As no one was prepared for this and Mr. Gillow would not even agree to the suggestion that Counsel's opinion should be sought, there was an impasse.

The church had remained out of use pending the work, services having to be held in the school.[11] The archival material is incomplete at this point and it is not entirely clear how the difficulty was resolved, but somehow it was decided at a parish meeting to put the church back into use anyway. It was three years before the work was finally completed and the church re-opened.[12]

A new carved pulpit was placed where the Leighton Hall pew had been (the pulpit was later moved, for reasons unknown, to the south

side). The pulpit, like the new pews, was made by Hatch and Son, of Lancaster. On it, fine brass plates were fixed, reminding the preacher of his responsibility by inscribing four New Testament texts in Greek, e.g. *'Woe is unto me if I preach not the Gospel!'* [13] Was this the vicar's idea or that of the non-conformist but learned donor, Mr E.B. Dawson?

Part of the Greek Text on the Pulpit Rail

The organ was also improved at a cost of £60. From the start all new pews were free. The splendid carved armorials from the old Leighton pew are now on a pew on the north side.

Holy Trinity Church,
WARTON.

SERVICES
IN CONNECTION WITH THE

Formal Re-opening of this Church,
AFTER ITS RESTORATION WILL BE HELD ON T.

ON THURSDAY, MAY 4th, 1893.
AT 3 P.M., AND 7-30 P.M.

PREACHERS
THE RIGHT REVEREND THE

Lord Bishop of Barrow-in-Furness
AT 3 P.M. AND

THE REV. A. HAWORTH,
RECTOR OF St. CATHERINE'S, MANCHESTER
AT 7-30 P.M.

The Collections will be in aid of the Restoration
Fund.

In May 1893 Dr Warem, the Suffragan Bishop of Barrow, in a neighbouring diocese, preached at the opening service. The extensive restoration gave the church the aspect it has kept to this day.

Addendum

It is interesting that memory of the matter of the pews was revived in recent years when the vicar, Brian Oddy, and Mr. James Reynolds, the successor of the Gillows, discussed the use of the new pew, and the latter agreed that it could be used unless required by the family. In a letter dated December 17th, 1969 he claimed that '*the inhabitants of Leighton Hall are deemed to have the right to the use of the pew*'. He had lent it, he said, to Lord Peel who had recently died and was happy that others should use it, but '*you will understand our desire to keep alive this old historic right that dates from the time of Sir George Middleton in the seventeenth century.*'[14]

St. John's, Silverdale

Silverdale was the only other township where there had been a Church of England place of worship before the nineteenth century. A chapel-of-ease, rendered necessary by the long and difficult path to the parish church of St. Oswald's, had been established in the seventeenth century.

There was a steady rise in the population of Silverdale following the arrival of the railway, so that between 1851 and 1881 the population doubled, and then rose by another 20% to its peak in 1891, and there were the summer visitors as well. The result was discussion about the need for a new church. In 1871 Silverdale was established as an independent parish including Lindeth, though civically this was still part of the township of Warton-with-Lindeth.

In 1879, stimulated by the building of the Methodist Church, a site committee was formed. In 1883 a new site was approved and money raised by public subscription. The principal subscriber was Henry Boddington of the Cove, a member of the brewing family. Mrs. Murton of Highfield was another generous donor and provided a variety of features including the Clayton and Ball east window in memory of her husband. The architect appointed was William Ball of the Manchester practice of Ball and Elce. Pevsner describes the church as *'a successful design by a hardly known firm.'* [15] It was consecrated by Bishop Fraser of Manchester in 1886 and during the rest of the century much was done to beautify it with stained glass, a carved reredos and an organ by Abbott and Smith of Leeds. The old chapel remained as a mortuary chapel, but in recent years has been converted into houses.

Alfred Hadfield, an Oxford graduate, was curate and then vicar, and was succeeded by John Lloyd Pain, formerly vicar of near-by Holme in Westmorland, also an Oxford graduate. He was appointed by the vicar of Warton, Thomas Holland Pain, and as both were scholars of Brasenose College, Oxford, and both were ordained in Chester diocese in 1856, one might conjecture that they were related or even twins. John Lloyd Pain almost saw the century out, dying in 1893. William Sleigh, B.A., who lived well into the next century, succeeded him from Trinity College Dublin.

St. John's, Yealand Conyers
Yealand Conyers was the site of the first new church in Warton parish. St. John's was built there in 1838 (and somewhat enlarged in 1861 and in 1882).

In 1854 John Deane Freeman, who had been minister at St. John's almost from the inauguration of the church, died and was followed by William Maw Shaw, the son of a Leeds Wesleyan minister, who was born in 1818. A scholar of Sidney Sussex College, Cambridge, he graduated in 1840 and was ordained in Toronto to serve as a missionary for the Society for the Propagation of the Gospel at Emily in Canada. He remained there from 1841 to 1845. Returning to England he was curate of Highgate, Middlesex, until he came to Yealand. He is recorded in Crockford's *Clerical Directory* as the author of *The Scriptural Harmony between Private Judgement and Church Authority,* published in 1874 by Simpkin at 4s 6d.

When Shaw died in 1889 Joseph Mitchell, who was a qualified medical doctor, succeeded him. Mitchell had entered St. Thomas's Hospital as a medical student in 1866 and held various hospital posts, gaining his M.D. in 1887. In 1870 he set up as a private practitioner in London, but also worked as Medical Officer of Health for St. Pancras including the workhouse there. His work gave him much experience of not only the physical but also of the spiritual needs of slum dwellers. He determined that he must devote his life to trying to help them. He began to study for Holy Orders and eventually gave up his medical career to devote himself to missionary and social work. In 1878 he took up a curacy in a large city parish at New Wortley in Leeds, becoming vicar in 1881. He found pleasure in the hard work there, but his wife's health suffered, so in 1889 he accepted the offer from the Hyndman Trustees of the living of Yealand, where his wife's health improved.

He, like previous incumbents, was a churchman of the Evangelical school, '*a keen advocate for Sunday Observance; an ardent supporter of Foreign Missions and a strict teetotaller*' as the obituary notice has it. It adds that '*He was however tolerant with those who differed from him*'. He retired to Sussex at the age of seventy-five because of ill health, but was buried at Yealand. Yealand became a separate parish in 1871.

Christ Church, Carnforth

The old tithe-barn was licensed for worship in 1850 and also served as a school. Thomas Dean, the vicar of Warton, conducted services there. In 1865 a curate was appointed for Carnforth, made possible by a grant from the Ecclesiastical Commissioners (who had taken over Cathedral properties). They added £120 to the vicar's stipend on condition that a curate was paid at least that amount.

After several curates had short stays, J.A. Fidler was appointed in 1869. He is entered in Crockford as Atkinson-Fidler, trained at Queen's College, Birmingham, and ordained deacon at Chester. A year later he was ordained priest at Manchester.

Christ Church, Carnforth before addition of Tower

In 1875 Carnforth became a separate parish, thus completing the division of the old Parish of Warton into four. Fidler became the first vicar and spent his whole ministry there. In 1871 a church building was begun, designed by Daniel Brade and Edward Smailes, Kendal architects. It cost £2,100 and was consecrated by Bishop Fraser of Manchester in 1873. It was later enlarged and a tower added.

James Erving, the Churchwarden already mentioned as having disagreed with the vicar of Warton over stained glass windows, said that Ismay Barns, one of the short-stay curates *'left this district in October 1866 ... he has ... high church notions his principal reason for leaving was the lending of school forms by school master to an Inn for a club dinner ... and thought the forms would be desecrated by being so used.'*[16] The school master in question was Henry Inglis Orr, a prominent Carnforth citizen. Barns tried to have Orr dismissed, a much criticised move.[17]

Erving disagreed with Mr Fidler also. It was over some *'alteration to the altar space.'*[18] Erving was not much of a theologian, and he always quarrelled with clerics anyway, but his remarks do suggest that there were some high church notions in the air, and probably indicate that churchmanship at Carnforth, as in Warton, was moving in that direction.

Borwick and Priest Hutton

These townships had no church of their own until the closing years of the nineteenth century, though there had been a private chapel on Borwick Green, but even that was closed by the end of the seventeenth century.[19] After that it seems that the people of Borwick were expected to get themselves to St. Oswald's. Thomas Dean, after he was appointed vicar of Warton in 1844, arranged for a service to be held in the disused tithe-barn of the Dean and Chapter of Worcester in Priest Hutton. These services continued, and in 1883 Dean's successor, Thomas Holland Pain, appointed Peter Knowles as curate of Warton on the understanding that he lived at Priest Hutton and conducted the services there. Knowles had trained at St. Bees College in Cumberland, had been ordained in 1868 and, when he came to Priest Hutton, had six curacies behind him, including Silverdale.

The Sharp family, already mentioned in connection with St. Oswald's, had removed from Lancaster to Borwick after a cholera outbreak. A fine mural monument at St. Oswald's records members of the Taylor and Sharp families. William Sharp had married Jane Taylor, whose family farmed there. Sharp became a solicitor and was heavily involved in the legal saga of the disputed will of John Marsden of Hornby.[20] William and Jane Sharp had nine children, including one called William.

William Junior, became a solicitor, moved to London and had a grand house in Albert Gate. He was childless and, apparently impressed by Knowles' work as curate, offered to build a church on land owned by his family between the two villages. He commissioned Paley of Austin and Paley (the firm's name between 1886 and 1895) to design the church. James Hatch and Son of Lancaster were the contractors. A photograph in the vestry shows workers posing at the partially built church. The first sod was cut in May 1894 and the church was dedicated on June 24th, 1896. William Sharp bore the whole cost in memory of his wife Clara, whose portrait relief forms a mural monument within. Other members of the family contributed items including the pulpit; the west window was given by William's brother, Edward. The east and west windows are by Ward and Hughes, the same artists who had worked on windows in St. Oswald's.

The Roman Catholic Church
St. Mary's, Yealand Conyers, was designed by Edward Paley, one of whose principal churches was St. Peter's Lancaster, which is now the Cathedral. Richard Thomas Gillow, (the Old Squire), great-grandson of the founder of Gillow's furniture firm in Lancaster, although no longer involved in the firm, made his home at Leighton Hall until his death at the age of 99 in 1906. He provided the present church building of St. Mary in Yealand Conyers. The church was built adjacent to the already existing presbytery and chapel. Completed in 1852 it has been described

as *'Ultramontane and Gothic, the creation of squire and priest.'*[21] It is said to have been built in response to the challenge made in 1838 by the building in Ye">aland Conyers, of the (rather less Gothic) Anglican church of St. John's.

St.Mary's Catholic Church
Yealand

There is said to have been a chapel, large enough to seat a hundred, established at Holme, just over the border into Westmorland, by *'the catholic gentlemen of Warton'* in 1843 for the use of immigrant workers in the textile mill there, but it is not clear how long it survived.[22]

Apart from that, St. Mary's remained the only Catholic Church nearer than Lancaster until 1926 when a church was provided in Carnforth. That is presumably why the average attendance, given in the returns for the 1851 census, was as high as 170, a large figure for a purely local congregation even allowing for the large household at the Hall, and for the alleged preference for Catholic tenants shown by its successive owners. The make-up of the 1851 congregation is not known, but in the mid-eighteenth century there were said to have been 54 attending from the parish of Warton, 27 from Bolton-le-Sands and 12 from over the border in Westmorland.[23] The pattern may well have been much the same in the nineteenth century.

There does not seem to have been any wide-scale movement of Irish immigrants into the parish and the church in Yealand was essentially what has been called a seigneural creation, heavily dependent on the successive Catholic owners of Leighton Hall. It had the same priest, William Henderson, from 1846 to 1887. In 1891, James Birchall, a thirty-year-old man born in Lancaster, was entered in the census as the priest.

148

The Society of Friends, Yealand Meeting House

By the mid-century it had become apparent that the Quaker community in Yealand had changed from being a fellowship of farmers

Friend's Meeting House Yealand Conyers

to a phase when many of its leading members were wealthy industrialists.[24] It is noticeable that the Yealand meetings were often able to give as much or more than the larger Lancaster meetings to such good causes as the:

> *'Negro and Aboriginals Fund', 'coloured refugees from Slavery in North America'* and *'the relief of Friends in North Carolina.'*[25]

It must have been a shock when the flax-weaving business of the wealthiest of them all, William Waithman, failed catastrophically in 1853, and he was declared bankrupt. Until then he had been among the most active of members. As a bankrupt he was disowned (no longer counted as a member) by the Society. That was customary, for it was felt that to cause loss to others by taking ill-considered risks to gain wealth was unacceptable.

What particularly shocked the Society was that he *'had recourse to increased assistance from his Bankers on a Special Security'*, so harming smaller investors where *'losses will be severely felt by those on whom they fall'*. His wife then wrote a dignified letter resigning her membership. She did not wish to remain in the society *'without her dear husband.'*[26]

The Quaker attitude to tithes and Church Rates continued to give offence to others. James Erving, as churchwarden, recorded in the early 1860s that Captain Yates, churchwarden for Yealand, and Thomas Dean, the vicar, summoned *'Ford, Batt and Preston (Quakers) for church rate'*. The three Yealand Quakers *'did not appear, judgement against them.'*[27] They must have been among the last to suffer before church rates were made voluntary.

Gradually, over the second half of the nineteenth century, a new spirit of innovation was waking the whole Quaker community from a long period of withdrawal and resistance to change which had characterised it in the eighteenth and early nineteenth centuries. The minute books of Yealand Meeting show signs that this change was being felt locally.[28] A perhaps minor instance was the agreement in 1853 that gravestones were to be permitted, a break with a long-standing tradition. Their size was, however, specified and they were to be of undressed freestone.

In 1854 steps were taken to increase the meeting's holding of books, and to move the small library to Roger Preston's grocery shop, so that the books might be borrowed by those outside the meeting. In 1875 it was agreed that at business meetings men and women should meet jointly. Men and women had always been seen as having equal part in the business of the meeting, but they had always until then met separately as George Fox had arranged, feeling that women would not speak out in the presence of men. There were even signs of change in the policy of automatically disowning any member who married out, married a non-Quaker that is. It was a policy that must have been partly to blame for the general fall in membership over the century.

Wesleyan Methodism
Silverdale Chapel

The Wesleyan Methodist congregations in Arnside and Silverdale had both been largely the work of Robert Gibson, a tenant farmer who settled at Arnside Tower farm in the 1830s.[29] Gibson died in 1873 but his sons carried on his work. In 1876 the Robert Gibson Memorial Chapel was opened at Arnside, and attention then turned to the creation of a chapel building for the flourishing community in Silverdale.

150

A Bolton cotton spinner, John Hebden, had come to live at Woodlands in Silverdale about 1873 and he proved a generous and active leader. He set aside an outbuilding for Sunday and weekday services. The congregation, which met in this preaching room as it was called, became part of the Lancaster Wesleyan Methodist Circuit.[30]

In 1878 a meeting was held to choose a site for a chapel. Hebden offered as a gift Stone Acre, a field almost opposite the then site of St. John's Church of England church. This proximity raised some doubt, but it was almost unanimously decided to accept. A building committee was set up which included Mr. Hebden, the Gibson brothers, *'one or two farmers'* and a number of gentlemen from Lancaster. It also included Joseph Summerfield, the stationmaster, and Robert Lambert, the blacksmith. William Wright, *'architect and Methodist'*, offered his services free of charge. Wright is mentioned in a history of the Sharpe, Paley and Austin practice of Lancaster in a paragraph concerned with the people who worked for the firm. He is described as a Quantity Surveyor in the work on Giggleswick School in 1886.[31] This ties in with the Gothic nature of the Silverdale chapel and almost suggests that it could be thought of as a minor work of the Paley and Austin firm, though done gratuitously. Wright's plans were accepted and tenders received totalling £1,500.[32]

The finished church (Trinity Wesleyan) was opened on October 29th, 1879. The design of the chapel was typical of the break away, in that expansive period of Methodist development, from chapel architecture to a more ecclesiastical style. The building was Gothic in character and furnished with a central communion table and a pulpit on the south wall. It has a remarkable window described by Pevsner as *'a sumptuous Dec. rose window in the façade.'*[33] It shows a wheel within a square. Did this symbolise Hebden's origins as a spinner? Stained glass in the east window was also given by Hebden and his wife. In 1883, by means of a bazaar at the Woodlands and a final gift by Hebden, the building debt was cleared. In 1885 the schoolroom was added and an organ installed.

Tewitfield Chapel, Priest Hutton
In the 1851 religious census Tewitfield Methodists recorded that there were 100 sittings in their chapel. Since the average congregation on Sunday evenings was said to be 106 (and 22 Sunday scholars) it is not

surprising, perhaps, that in 1886 the old chapel, built in 1824, was enlarged by adding another storey. The original chapel was by then being described as a barn *as simple and comfortless as anything in the area*.[34] Since Tewitfield itself was merely a small part of Priest Hutton and the population of the whole of that township grew only from 234 in 1851 to 242 in 1891, the chapel must have been drawing its congregation from a wide area. It seems, indeed to have been a particularly lively congregation, not only active in its own affairs, but supplying a number of travelling preachers.[35] The enlargements to the chapel were to a design of William Wright. This seems to be the same person who designed the Silverdale chapel, but the Tewitfield chapel, being a mere enlargement of the original barn like building, could not be so Gothic.

Warton Methodist Church

According to the centenary history of the Wesleyan church in Warton there were Methodists in the township at least from the opening decades of the nineteenth century. By 1838 the group had built a chapel for themselves. It was not a large group. In the 1851 census average Sunday attendance was given as 12 and in the next few years it fell even lower. In 1858 there were said to have been only two members. Nevertheless if the church never had a large congregation in the nineteenth century, neither did it fade away. In 1868 the membership had risen again to 10. By 1881 the small congregation had finally managed to clear off the debt incurred when the chapel was built.[36] No obvious reason has emerged why the group in Warton remained small. Perhaps there were simply too many congregations in very close proximity; not only the very flourishing congregation at Tewitfield, but also the others described below in Carnforth, Borwick and Yealand Redmayne.

Carnforth

When the previous volume of this history was written it was thought that there was no record of the establishment of Methodism in the township of Carnforth.[37] Now an account has been found which fills the gap. A newspaper article on the Jubilee Celebrations of the Sunday School held in 1891 records an address by Mr. Unsworth, a long-term member of the congregation. He said that *there being no written history of the cause* he had *interviewed one or two friends*. What emerged was, of course, only what was recalled by a few elderly people some fifty years after the event, but it tells a story very typical of the establishment of Methodism in small communities all around; a story not so much of direct conversion by itinerant preachers as of an individual who had already been converted elsewhere moving into the township and opening his house to a small group ready to receive his message. It was what is known to have happened at Silverdale and Tewitfield and possibly, though this is not so clear, in Warton too.

What the elderly individuals related was that Methodism had been brought to Carnforth (at an unspecified date) by Stephen Harrison of Settle who came to live at Brow Foot Farm and opened his house for meetings. Then, Mr. Unsworth went on, '*About 51 years ago*', which would have been 1848 or so, a Mr. Thomas Stephenson offered his large kitchen at Carnforth House as a Sunday School. The kitchen soon became too small and new premises were found in what later became '*Mr. Wood's blacksmith's shop*', and the new Sunday school was opened in August 1849 by '*David Greenberry, a converted ex-prize fighter*'. Perhaps this was the David Greenberry (Granberry in the Lancaster Guardian) who is said to have had much influence on General Booth of the Salvation Army in his youth. Greenberry was not a prizefighter, but was said to have had all the appearance of a country squire. By 1870 even this new Sunday School was proving too small for '*the 70 or 80 scholars on the books*'.[38]

It was in that year that a chapel was built on Lancaster Road. The new chapel was able to seat a congregation of 250. The previous year three memorial stones had been laid, a ceremony at which a useful £121 3s 4d was '*placed on the stones*' to add to the £340 already raised by subscription. Mr. Barton, manager of the Iron Works, had given £5 (not over and above generous since at least five people had given £20 and over, but after all Mr. Barton was not a Methodist). The men from the Iron Works gave £7.[39] The Methodist church continued very active in Carnforth, as did the Sunday School. The Methodist church may well have been one of  the most important inspirations for the various temperance movements in Carnforth. Mr. Unsworth in his Jubilee address certainly thought so.

153

The Methodists had, he said, '... *done the greatest share of temperance work in the town*'. They had also, he threw in for good measure, initiated the Carnforth Brass Band and a Drum and Fife Band in connection with the Band of Hope.[40] Sadly the church building no longer survives.

Yealand Redmayne, Brackenthwaite

The small Methodist group described in the 1851 census met in the house of Thomas Burrow Bush. In the main census Bush is entered as an agricultural labourer of 31 years born in Yeoland, with a wife, Ellen, who had been born in Levens, Westmorland. The Kendal circuit plan shows that there was a Methodist group in Levens. It could be that at some point Bush had been hired on a farm there and been converted. If so the Yealand group might count as another example of how Methodism was brought to small communities by an incomer converted elsewhere. The group is always referred to as at Brackenthwaite. One assumes that Bush, as an agricultural labourer, was living in a tied cottage on the Brackenthwaite estate. It would have been difficult for him to hold a non-conformist meeting in the face of opposition from his employer, but in 1851 Brackenthwaite was owned by Mr. Waithman who, as a Quaker, might well have had some sympathy with a fellow dissenter. Brackenthwaite continues to be mentioned in the circuit plan until 1855 (when it was bracketed with the Warton group). After that no more is heard of it.

Borwick

In 1859 the circuit plan mentions a group at Borwick that held a meeting every week (this was not the Tewitfield meeting in neighbouring Priest Hutton for that is mentioned separately). The Borwick group was still being mentioned in 1868. As far as can be traced no account of this group was ever written down. One mention of it has been found in a newspaper article in 1869 that reported that the group met weekly in a building constructed out of two cottages and of '*very limited dimensions*'.[41] There was never a purpose built chapel, but the group survived beyond the nineteenth century.

Primitive Methodism, Millhead

As well as the Wesleyan Methodist group in Warton another branch of Methodism became established there among the ironworkers in Millhead. Primitive Methodism resulted from a dispute over the holding of American style Camp Meetings in 1807. These were forbidden by the rather conservative Methodist Conference, fearful of imputations of political sedition during the Napoleonic war. Two preachers, Hugh Bourne and William Clowes, disregarded the prohibition and held such a meeting on Mow Cop, a hill in Staffordshire, and were ejected from the connexion. They formed a new one called Primitive and this spread almost as widely as the parent body. Its membership was more radical in political and liturgical views than the Wesleyans, and was also mainly of a lower social order. It seems probable that this movement was brought to the area by the ironworkers from the Midlands, though there is a gap in information between the arrival of the first ironworkers in 1864 and the building of the chapel in 1873. The foundation stone was laid by James Williamson Junior (this would be the son who later became Lord Ashton).[42] Williamson himself was an Anglican, but he apparently thought working class religious dissent was worth encouraging as tending to produce hard-working and loyal employees.[43] The Millhead chapel survived the Methodist union in the twentieth century, but closed in the 1940s.

The Congregational Church, Emmanuel Chapel, Carnforth

In 1866 an agent of the Congregational Union from the High Street Congregational Church in Lancaster '*laboured for nine months*' in Carnforth with no result '*because of the changing characteristic of the people.*'[44] The Emmanuel congregation started later as a withdrawal from the Methodists. The story has been learnt from the late Ruth Baddeley, author of the Jubilee history of the church.[45]

Two very personal issues were apparently involved. The first was the desire of a Mr. Stephenson of Carnforth to marry his deceased wife's sister; a hot political issue at the time as evidenced by W.S. Gilbert's famous words in *Iolanthe*, '*And prick that annual blister, Marriage with deceased wife's sister*'.

By the marriage act of 1835 all such marriages had been declared void. Ministers of the Church of England would not perform the ceremony, but Methodist churches seem sometimes to have taken a more relaxed view. At any rate Mr. Stephenson left the Anglican church and joined the Carnforth Methodist Church, of which he became a prominent member.

155

The second issue was the breaking of a marriage engagement between a daughter of the Stephenson family and the son of another prominent Methodist family. Thomas Stephenson, a draper and a prominent citizen in Carnforth, felt he could no longer be associated with the chapel. The young man, he learnt, had been *'dallying elsewhere'* and had, indeed, fathered a child.

Mr. Stephenson and a group of friends began to meet in a room over the stable of his shop in Market Street that was used, during the week, by his seamstresses. Adam Scott, minister of the Centenary Congregational church in Moorgate, Lancaster, became interested and so did a leading member of his congregation. This was E.B. Dawson, of Aldcliffe Hall, who had considerable property in the Carnforth area. In May 1879 a room was rented, furnished, and opened for worship by Adam Scott. On Boxing Day that year the Sunday School tea party and concert was held.

Scott, in opening the proceedings, asserted that *'They had not begun work in the town of Carnforth in opposition to any other Christian church (hear, hear) and that, through the kindness of the vicar of Carnforth, they met for their entertainment in the National School'*.[46]

Dawson gave land on which a school chapel, which could seat 200-250 people, was erected. It was formally opened in October 1880.[47] In 1882 it was felt possible to invite a minister of their own and W.H. Towers, a farmer's son from Nether Kellet who had studied at the Nottingham Institute, a training college for preachers, was appointed. He moved on to Manchester in 1886 and was succeeded by the Rev. J. Harrison who was still in charge at the end of the century. In 1889 another classroom was added, largely financed by Dawson. Before long the building of a new chapel was planned. This was designed by Dawson's son, Howard, a 32 year old architect, who did not survive to complete it.

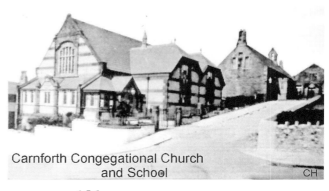

Carnforth Congregational Church and School

The estimated cost was £1,000, towards which E.B. Dawson was the principal subscriber. The new church was opened in 1897 in Hawk Street. The old church continued in use for the school.

The Salvation Army

A new denomination had appeared in the 1860s with William and Catherine Booth's development of open-air preaching and the use of military titles. The Salvation Army visited Carnforth in 1882, and later began meeting in what were called barracks, a wooden barn behind Hunter Street. A well-supported first meeting there, followed by a parade, was reported in 1886. Another report spoke of 22 *'little soldiers'* parading around the village before a public meeting.[48]

In the 1891 census there was a Salvation Army Officer, Elizabeth Barber living at 8 Booth Street. She was unmarried, aged 22, and living alone. It seems she married shortly after, for in November 1891 the death, at the age of 24, of the wife of Captain Watson of 8 Booth Street was recorded. The newspaper article only says the illness was *'very short'*. The funeral was said to be very simple; no hearse, the coffin was carried on a wagonette. On top of the coffin were laid the dead woman's bible, bonnet and tambourine. The young death seems to have made a big impression. Three hundred people followed the coffin to its burial place in Warton.[49] This was the first Salvation Army funeral held in Warton.

The work continued and the names of other officers working in Carnforth are recorded from time to time in the newspapers. The Salvation Army did not restrict their activities to Carnforth. It seems to have been a custom to visit (with the band) Silverdale and sometimes Arnside and Storth, at Easter and Whitsuntide.

---

[1] J. Rawlinson Ford, & J.A. Fuller-Maitland eds., *Lucas's History of Warton Parish (compiled 1710-1740)* (Kendal: Titus Wilson & Son, 1931) p.27.

[2] Trinity College, Cambridge, *Rectoria de Warton*, a terrier (a photocopy is held by the Mourholme Local History Society).

[3] Mourholme Local History Society Book Goup, *Warton 1800 – 1850: How a North Lancashire Parish Changed* (Mourholme Local History Society 2005), pp.144-161.

[4] James Erving of Thwaite Gate, Carnforth: notebook with memoranda on international news and local and family events in Carnforth and Rochdale 1838-73. 1857, p.187. Lancashire Record Office, DP494/1 acc 9158.

[5] Ford & Fuller-Maitland, *Lucas's History of Warton*, p.12.

[6] James Erving of Thwaite Gate, Carnforth: notebook, 1857, p.187. Lancashire Record Office, DP494/1 acc 9158.

[7] *Westmorland Gazette*, August 18th, 1888.

[8] Warton Parish, Churchwardens' Accounts, Lancashire Record Office, PR 572.

[9] Kenneth Beaulah & Hans van Lemmon, *Church Tiles of the Nineteenth Century*, (Shire Publications Ltd., 1987), p.184.

[10] *Westmorland Gazette*, August 18th, 1888.

[11] School Log Book Archbishop Hutton's School Warton, April 1889, Lancashire Record Office, PR 3332 acc.5192.

[12] Press cuttings from Lancaster and Westmorland papers, formerly in the church archives and now in the possession of the Mourholme Local History Society, give detailed reports on the consistory court and parish Meetings.

[13] *The Bible, The Authorized King James Version*, "The First Epistle of Paul the Apostle to the Corinthians," 9:16 (First published in 1611).

[14] James Reynolds, letter concerning pew in Warton Church, 17th December 1969. Warton Parish Church archives.

[15] Nikolaus Pevsner, *Buildings of England: North Lancashire* (Penguin, 1969).

[16] James Erving of Carnforth: notebook, 1867, p.227. Lancashire Record Office, DP494/1 acc 9158.

[17] *Lancaster Guardian*, June 2nd, June 9th; June 23rd, 1866.

[18] James Erving of Carnforth: notebook, p.269. Lancaster Record Office, DP494/1 acc 9158.

[19] William Farrer, & J. Brownbill, eds., *Victoria History of the County of Lancaster*, vol.8 (Constable, 1914), p.175.

[20] Emmeline Garnett, *John Marsden's Will, the Hornby Castle Dispute, 1780-1840* (Hambledon Press, 1998).

[21] J.A. Hilton, *The Catholic Revival in Yealand, 1782-1832* (Preston, 1952), p.1.

[22] K. Laybourn, *A Comparative Study of Holme and Burneside* (M.A. Thesis, University of Lancaster, 1969), p.82.

[23] Hilton, *The Catholic Revival in Yealand*, p.4.

[24] Angus Winchester, *Yealand Quakers: The History of a Country Meeting* (Philoscopus Publications, 1993).

[25] Lancaster Monthly Meeting, Minute Book, 12 May 1852 – 9 December 1863. Lancashire Record Office, FRL 2/1/1/19.

[26] Lancaster Monthly Meeting, Minute Book, 12 May 1852 – 9 December 1863. Lancashire Record Office, FRL 2/1/1/19, March 1855.

[27] James Erving of Carnforth: notebook, 1861, p.207. Lancaster Record Office, DP494/1 acc 9158.

[28] Yealand Preparative Meeting, Minute Book, 1844. Lancashire Record Office, FRL 8/1/1/.

[29] Mourholme, *Warton 1800-1850*, pp.156, 157.

[30] Silverdale Methodist Church Council, *Silverdale Methodist Church, a Short History 1879-1979*, Lancaster Reference Library, Local Pamphlets J6 LAN/SIL.

[31] James Price, *Sharp, Paley and Austin: a Lancaster Architectural Practice 1836-1942* (Lancaster: Centre for North-West Regional Studies, University of Lancaster, 1998), p.10.

[32] Silverdale Methodist Church Council, *Silverdale Methodist Church*, Lancaster Reference Library, Local Pamphlets J6 LAN/SIL.

[33] Pevsner, *Buildings of England: North Lancashire*.

[34] *Lancaster Guardian*, March 13th, 1886.

[35] Wesleyan Methodist Circuit Plans, Lancaster Record Office, Mla, 1/1/5.

[36] Eva Needham, *Yes in Christ: Warton Methodist Church 1838-1938* (1988).

[37] Mourholme, *Warton 1800-1850*, p.157.

[38] *Lancaster Guardian*, July 29th, 1899.

[39] *Lancaster Gazette*, July 10th, 1869.

[40] *Lancaster Guardian*, July 29th, 1899.

[41] *Lancaster Gazette*, July 10th, 1869.

[42] *Lancaster Guardian*, April 26th, 1873.

[43] Phillip J. Gooderson, *Lord Linoleum: Lord Ashton, Lancaster and the rise of the British Oilcloth and Linoleum Industry* (Keele University Press, 1996), pp.93, 156.

[44] Ruth Badley, *Emmanuel Congregational Church, Carnforth 1880-1980* (1980), p.1.

[45] Badley, *Emmanuel Congregational Church*, p.2ff.

[46] *Lancaster Guardian*, January 3rd, 1880.

[47] *Lancaster Guardian*, October 30th, 1880.

[48] *Lancaster Guardian,* April 9th, 1887.
[49] *Lancaster Guardian,* November 7th, 1891.

Chapter Eight

PUBLIC HEALTH AND PRIVATE MEDICINE

Perhaps to talk about private medicine in the nineteenth century is somewhat confusing. Today, private medicine has come to refer only to the medical help which a person pays for individually, and to exclude similar help paid for indirectly through the National Health Service.

In the nineteenth century the attendance of a doctor in sickness was always something that had to be paid for by the patient (though he might get help from charity or personal insurance with a Friendly Society and the like). The only exception was the medical care allotted to paupers through the Poor Law system. Public Health, then as now, referred to general measures taken at a public level to ensure better health for the nation, measures such as improved sanitation, safer drinking water, cleaner air and, the first of the personal protection projects, vaccination of individuals against smallpox. Doctors in the nineteenth century were becoming more and more involved with these measures and the government, having passed compulsory legislation, had to man the new services and so to pay a salary or fees to private doctors to take on such public work as Medical Officer of Health to a sanitary district, Poor Law Doctor, Appointed Factory Doctor and Public Vaccinator.

Private Medicine: The Medical Act 1858

The medical profession was coming under closer central scrutiny. Medical training had undergone thorough review by the Select Committee on Medical Education of 1834. Its report, together with agitation from within the profession, led ultimately to the Medical Act of 1858. The professional aim of the doctors in their support for this Act (though they did not speak with one voice) was the protection of the public by the improvement of medical training and by insisting on the professional validation of claims to being qualified to practice medicine. There was also, not unnaturally, a strong wish to preserve their profession from competition from those who had avoided the expense of training. The Act gave power to what came to be known as the General Medical Council to approve training courses, define qualifications and also to act as the arbiter of professional ethics. One single public register of all legally recognised practitioners was to be kept; admission to the register was to be authorised by the General Medical Council, which was subject only to the Privy Council. (Lamentably, a practitioner could be recognised even if he only had a qualification in either medicine or surgery; he did not need both). Self-organized, *ad hoc* training was out, as was training through apprenticeship alone. To the intense chagrin of doctors, the mere practice of healing by the non-registered was not made illegal provided no false claim to qualification was made.

By the second half of the nineteenth century, many country practitioners, certainly those in the north of England, had a top class medical degree: the M.D. from Edinburgh, Glasgow or, in an increasing trickle, from the new London University. For a time an M.D. could still be purchased from Aberdeen or St. Andrew's University by paying a modest fee and having the recommendation of two colleagues, as Edward Jenner had done.[1]

It became more and more common for doctors to be both medically and surgically qualified, that is as Licentiates of the Society of Apothecaries (L.S.A.) and Members of the Royal College of Surgeons (M.R.C.S.) they became, in fact, general practitioners. They also commonly, either to gain experience or to eke out their income or both, took up paid public appointments of various kinds, such as that of Poor Law Medical Officer. It was legally necessary to have both qualifications to obtain that appointment, as it was to be a factory doctor, physician to a public lunatic asylum, surgeon to a hospital, and a doctor working for insurance companies or friendly societies. It is hard to over-emphasize the impact such a requirements made on health care and medical practice.

Medical Practitioners in Warton Parish
As the century advanced it becomes possible to trace individual practitioners working locally through the new Medical Directory as well as through local trade directories and the census returns. All the doctors were reasonably qualified according to the standards of the time, and some highly so.

Dr. Peter Allen of Yealand Conyers

It is not known exactly when Dr. Allen came to the parish, but the

No. 3 Ivy Cottages, Yealand Conyers

1861 census records a Dr. Allen at number three Ivy Cottages in Yealand Conyers living with his wife and mother-in-law. He kept two resident house servants, an indication of a comfortable lifestyle. During the time he was in Yealand he moved from Ivy Cottages to Laurel Bank. He stayed in Yealand until 1868, and then went to London, becoming a consulting surgeon at St. Mary's Hospital. He developed typhoid fever and died in February 1874 at the age of only 47 years.

It is intriguing to wonder how it was that someone like Peter Allen came to an out-of-the-way country practice in Warton parish. Was there, perhaps, some connection with the area? His career here was not entirely happy. He had been appointed as Medical Officer to the Lancaster Poor Law Union but in 1858 was accused by the Guardians of failing in his duty. The story can be followed, more or less, in the pages of the *Lancaster Gazette*.[2] It concerned Robert Fell, a young farm servant in Yealand Redmayne who had his finger trapped in a winnowing machine. As far as one can tell at this distance of time Allen's emergency treatment, by amputating a finger that was already almost completely severed, was both appropriate and prompt; the argument that arose was over whether he should have refused follow-up treatment until the Guardians had promised to pay for all treatment. It was all a little absurd because, in the course of a seven hour formal enquiry, it turned out that Robert Fell never wanted free treatment, in fact was indignant at being thought a pauper. Perhaps Allen's real fault was not having listened to his patient. The Poor Law Commissioners in London wrote to him calling for his resignation, which he promptly tendered.

The Lancaster Poor Law Union then advertised for a new fully qualified doctor to become Medical Officer to the Northern Division, at a salary of £20 per annum (and certain extra fees).[3] The appointment was held for a while by two further local doctors, Dr. Wm. Jackson of Bolton-le-Sands (of whom more below) then by a Dr. George D. Hunt, of Warton, but in 1865 Dr. Allen was re-appointed. It does seem that Dr. Allen's original transgression had been a technical lapse but not a heinous offence.

Dr. James Matthews of Yealand Conyers

Dr. Matthews followed Dr. Allen at Laurel Bank in 1868. He had studied at Guy's Hospital, qualifying in 1862. He obtained a further qualification in Dublin in 1869. After a while in Laurel Bank he moved

up the road to live and practise from a larger house, Clifford Hall. The surgery itself was a separate one-storey building with two rooms, a waiting room and its own entrance from a side road, Dykes Lane. There was a lamp at the entrance behind a sheet of red glass, which, when lit, indicated that the surgery was open. The glass panel was still there in 1990, but Clifford Hall has now

Laurel Bank, Yealand Conyers

been converted to separate dwellings and the surgery building demolished. Dr. Matthews' practice covered a fairly wide area, but was mostly concentrated within a four mile radius which included the seven townships of Warton parish, together with Burton-in-Kendal and Holme.

He called other doctors in for consultations, some local and also some from afar. For example, Dr. Whitehead of Manchester was called to see Mrs. Gillow of Leighton Hall. In 1868 Dr. Matthews accompanied Mrs. Gillow to Clifton in Bristol, possibly for spa treatment there. He also attended the pupils and staff at Burton House, a private school run by a Mrs. Nutter. It seems likely that Dr. Matthews dispensed medicines for his own patients. There was a chemist and druggist in both Milnthorpe and Carnforth by 1879, but neither would have been easy to reach. It was in any case customary for rural patients to collect their own medicines from the surgery. Dr. Matthews was also surgeon to the Carnforth Iron Company, medical referee for the Provincial Insurance Company and for the Briton Medical Assurance Company, Medical Officer to the Lancaster Union, Public Vaccinator and Appointed Factory Doctor.

A certificate given in 1875 by Dr. Matthews, as the Certifying Factory Surgeon, concerns a girl, Margaret, who was seeking employment at Holme Mills. Dr. Matthews' task was to give his opinion on her age – her parents were very unlikely to have troubled to have obtained a birth certificate in those days. He gave it as his opinion that she was at least eight years old, and was not incapacitated by infirmity from working '*for the time allowed by the act.*'

As can be seen in the illustration below the certificate is headed: **Factory Regulations Act, 7 Vic[toria] c. 5.** (i.e.1844).

It is a good reminder of the limited power of the 1870 Education Act or the Factory Acts to keep children in school and out of the mills.

Dr. Matthews' Day Book, running from January 1st, 1868, to January 6th, 1869, has survived in private hands. The book tells nothing of Dr. Matthews' routine consultations with patients or of his methods of diagnosis, but it does show that his work included setting fractures, lancing abscesses, syringing ears, tooth extractions, even amputations after an industrial accident. He delivered one, two or more babies a month. He does not record much detail about the births, or whether there was a midwife in attendance too. In the year covered by the Day Book only one neonatal death was recorded. He prescribed cough mixtures, antacids, tonics, purgatives and considerable amounts of opiates, though probably not more than was customary at a time when opium was the only reliable pain reliever (even aspirin was not available till the very end of the century). The only medicines among those listed that in any way attacked the basis of the disease, rather than merely lessening symptoms, were colchicum (which still has its place in the pharmacopoeia for the treatment of gout) and sulphur ointment for scabies. Only in his rôle as public vaccinator against smallpox had he anything specific to offer in infectious disease. Otherwise he could only have offered diagnosis, advice and the reassurance of his presence. The latter he could, and apparently did supply. He was permanently on call, all night and at weekends including Sunday. Only one entry betrays impatience. He was called out for a journey of several miles at night and recorded it in medical dog-latin as '*Iter* [journey] *and botheration.*'[4]

Dr. William Jackson and Dr. Edward Sidall Jackson
In 1860 the *Lancaster Guardian* reported that Dr. Jackson had been involved in a minor accident in Warton; his horse had fallen in the shafts and the passengers had been thrown out of the trap. Obviously there were hazards on the roads for country practitioners. The 1861 census shows William Jackson living at Waterloo Cottage in Bolton-le-Sands and practising as a surgeon. He was aged 33 at the time, had been born in Warton and had qualified as a Member of the Royal College of Surgeons, but does not seem to have held any qualification as a physician. He and his wife Sarah employed two domestic servants. They had three children; the eldest was six years old and had been born in Bolton-le-Sands suggesting that Dr. Jackson had been there at least since 1854. The next son, Edward Sidall, was four years old at the time. His career is considered next.

Unquestionably the main doctor in the area towards the end of the century was Dr. Edward Sidall Jackson of Market Street, Carnforth. He was doubly qualified from Edinburgh both as M.B. (Bachelor of Medicine), and C.M. (Master of Chirurgery, which was the preferred name for surgeons in Scotland). Both qualifications had been earned in 1879. In 1900 he obtained the higher qualification of M.D. (Doctor of Medicine), also from Edinburgh. He first partnered, and then succeeded, his father William who died in 1892. He was appointed Medical Officer of the Bolton-le- Sands and Carnforth District of the Lancaster Union. He employed a succession of assistants. The practice was based in Carnforth. In 1902 he moved from the old surgery in Market Street to Robin Hill, a new-built house and surgery in the same street. Robin Hill was to continue as a doctor's home and surgery until September 1956 (though minus the glass cases of stuffed birds which were a well remembered feature of Dr. Jackson's waiting room).[5]

There is a small notebook, which has survived from the Jackson practice with '*Prescriptions*' written on the cover. Inside it is stamped on the first page '*1869*', so it must originally have belonged to Dr. William Jackson of Bolton-le-Sands, then to Dr. E.S. Jackson, then to his successors.[6] The information it provides is unfortunately limited. Sometimes the patient's name has a brief address beside it and from that it can be seen that the area covered by the practice included the various townships of the parish as well as Burton and even over to Aughton four miles to the east.

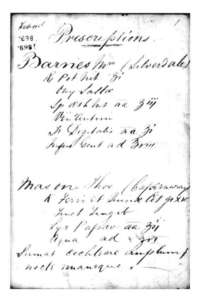

His heavy workload included a high proportion of accidental injuries – only too common as has been said in earlier chapters - on the railways and in the ironworks. A surprising amount of accident and emergency medical care was associated with increasing road traffic. Even Dr. Jackson was thrown from his trap (like his father before him) when the reins broke, but he does not seem to have been injured.[7] A few examples will illustrate the road accident cases to which Dr. Jackson and his colleagues were called.

Dr. E.S.Jackson of Carnforth

A Silverdale lad, William Robinson, was kicked in the head by a horse belonging to Capstick the butcher. He was reported to be in a critical condition under the care of Dr. Jackson.[8] G.B. Adamson, hairdresser of Carnforth, was thrown over the handlebars of his bicycle *'with great force'* when the rubber tyre came off near Morecambe; he had a broken arm and bruises. A man driving a young horse from the gasworks at Carnforth lost control and crashed against a shop. He was taken to Dr. John Joseph Butler's surgery in New Street.[9] One other example may suffice. A trap party from Morecambe was going to a sale when a horse bolted near Howard Cottages by the wooden bridge over the River Keer. Seven adults and two children were injured. One woman is said to have been seriously injured. Mr. Edward Parker, manager of the Midland Wagon Department who lived in one of Howard Cottages, stretchered the injured to the Albion Temperance Hotel, Carnforth.[10] Dr. Jackson and his assistant, Dr. Winter, attended promptly. Later in the week it was reported that Miss Pilling, the woman with the serious injuries, was still in a very critical state.[11]

To mention only these well-known practitioners might give a false picture of the situation. The names of other doctors come and go in the records. In the 1871 census, Dr. Matthews had a 20-year-old assistant, George Simpson, living with him. It was common for young doctors to seek employment here and there as assistants to gain experience, accumulate capital and then buy their own practice. Since they would only be in any one place for brief periods, information about them is usually lacking – usually unrecorded in trade directories, census records or newspapers. The Medical Directory of 1889 does place Irish-born Dr. Butler in New Street, Carnforth. Dr. Butler was to become prominent as a member of Carnforth U.D.C. The 1891 census for Silverdale shows a Dr. Frederick Dinwoodie, described as '*M.D. and surgeon*'. He had been born in Appleby and in 1891 was a 47 year-old widower who lived at Lindeth View and was cared for by a housekeeper. He has already appeared in these pages, though not by name, as the doctor who dealt sympathetically with a confused old man who attempted suicide in 1892 (see chapter six).

Paying for Treatment

The income of local doctors came basically from the fees they charged plus payment for prescriptions. There is no clear and comprehensive schedule of charges available, only odd entries such as that Dr. Matthews in the 1860s asked 6s for an inhaler and 12s for a ring pessary. When he had to amputate William Barnes' left arm after an industrial accident he charged £3. Barnes was working as a labourer for a coal company at New England, a small settlement on the canal in Priest Hutton. Dr. Matthews fee of £3 would have been an overwhelming sum for a labourer whose weekly wage might well have been a third of that or less and who was presumably going to be off work indefinitely. One hopes the company paid. In general bills were sent out to patients, the fees charged being tailored to their assumed financial standing; wealthy patients were charged much more for services than those on lower incomes.

Most practitioners had a scale of fees, say 1s 6d per mile travelled; attendance on a pauper 1s, on a labourer 1s 6d, a tradesman 2s 6d; perhaps 10s 6d to £1 1s 0d for a confinement.

Incomes of £150 - £200 per year in the country and £300 - £400 in the towns were common for doctors. Few came to a comfortable income before about 40 years of age. Most were overworked; on call all hours for fifty-two weeks a year.[12] Being civil to affluent snobs, bearing with slow payers, treating scores of sick who never paid, all added up to a stressful, gruelling life. A writer on medical history has said:

> '*Two things above all were essential for the success of a country practitioner: a good reputation and a good horse.*'[13]

The importance of Friendly Societies in helping to tide people over in times of sickness goes well back to the first half of the century.[14] Their importance continued to grow. At the end of the nineteenth century Friendly Societies were '*the largest exclusively working class organisation in Britain.*'[15] Membership in 1900 totalled about 5.6 million in Great Britain. The local newspapers of this period carry many items about these societies, so it is reasonable to assume that many patients covered themselves and their families for medical costs in this way.

Then there was the Poor Law system. One entry in Dr. Matthews' daybook was overwritten '*pauper*', presumably meaning that the Overseers would pay. Dr. Matthews had different account numbers for some large estates, so that he could bill the proprietor for service to family and estate people. Another system of numbering does seem possibly to allow for claims against an insurance scheme such as a Friendly Society.

Hospitals

Even if the work of local medical practitioners did not change enormously in the last years of the century, there were changes in what might be called the back-up and ancillary services. Though the greater part of medical work was undertaken by the general practitioners treating patients at their surgeries or in the home, yet increasing amounts of medical care were being undertaken at the Lancaster Infirmary, first in its old building in Thurnham Street and then, from 1896, at the New Royal Infirmary.

Lancaster Infirmary 1901

During 1854 there had been 29 surgical inpatients and nine deaths; in 1858 there were 53 surgical cases, of whom eight required operation, all making good recovery. In 1873 there were 121 admissions, 64 of them surgical, of whom 11 died. From 1886 surgical practice became more accurately documented, especially from 1896 when records of routine anaesthesia appear - this was the year the New Infirmary opened on the 24th of March and the first honorary anaesthetist, W. Dodgson Barrow, was appointed.

That year 140 operations were carried out, with 125 anaesthetics undertaken.[16] In 1889, work people contributing to the Lancaster Infirmary weekly collection included Midland Rail Company employees in Carnforth £2, Carnforth Passenger Department of Furness Permanent Way £3.[17]

There were moves to set up hospitals in the Warton district. In 1878 at the inquest on James Thomas Hinde, who had died after a mismanaged first aid treatment for a railway accident (see Chapter 2), the Coroner said that the Railway Company should have a cottage hospital at Carnforth to save patients being jolted to Lancaster.[18] In the 1897 Jubilee Year it was proposed that to commemorate Queen Victoria's 60 year reign, a cottage hospital should be built which, it was felt, would have allowed the parish doctors to extend the scope of their work. Both proposals came to nothing.

There were even more persistent, and partially successful, attempts to erect a Fever Hospital. Its story can be read in the reports of the District Medical Officer for Lancaster Rural Sanitary Authority[19] and in contemporary newspaper reports.

The waves of infectious diseases were seen as a continual reproach to the public health authorities. Compulsory notification of the more virulent infectious diseases and the provision of an isolation hospital were two measures repeatedly demanded. The 1887 Silverdale township meeting discussed proposals to build an infectious diseases hospital at Silverdale, but rejected it in favour of a small cottage hospital at Carnforth.[20] In the end it was agreed that a portable hospital with six beds was to be sited in a field in Carnforth (it was to serve the whole Rural District, which was why it had to be portable). It was bought and erected in 1888 and moved from place to place several times;[21] in an outbreak of fever in 1890 there was even a possibility that a second portable hospital might be needed.[22]

The Medical Officer wanted the hospital to be for the Warton sub-district only, which he thought *'quite large enough to require the exclusive use of it'*. He added that *'the cost of transport ... renders it practically useless for the other portions of the district'*.[23] In 1891, when Carnforth was visited by an epidemic of measles followed by one of scarlet fever, it was reported that there had been better control achieved by using the hospital, which now had a kitchen and pantry adjoining it. In 1892 the hospital at Carnforth was unoccupied, according to the Medical Officer, *'chiefly on account of the damage, expense and delay attendant on its removal'*.

In 1894, the hospital was again put in order for fever cases by the new Carnforth Urban District Council (though it was noted that parents were refusing to allow their children to be moved there). The portable hospital finally succumbed to the severe storms at the end of 1894. By 1899 arrangements had been entered into with Lancaster for transferring all cases of infectious disease to the isolation hospital there.

For other specialised hospitals Warton parish had to depend on county provision. The County Lunatic Asylum had been opened in Lancaster in 1816 and the Royal Albert Asylum for Idiots and Imbeciles of the Northern Counties was added between 1864 and 1870.[24] No offence was meant (and possibly not all that much taken), at this date, by the blunt titles of the two hospitals; it was simply standard usage, and the opening of the Royal Albert was obviously seen as an occasion for jollification.

School children took an unofficial day off to see *'the laying of the foundation stone at the new Idiots' Asylum in Lancaster.'*[25]

Nursing
An important ancillary service increasingly available was the professional nursing care which could be offered by District Nurses, that is nurses paid for out of public money to nurse the poor. Schools were being established for their training, the earliest in Liverpool in 1863.[26]

No record of any such treasure in Warton parish itself has been found. There was no midwife living in the parish either. Most deliveries still took place at home. A doctor might be present and, since 1886, training in midwifery had been compulsory for medical qualification. The delivery was more likely to be supervised by a woman from the village than by a doctor, but she would most commonly not be formally trained, but rather a neighbour who had gained experience on the job. Training in midwifery had been available from the 1860s, but it was not till 1902 that training was legally required for those practising midwifery for gain, and even then sufficient previous experience without training was enough for registration.

Private Medicine: Conclusion

Undeniably great advances in health care had been made through the century. The better training and the setting of standards for the medical profession, the application of developing biological sciences and even more importantly, a background of better nutrition and improved public health measures, had all played their part. They also pointed the way to further improvement that continued through the twentieth century.

The country general practitioner in areas like Warton had status and a reasonably good standard of life gained by gruelling work. However it has to be admitted that, as yet, what curative medicine had to offer remained disappointingly ineffective.

Public Health: Cholera and the Public Health Acts

Over the years Warton parish, like everywhere else, felt the effects of the new technology and the new attitudes of the Victorian age. The nation as a whole had been aroused to make *An Attack on Filth* (the capital letters almost write themselves). As described in an earlier volume of this history,[27] the first major shock to complacency was the coming of cholera in 1831.

It was followed by the publication in 1842 of Dr. Chadwick's monumental report on the *Sanitary Conditions of the Labouring Population*.[28] His findings were shocking enough to shake all complacency and in 1848, a Public Health Act was finally passed. It set up a central General Board of Health and empowered local authorities to establish boards of their own (but compelled them only if the annual death rate was above twenty-three per thousand over the preceding seven years). The boards were to have powers over sewers and drains and water supplies, also the regulation of slaughter houses, all offensive trades and all nuisances, as the phrase was; to decide if houses were fit for human habitation, to provide burial grounds and more besides. The first efforts rather naturally went to improving conditions in towns. Chadwick's report had not exonerated the countryside, but the effects of bad sanitation there were not as dramatically noticeable as in the towns.

A further Public Health Act of 1872 specifically included rural areas and was mandatory. In accordance with its terms a Lancaster Rural Sanitary Authority was established in 1873.

Its area of administration was that of the already established Poor Law Union, and so included all the townships of Warton parish. In 1874 the Authority appointed a Medical Officer of Health, Dr. John Harker. In the first instance he was given a salary of £75 per annum. The salary was plainly felt to be an imposition on the rates, for two years later there was an attempt to reduce it to £10 on the ground that his services had not benefited the district '*to an extent equivalent to £75*'.[29] A compromise was reached at £50.

An Inspector of Nuisances, Mr. Jeremiah Jowett, had been appointed the previous year with a salary of £150 per annum (but the holder of the office had to double as the Authority's Surveyor and was a full time employee). Mr. Jeremiah Jowett is one of the district's unsung heroes. He held his post for over 25 years, despite constant trouble with his breathing, and died in harness in 1898. His obituary claims for him responsibility for the sewage works at Carnforth, Ellel, Bolton-le-Sands, Scotforth, Skerton, Warton, Slyne, Glasson and Heysham. This is a less than adequate tribute. It does not reveal, as contemporary reports do, the indifference and often downright opposition he had to contend with from authorities who were less than convinced that public money should be spent on sanitation. Nor does it speak of what was perhaps his major achievement, a painstaking determination to follow up any infringement of each new regulation, whether to do with sanitation, water supply, housing or animal care.

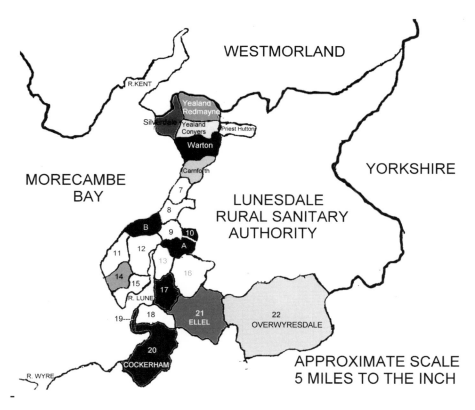

Townships in the Lancaster Rural Sanitary Authority 1873.

Key

1-6. Townships in Warton Parish.

7 Bolton-le-Sands	8 Slyne with Hest
9 Skerton	10 Bulk
11 Heysham	12 Heaton with Oxcliffe
13 Aldercliffe	14 Middleton
15 Overton	16 Scotforth
17 Ashton with Stodday	18 Thurnham
19 Cockersand Abbey	20 Cockerham
21 Ellel	22 Overwyersdale

Sewage

What was achieved in Warton parish by this new authority? - certainly not mains drainage for the whole area. That would have been an absurd ambition in any case in a rural area and has still not been attempted. Outlying villages, though they now use water-borne disposal of sewage, still depend on septic tanks, the hygienic modern development of the old cesspit.

Indeed in the nineteenth century sewers, when they were installed, were sometimes a liability rather than an asset. Carnforth's problems in the 1860s with badly designed sewers and a shortage of water to flush them has already been mentioned (see Chapter Four). Warton township had long had a sewage system of a sort, but a description of it as late as 1902 was not encouraging. The Inspector of Nuisances had long been complaining about it, but still:

> '*It consists practically speaking of two separate sections ... The north sewer discharges into a tank in a field. This tank is emptied once a month by a contractor. But as the sewer receives not only the drainage of houses, but also the surface water ... in rainy weather ... its overflow is continually creating nuisance*'.

The south sewer was no better since:

> '*... water closet drainage, as well as road and ground water, discharges into an open tank ... only a few yards from the dipping place, which is an important source of local water supply.*'[30]

SELF-ACTING
EARTH CLOSET

Of much more help to the rural district in achieving better sanitary conditions was the long running battle to get ill-maintained and foul privy middens up-dated at least to the less offensive earth-closets (or ashpits as they were usually called). A privy midden is simply a bench with a hole over a muckheap. In an earth closet, ash or sieved earth was added so that the contents of the container became less foully soggy and more friable and so could be cleared with a minimum of offence - that is provided care was taken to keep rainwater and ground water out, which Mr. Jowett, the invaluable Inspector of Nuisances, found was not always the case.

Sanitation

Good earth closets are a reasonably satisfactory system in country areas, as many older people know. Even in 1920 there were far more privy closets in rural Lancashire than water closets.[31]

There were problems, though, in maintaining earth closets. There was the difficulty of obtaining enough earth or ash for proper functioning. As the Medical Officer of Health acidly remarked about Millhead's arrangements '... *these places cannot be called dry earth closets unless they are supplied with dry earth, which they are not.*'[32] Later in the century earth closets, especially in Carnforth, were beginning to be replaced by pail closets: metal receptacles that did not have to be emptied on site, but could be closed, removed and replaced. Both systems, however, depended on regular servicing. The task was put out to contractors and apparently, by the beginning of the next century, the villages could hope to have this done at least every two months.

Silverdale received especial approval, for there '*an apparatus*' had been purchased for use by the contractors for emptying cess pools which they were bound to do monthly.[33]

Lindeth, the small settlement that was neither quite Warton nor quite Silverdale, was perhaps more typical of isolated parts. The Sanitary Inspector drew the attention of his authority '... *to the indefinite manner of house refuse removal*'. He found that no particular time was specified for removal.[34] A further problem was where the contractors were to put the contents. As has been mentioned, even Warton's sewers led into an open tank sited next to a dipping place, (in other words the spring on the Weir, from which drinking water came). The indignant Inspector of Nuisances found that local inhabitants were complaining that when the tank was (infrequently) emptied the contents were simply spread out to dry on site. '*Arrangements will have to be made to have it carted right on to the land*' he commented.[35] That would have been accepted practice at the time, even if not quite in accord with modern ideas. We no longer think of untreated sewage as suitable for tipping on the land even in rural districts.

Water

In the same way, an improved water supply, more or less adequate for a small country district, was slowly achieved. Until the 1870s all water in the district came from the natural resources of wells, springs and rainwater off the roofs. Naturally it tended to fail in times of drought and the problem increased as the population grew. Crisis was probably delayed by the unrelated fact that thatch was giving way to slates as roof covering, so that run off into tanks increased, but there was no other way of increasing supply. Even the Thirlmere/Manchester pipeline was of no avail since no township was connected to it.

A Water Act of 1878 laid a duty on Rural Districts to see that every dwelling house had an available supply of wholesome water, but there was no suggestion that this must be piped water. It was however indicative that a different attitude to water supplies was growing. Ever since the cholera epidemics it was increasingly realised that water, however clean it might look, might still be a source of disease. Real attempts were made to improve its quality. Rain tanks could no longer be installed without a filter to remove at least the macroscopic dirt. Supplies suspected of being the source of infection were checked, and, if thought to be contaminated, could be closed. It was something but, in the eyes of the Medical Officer of Health, not enough. As late as 1915 he was saying that ' ... *less than half the houses in the district have a constant and pure water supply.*'[36]

The Final Decades: 1875 to 1900: the State of the Parish

It was an important duty of a Medical Officer of Health to make annual reports on his district. His reports, along with those of the Sanitary Inspectors, ensured that much more can be known about the health of the parish than in earlier years, and supply a picture of the effects on people's health of all the changes outlined in this chapter.

Local reports must, of course, be read in the light of the changes affecting the country as a whole. The Registrar General, from the time of the establishment of the office in 1837, published each year death rates, that is the numbers dying per thousand of the population. Death rates can be used to compare the health of a nation over a period, even though they are a fairly rough measure of health, since they take no account of morbidity, that is illness not leading to death.

Throughout the second half of the nineteenth century death rates were falling. In the decade 1850 to 1860 the average death rate for England and Wales was 22.2. In the last decade of the century it was 18.2.[37] Lancashire, with its agglomeration of large unhealthy towns always did rather worse than average. In 1850 in Lancashire, the death-rate was 24.3; this was *the worst record of any county in the kingdom*.[38] Rural areas did rather better. The Warton area where the M.O.H. could report an average annual death rate for this last decade of a mere 14.88 was doing well.

Among the annual reports of the Medical Officer for Lancaster Rural Sanitary Authority, one which has survived is for the year 1876, only three years after the sanitary authority was created.[39] It affords a window into the health of the rural district half way through the second half of the nineteenth century. From it, for the first time, some details of the range of disease facing local doctors can be obtained. In the Warton district, out of the 96 deaths, 46 (48%) were of children under five years of age. That was high even for a time when children were at particular risk. It had been an epidemic year for whooping cough with eight deaths; without these the percentage is a more usual 40%.

Table 9.1 gives the deaths in that year from 13 common causes of death. Not all causes of death have been included, but the figures tend to confirm what was postulated for the earlier years of the century; that is the major importance of infectious diseases as a cause of death (especially as a noticeable proportion of the deaths from heart disease and kidney disease would have been the result of damage by infectious disease).

Dr. Harker, who compiled the report, was heartened by finding fewer deaths in 1876 than 1875 and asserted: *'This diminution is mainly owing to sanitary improvements'*, but he added that there was scope for improvement especially in Warton, Bolton-le-Sands, Slyne and Skerton. He may have been wrong in thinking a lowered death rate from infectious disease quite so immediately connected with improvements in sanitation, but it was very much the thinking of the time.

Table 9.1

Disease	Deaths under age 5	Deaths age 5 and over	Total Deaths
Scarlet Fever	4	0	4
Diphtheria	0	1	1
Whooping Cough	8	1	9
Typhoid/Enteric Fever	2	2	4
Diarrhoea	3	0	3
Phthisis	1	6	7
Tuberculosis (other)	6	3	9
All infectious diseases	**24**	**13**	**37**
Pneumonia	1	1	2
Bronchitis	3	3	6
Cancer	0	2	2
Bright's Disease	0	1	1
Heart Disease	0	4	4
Premature Birth	0	0	0
Other Causes	?	?	44
All non-infectious diseases	**?**	**?**	**59**
TOTAL	**?**	**?**	**96**

From the M.O.H.'s Report for the Rural Sanitary Authority (Warton District) for 1876

> **Note**: Phthisis = T.B. of lungs
> Tuberculosis (other) includes T.B. meningitis and T.B. of bones
> Bright's disease = all forms of kidney disease

The high death rate from all forms of tuberculosis would have been more likely to respond to improved nutrition, reduction in overcrowding and elimination of T.B. from cattle. In his report the M.O.H. divides tuberculosis into phthisis (lung disease) and other forms, which would have included meningitis and the crippling tubercular infection of joints. The six deaths in children and three in adults in this category would most probably have been contracted from contaminated milk.

To give the M.O.H. his due he was aware of the danger. In his 1898 report he noted that '*The cattle of this neighbourhood are highly tuberculous*', and from then on did what he could, but real control was beyond local effort. The elimination of tuberculosis resulting from infected milk was eventually one of the successes of public health, but it took a national effort and was not achieved until the twentieth century.

The late nineteenth century decline in the death rate from scarlet fever on the contrary seems to have had nothing to do with man's efforts. There was no effective medical treatment until the coming of antibiotics, and isolation, the nineteenth century stand-by, was of doubtful use in controlling epidemics. It was nature itself that took a hand. For no known reason scarlet fever simply took on a much milder form. Deaths per year peaked in 1863 at a total of 30,000 for England and Wales, and thereafter fell uninterruptedly. After 1894 there are no deaths from scarlet fever in Warton district recorded by the M.O.H.

From the 1850s diphtheria, which had previously been overshadowed by scarlet fever, began to appear in epidemic form. The epidemics were never on the scale of scarlet fever, though because it is such a lethal disease it overtook scarlet fever as a cause of death. In the Warton district there were repeated small epidemics, but fortunately never more than one death in a year, more usually none.

Measles, because it was more frequent, could be a greater killer. In 1890 eight children died of measles in Warton, and though it never struck again at that level, epidemics came round regularly and deaths still occurred. When there was an outbreak the M.O.H. could, and did, close schools. All the schools in Carnforth were closed for a time in the winter of 1894.[40] The next winter they were closed again for three weeks, along with Warton Infant School.[41] Whether the move had any effect on the epidemic is open to doubt.

The M.O.H's faith in sanitation as the key to health would have been most justified in the case of intestinal illnesses, particularly in the form of summer diarrhoea, that attacked so many children. Certainly deaths from intestinal infections did progressively decline throughout the last decades of the century, though there could still be bad years. In 1892 there were 15 cases of typhoid in the rural district, eight of them in

Warton sub-district (five in Carnforth and three in Millhead). The source was never found. Warton finished the century on a high note. In 1899 it was the only sub-district where there were no deaths at all from infectious disease.

[1] Irvine Loudon, *Medical Care and the General Practitioner 1750 - 1850,* (Clarendon Press, 1986), p.38.

[2] *Lancaster Gazette,* June 5th, June 12th, July 10th, 1858.

[3] *Lancaster Gazette,* July 31st, 1858.

[4] B. & J. Clarke, "Dr Walling and Dr Matthews, Two Yealand Conyers Doctors," *Mourholme Magazine of Local History,* (No.2 1990).

[5] John Findlater, "Robin Hill: No. 24 Market Street, Carnforth," *Mourholme Magazine of Local History* (No. 2 1994), p.1.

[6] Prescription Note Book, Dr. W. Jackson & Dr. E.S. Jackson, begun in 1869. Now in the possession of Dr. John Findlater.

[7] *Lancaster Guardian,* May 22nd, 1897.

[8] *Lancaster Guardian,* July 2nd, 1887.

[9] *Lancaster Guardian,* February 3rd, 1894.

[10] *Lancaster Gazette,* June 4th, 1890.

[11] *Lancaster Guardian,* June 7th, 1890.

[12] Loudon, *Medical Care,* p.38.

[13] Loudon, *Medical Care,* p.116.

[14] Mourholme Local History Society Book Group, *Warton 1800-1850: How a North Lancashire Parish Changed* (Mourholme Local History Society, 2005), pp.173-4.

[15] David Gladstone, ed., *Before Beveridge; Welfare Before the Welfare State* (Choice in Welfare No 47) (London: Institute of Economic Affairs, 1999), p.5.

[16] Philip Cartwright, *History of Anaesthesia in Lancaster,* (n.d.), p17.

[17] *Lancaster Gazette,* December 14th, 1889.

[18] *Lancaster Gazette,* September 7th, 1878.

[19] Annual Reports of Medical Officer of Health, Lancaster Rural District, 1889-1919. Environmental Health Department, Morecambe Town Hall.

[20] *Lancaster Guardian,* March 26th, 1887.

[21] Annual Reports of Medical Officer of Health, 1896.

[22] *Lancaster Guardian,* March 7th, 1891.

[23] *Lancaster Guardian,* March 7th, 1891.

[24] *Lancaster Guardian,* September 9th, 1870.

[25] Yealand Preparative Meeting, *Log Book of Yealand British School,* (Yealand Friends' Society, 1868), June 17th.

[26] Ruth Hodgkinson, *The Origins of the National Health Service,* (Wellcome Historical Library, 1967), p.287.

[27] Mourholme Local History Society Book Group, *Warton 1800-1850,* pp. 168-169.

[28] Edwin Chadwick, *Report on the Sanitary Conditions of the Labouring Population of Great Britain* (originally published 1842, reprinted, M. W. Flinn, ed., Edinburgh University Press, 1965).

[29] Minute Book of Rural Sanitary Authority, entry for May 16th, 1876 p.122. Lancashire Record Office, SAL/1.

[30] Surveyor and Inspector of Nuisances Reports, 1898-1902, Lancashire Record Office, RDLa/12/13.

[31] Annual Reports of the County Medical Officer of Health, Lancashire Record Office, PHR.

[32] Annual Reports of Medical Officer of Health, 1892, Lancashire Record Office, PHR.

[33] Annual Reports of Medical Officer of Health, 1909, Lancashire Record Office, PHR.

[34] Sanitary Inspectors' Reports 1906-1911, 27th October, 1906, Lancashire Record Office, RDLa/12/7

[35] Surveyor and Inspector of Nuisances Reports, 1899-1901, 20th October, 1900, Lancashire Record Office, RDLa/12/11.

[36] Annual Reports of Medical Officer of Health, 1915, Lancashire Record Office, PHR.

[37] Anthony S. Wohl, *Endangered Lives: Public Health in Victorian Britain* (Methuen, 1984), p.11.

[38] E.C. Midwinter, *Social Administration in Lancashire 1830-1860: Poor Law, Public Health and Police* (Manchester: Manchester University Press, 1969), p.74.

[39] Annual Reports of the Medical Officer for Lancaster Rural Sanitary Authority, 1876. Photocopy kindly given to the archives of the Mourholme Local History Society, by Dr. John Dyer.

[40] *Lancaster Guardian,* November 23rd, 1894.

[41] *Lancaster Guardian,* December 21st, 1895.

Chapter Nine

GROWING UP IN WARTON PARISH

Infancy

Infancy was a time of danger in the nineteenth century. A newborn's chance of dying before its first birthday was high. Even in the last decades of the nineteenth century the national infant mortality (that is the number of babies dying before one year of age for every 1,000 born alive) averaged 150. A comparable figure today would be under 10.

Rural areas, it is true, always tended to do rather better than the rest, and Warton was no exception. In the 1890s the Medical Officer for Lancaster Rural District reported an average infant mortality of only 117.[1] All the same, since 106 babies were born on average each year in the parish, that meant twelve baby deaths to mourn.

The Medical Officer did not indicate, in these summaries, what caused their death, but the fact that the rate varied greatly from year to year – a mere four in 1895, but 34 in both 1893 and 1894 - does suggest epidemic diseases. In this age group among the most likely causes would have been the illnesses grouped as diarrhoea – a natural result of imperfect water, contaminated milk and the difficulty of preserving food

when there was no refrigeration. Babies who, for any reason, could not be breast-fed, were at particular risk. The design of baby bottles was often very poor. A popular one was the Alexandra, named after the Princess of Wales. It had a narrow metal tube welded into the neck to admit air to improve the flow of milk. It was quite impossible to keep the tube sterile. Doctors labelled it the *'killer'*.[2]

Childhood

In well-to-do Victorian families childhood was, despite the obvious differences, not in essence different from childhood today; that is to say, childhood was accepted as a period set apart for play and learning before adulthood and the need to earn a living closed in.

Very little of this applied in households living on the uncertain wages of a labourer or a farm worker. Anything their children could earn for themselves lessened the burden on the family income. Book learning might be valued, but was not always achievable. It was not so much the school fees that deterred parents. Although until almost the end of the century even the state schools charged a fee, it was often no more than a penny or two a week, and by the end of the century even this was being waived in many cases. It is known that in 1891 schools in Carnforth were asking for a fee of 2d for older children, but less for the lower standards and nothing at all for infants.[3] The difficulty was rather that school attendance meant the child was no longer a potential wage earner.

School and Work
It is no wonder that there is evidence that quite young children in the parish were working. In 1868 the children of Silverdale were instanced as the victims of exploitation in a parliamentary report into child labour. The inspector sent down into this part of the world was given some alarming information about cockling on the sands. It was not the physical dangers that struck him, but the moral dangers. Cockling, he wrote, *'appears to combine all the worst abuses of agricultural gangs, with some particular aggravations'*.

Girls cockling
Morecambe Bay

Children, he found, were early taken out on the sands by their parents, and by seven years old could be adding substantially to the family income. He heard of still younger children employed at home in '*picking*' shrimps. Consequently, he said, the children grew up '*in a state of ignorance and heathenism*'. Moreover, groups of boys and girls working together on the sands led to '*great evils*'. The children's language was '*in the highest degree obscene and profane*'.[4]

The inspector may have been over-reacting, but it is true that, the year before he wrote, the head master of Yealand Friends' School was having trouble with his Silverdale pupils who were guilty of '*rough behaviour*' and '*vulgar talk*' on their way home[5] and on another occasion of using '*bad language to the girls when going home.*'[6] Silverdale children walked three or four miles to school each day, and no one seemed to think that adult supervision was necessary. A certain amount of '*rough behaviour*' was probably inevitable.

It was not only Silverdale children who missed school for work. Surviving school logbooks are full of complaints about children working. Farm work was what usually kept the boys off school. A calendar of the farming year could be kept from the logbook of Yealand British School: March: potato planting; April: peats, potato planting, peeling bark, picking stones and weeding; May: sheep washing; June: thinning turnips; July: hay-making; August: harvest; September: picking fruit; October: potato lifting; November: turnips. For the girls it was minding babies, helping mother clean down, or simply wanted at home.

School and Play

It was not only work that kept children off school. Yealand logbook also records a good deal of plain truancy. Children went sliding on the ice or lit bonfires and came late to school; when '*the hounds were out*' the boys ran after them. Also there were, of course, times when the children were just plain tiresome; they picked nuts and scattered the shells about the schoolroom,[7] the boys swung on the yard gate, or chipped the seat in the playground shed with their knives. Other crimes recorded were the breaking of a window with a catapult (which led to all catapults being confiscated),[8] playing with gunpowder in the classroom for which the boy was '*rebuked*'[9] and smoking. In 1876 the head master was horrified to find that most of the older boys smoked pipes and reprimanded them.[10] The girls seem to have been more conformist, or better at not being found out. The only misdemeanours recorded were disturbing the silence of the Meeting House by rushing noisily about in the playground and coming in late for afternoon school.

However, not all was disobedience and punishment. The schools allowed, or at least winked at, other amusements - going on the Warton Club walk and to the Lancaster Cheese and Cattle Fair, or to the Agricultural Show at Burton. In 1869, so many pupils of the Yealand Friends' had gone to a circus in Carnforth that those who remained were sent home,[11] and the whole school had to be closed in the afternoon. In 1881 Carnforth National School closed for one afternoon so that the children could attend the wedding of the vicar, Mr J.A Fidler,[12] and in 1897 the head master very sensibly gave all the pupils a half day holiday on a freezing February day so that they could go and skate on the canal.[13]

The impression is that all these entertainments were not so much amusements for children, as adult amusement in which the children joined. There were however some amusements primarily for children; especially the Sunday School treats.

What the children played when left to themselves is harder, indeed almost impossible to find out. It is to be supposed that well-to-do children would have been supplied with toys such as can be seen in the Lancaster Museum of Childhood, and one hopes that some at least of those who could not afford these delights had home-made toys, such as whipping tops, rag dolls and five stones. They are not the sorts of things to survive and no mention of them has been found in the newspapers or in the school logbooks (apart from the catapults that were confiscated). Even balls are not mentioned.

It was for throwing stones that the boys got into trouble. Sometimes they aimed at each other or at passers-by, but stone throwing seems also to have developed at times into an organised game. It is given a name of its own, '*duckstones*', in a newspaper article of 1887. As far as can be made out from this it was not ducks-and-drakes that was being played, but a game known elsewhere as duck-off, which consisted of trying to knock a stone off a distant perch. During one game George Fretsom of Warton was hit so hard on the head by a stone that had '*rebounded off a wall*' that a doctor had to be called.[14] In 1894 some Carnforth boys put their skill with stones to use. The Lancaster Cycling Club complained of '*urchins*' in Carnforth throwing stones at the riders with '*too dexterous aim*'.[15]

Children at least had plenty of space to play in fine weather; they were left free to roam fields and woods, and even the roads could be play-places in those days before motorised transport. Rainy days could be a problem in small crowded cottages. In 1888 Dr. Parker, the Medical Officer of Health, made a special visit to Millhead in connection with an outbreak of scarlet fever. The day of the visit was '*very wet*' and he found that '*in nearly every privy children were playing*'. He commented judicially that even the cleanest privy '*cannot be considered a proper place for children to spend any length of time*'; many of the privies, he added, were not at all clean but in an extremely offensive state.[16]

Punishment

Physical chastisement was the usual punishment and never seems to have been queried, though in 1866 Mr. Orlando Pearce, headmaster of Yealand Friends' School, instituted what was in essence a system of stars in the hope, as he wrote in the logbook, of '*reducing the amount of corporal punishment*'.[17] Whether he succeeded is not known. The plan is not referred to again.

One head took violence beyond what even the opinion of the time thought right. In 1878, Carnforth was up in arms because the head master of the National School, Mr. Clarke, hit a pupil, James Heslop, over the ear. The boy went into a series of convulsions and 36 hours later was dead. The fits were attributed to his suffering from worms (an accepted cause of fits in those days). No case was brought against Mr. Clarke, but the governors very promptly issued a recommendation that corporal punishment was to be avoided as far as possible and, if it was used, a written record must be entered in a book kept for the purpose.[18] The shock of the death of poor James Heslop presumably wore off and corporal punishment continued, as many know to their cost – or to their benefit!

Children in Trouble

Children who got into more serious trouble and came before the courts were also likely to be punished by a birching. This was formally ordered by the magistrate, and the parents had a right to be present; after 1872 the maximum number of strokes that could be ordered was 12. All children, however young, were tried in the same court as adults. The malefactor who damaged Hartley's shop front in Carnforth turned out to be only *'about five years old'*. He had been trying his knife out and had caused five shillings worth of damage. Good sense prevailed. The parents agreed to pay the cost and Mr. Hartley withdrew the charge.[19]

In the case billed in the newspaper as *'Orchard Robbery in Warton'* the two boys up before the court were aged eight and six and had been formally charged with the theft of plums from the orchard of an old man, Mr. Stainton. It turned out to be rather more than mere scrumping. There was, just as there might be today, a gang of local boys who were harassing Mr. Stainton, and had been setting the little boys on to steal his fruit. The parents had done nothing to control them. The parents were ordered to *'speak to the boys'* and to pay costs of 11s 6d each. One of the parents said truculently that he hadn't got that much and that it would be a long time before he paid it. He was told that if the fine was not forthcoming he would go to prison.[20]

The usual punishment for stealing was the birch. Four boys who stole toffees from Mr. Mashiter's shop at Carnforth,[21] two boys who stole *'tame fowls'* from the Shovel Inn in Carnforth[22], and two boys who stole eggs from a farm,[23] were all birched. An 11 year old girl, Agnes Milligan, was dealt with as an adult would have been. She was a domestic servant at the house of Mr. George Thistleton, a Borwick vet, and was charged with arson (she had found the hay in the haymow ablaze and the family had accused her of setting light to it herself). She was remanded in custody and was reported to have '*cried bitterly at the thought of being parted from her father*'. Her employers may, it seems, have tricked her into a confession. Nevertheless, off to prison this child had to go to await trial.[24]

Schools

It might be supposed that that the Education Act of 1870, which took the first step towards making education compulsory (and ultimately free) for all children, would have made a dramatic difference to children's schooling. It did, of course, change things, but not, in Warton parish at any rate, in any sudden way.

Long before the act came into force, the provision of elementary school places had, for various reasons, been charitable, Christian and social, and had been everywhere increasing. They could not yet, however, be supplied directly by the state. State education was equated in people's minds with a purely secular education and that was unthinkable for many. Education, it was held, must involve religious education and that must, of course, be supplied by teachers of a right way of thinking. The result was a battle between the established church and dissenting churches for the control of education. The battle may not have been edifying, but it did ensure that considerable efforts were made by all the denominations to supply schools.

The efforts came to be co-ordinated by two great educational societies, the National and the British (or more formally the *National Society for Promoting the Education of the Poor in the Principles of the Established Church* and, for dissenters, the *British and Foreign School Society*). Ever since 1833 the state, though barred from creating its own schools, had been making increasing educational grants, not directly to schools, but discreetly filtered through the two societies – each receiving grants proportional to the amounts they themselves could raise. It was only very cautiously that the 1870 Education Act moved outside this system. It laid down standards of how many school places were to be supplied in any district, and only if the target was not met by denominational schools would it intervene. In such a case a district could be compelled to elect a local School Board with the power and duty to set up sufficient schools, the cost of which was to come out of the local rates. Such School Boards and the Board Schools they created were very necessary in many parts of the country, particularly in the growing industrial towns. There, the denominational schooling had proved very inadequate indeed, but in Warton parish population growth had been moderate, and the denominations had managed better. When in 1873 the Education Department demanded returns from all districts on the number of school places available, Warton parish passed muster except in one township and that, rather unexpectedly, was not the growing industrial township of Carnforth, but the old central township of Warton-with-Lindeth.

Archbishop Hutton's Grammar School, Warton

Warton Township was told it must supply a new school with places for 100 boys,[25] yet the township was the site of the grammar school founded by Archbishop Hutton in 1594 and still in use. The problem was that, as a grammar school, Archbishop Hutton's did not count as providing elementary education. The difficulty was solved, not by building a new school, but by re-classifying Archbishop Hutton's as a public elementary school. Educationally the change would not have been great, for the school was already supplying basic rather than grammar school education. When a parliamentary commissioner visited the school in the 1860s he found the pupils were all under 12 years of age. On the day he visited there were only 11 children in attendance, including *'one or two girls'*. Seven of these were able to read *'tolerably'* in easy lesson books. Three were able to answer questions on the multiplication table. Two *'with some difficulty were induced to write figures on the slate from dictation'*. No classics had been taught for *'a good while'*. In the last five years only three or four pupils had been taught algebra, three each year had learnt mensuration (calculating area) and three had learnt bookkeeping.[26]

On grounds other than educational, the school would have felt a difference. Under the new Act the right of parents to withdraw children from religious instruction on the grounds of conscience was guaranteed.[27] Previously Archbishop Hutton's had felt able to insist, at least on paper, that the children were:

> *'to attend service at the Parish church twice every Sunday and also public prayers in church on All Saints Day and on Wednesdays during Lent.'*[28]

However, the trustees gave in. If they tried to keep Archbishop Hutton's as an independent grammar school then either they would have to raise the money for a new elementary school, or allow a School Board to build such a school for them (and charge it on the rates). Moreover, in such a board school, the Act had laid it down that *'no catechism or religious formulary which is distinctive to any particular denomination shall be taught'*. If Archbishop Hutton's remained a denominational school it could at least teach religion in its own way, as long as no child was forced to attend the teaching. The trustees took the plunge, and on Monday January 29th, 1877, Archbishop Hutton's was re-opened as a public elementary school under a new master, Mr. Arthur Perfect.

Yealand Friends' School

The Society of Friends in Yealand Conyers had run a school there since 1709. The school was already functioning as a British School in 1867, as a surviving logbook begun in that year shows.[29] Friends would have had little difficulty in accepting the requirement that children could be withdrawn from religious instruction on conscientious grounds. The school had always accepted pupils of other faiths,[30] and the logbook shows that headmasters placidly accepted that on certain feast days Catholic and Anglican pupils would be at church and so not come to school.

The New Schools

The two older foundations would not have enabled the parish to comply with the requirements of the 1870 Act, if it had not been for the newer schools founded by local enterprise in conjunction with the two great educational societies. The National Society was the first involved. It had already helped to found a school in Yealand Redmayne in 1842,[31] and it went on to help in the founding of a school in Carnforth in 1850.[32] The National Society also gave help in founding a school in Silverdale in 1854 and one in Priest Hutton in the mid-1860s. Apart from the Friends' School in Yealand Conyers only one school came under the protection of the British Society in 1873, a school for girls and infants in Warton village which was opened in 1865.

192

Yet to speak of these schools as National or British does not, perhaps, do justice to the enormous amount of local effort that went into funding them. Schools could, and did, charge fees, both before and after 1870, but such school pence could not cover costs. Figures have been found for only one school.[33] In 1872 the accounts of Carnforth National School showed that 35% of the annual cost of the school was raised from fees. The actual sum was £72 and since there were, according to the Education Department, 284 children in the school, this works out at between a penny and two-pence a week per child. The government grant amounted to another 30%. The remaining 35% came, it must be supposed, from private effort, including the £500 raised by a bazaar in 1861.[34]

The Infant School in Warton was built entirely at the expense of Mr. and Mrs. E.B. Dawson, philanthropic and influential Congregationalists. At the laying of the foundation stone Mr. Dawson said that his only motive in creating the school was *'that it might be a blessing to the children and the people of Warton.'*[35] In his school, he promised:

> *'The scriptures would be taught, not on any denominational basis, but only in an elementary manner as befitted the minds of infant scholars.'*[36]

More often, however, many smaller givers united to create and maintain the schools. The efforts of these small-scale givers is the more remarkable in that not all would benefit directly from the schools they helped to found. Elementary schools at that period were for the children of those termed the labouring classes, though many artisans, shop-keepers and clerks also sent their children to them. The charitable donors might well have preferred to educate their own children at home, or send them to private establishments.

The Congregational School, Carnforth

One completely new school was founded later by the Congregationalists in Carnforth. This school, too, owed much to Mr. Dawson, who donated a site in Hawk Street, but the congregation raised much of the money themselves - £400 in subscriptions alone, not to mention such subsidiary aids as money from concerts and tea-parties.[37]

In a very practical spirit they put up a dual-purpose building, a *'school-chapel'* it was called, and equipped it with *'Mr. S. Meade's reversible desks usable by children, adults and as tea tables'*. A sliding partition allowed the hall to be used as one large meeting place or transformed into two classrooms.[38]

The Continuing Fight Against School Boards

In 1882 Carnforth had reason to fear it might be saddled with a school board. School places had not been keeping pace with the growing population. The governors of the National School called a public meeting:

> *'so that'* as the Lancaster Gazette put it, *'the ratepayers and others interested might have an opportunity ... of keeping off what at present seemed to be inevitable, namely, the formation of a School Board.'*[39]

The newspaper makes interesting reading. It seems to have been a largely silent meeting. One man, a Mr. Wrightson from the Iron Works (subsequently Manager and Secretary), did suggest that some rate-payers might actually prefer having a school board to giving still more money to the school managers. No one supported him; no one even seems to have spoken against him. It was obvious, as even Mr. Wrightson allowed, that people simply did not want a school board whatever the arguments. A committee was set up to consider ways and means of raising the necessary funds. By the next year enough money had been raised to enlarge the school by the addition of an extra storey so that it could accommodate 100 more pupils, or 700 in all.[40] Also, though this was never mentioned at the meeting, the Congregationalist British School was already being built, and must have helped stave off a school board. By 1886 it was able to add 250 places to the National School's 600.[41]

There was one last threat of a school board. In 1891 the law had finally brought to an end the anomaly that, though education was compulsory yet it did not have to be free. An Act of that year, though it did not quite venture to say that all places were to be free, did say that if any parent petitioned for a free place then it must be supplied. Silverdale School, like all the other local schools, had been lowering its fees progressively. By 1892 all infants were being taught free, and no parent needed to pay for more than two children however big the family.[42] This was not enough for some of the inhabitants. At the end of 1892 29 Silverdale parents petitioned for free places for their children (or at any rate 29 signatures appeared on the petition). The Education Department instructed the managers to see that free places were available, or else action would be taken '*under section 5*'; in other words a school board would be set up.

In January 1893 a meeting of Silverdale ratepayers was called. Reading between the lines of the report in the newspapers one feels that the protest was mostly about what were seen as poor standards of teaching in the school. When the meeting had cooled down, it was obvious that nobody wanted a school board, and nobody had any basic objection to free education. The protesters dropped their complaints about the teaching in the school and the managers promised that all places in the school would be free - provided only that subscriptions were raised all round. There the matter rested until, in 1902, another Education Act abolished all school boards and gave supervision of both primary and secondary education to the Local Education Authorities of counties or county boroughs.

All these schools, in one form or another, lasted till beyond the end of the century, though by the 1890s the small Church of England school at Priest Hutton was struggling. In 1895 the inspector reported that he found it '*inefficient*' and said he was not prepared to recognise it as '*a public elementary school*' unless a certificated teacher was employed.[43] This would have meant a substantial commitment for so small a community.[44] It must have been managed for there was still a school, with 41 children in attendance, in 1918.[45]

The National schools at Carnforth, Silverdale and Yealand continued successfully. Archbishop Hutton's remained in the original building that had served it since it opened in the sixteenth century (though altered and improved). It was not till 1902 that it moved into new purpose-built premises in the main street. The Friends' school in Yealand closed as a public elementary school in 1896, but continued as a private school under a Quaker headmaster. It is not entirely clear what led to this decision. It seems to have been partly because there was difficulty in finding managers among Yealand inhabitants. It also followed an unfortunate disagreement with Mr. George French, the head master. The records of the Friends' Society discreetly give no details of the disagreement, but the logbook reveals that feelings ran high enough for Mr. French to countenance his class hissing the managers when they visited. The Congregational school lasted out the century, before moving in 1902 to North Road.

Private Schools

There are records of three private schools in the parish between 1850 and 1900. It seems from the 1851 census that four enterprising young ladies from Manchester had set up a school in Lindeth Cottage. They had eight boarders, but nothing is known of their qualifications to teach. At the time anyone could open a school without any formal requirements. The school had vanished by the time of the 1861 census.

Miss Pickford's School

There were two long-lasting private schools in the parish. Miss Emma Pickford ran a boarding school for young ladies in Haws Hill in Carnforth. Her school is mentioned in an 1866 directory,[46] and was still there at the time of the 1891 census, in which Miss Pickford features as a 59 year old private school teacher living at 2 Haws Hill. She is still mentioned as running a school in a directory of 1901, by which time she would have been almost 70.[47] Little indication of what was taught in her school has been found, but it is known that in 1882 some of her pupils sat the Cambridge University Local Examination,[48] which suggests the school aspired to something beyond the mere imparting of accomplishments to young ladies.

A private school (for boys) in Yealand Conyers was definitely a high flyer. It was founded in 1874 by a Mr. Walter Blanchard, who claimed for it not only that it was situated in a healthy district such as must appeal to a careful parent, but also that it was celebrated for its academic successes. Moreover it had a resident teacher of music and modern languages.[49] From the newspapers it is known that Mr. Blanchard was offering instruction in Latin, French and German, mechanics, geometry, algebra, mensuration, history and geography. The success of his pupils in public examinations received notice in the newspapers. The Gazette in 1885 recounts how one of the pupils, W. Birkett:

> *'reached the standard of merit which is accepted both by the General Medical Council and the Incorporated Law Society as a proof of a good general education.'* [50]

By 1897 Mr. Blanchard had moved his highly successful school to Lancaster. Nothing has been found about the level of the fees at either school.

Teachers and the Taught

It is hard to find out what the Victorian children of Warton parish were being taught in the elementary schools. The curriculum would have been much the same in all, for it was inevitably heavily influenced by what subjects would earn the biggest grant. One might have hoped to get some insight into the teaching from the surviving reports of H.M. School Inspectors, but unfortunately much of the period came under the notorious 1862 Revised Code. In the interests of economy this had introduced a very strict Payment by Results scheme. It decreed that school grants were to be dependent on how many children passed a series of graded examinations in reading, writing and arithmetic. Very naturally, hard-pressed schools concentrated on these basics to the detriment, many thought, of a wider education.

The views of the Inspectors, who were given the tedious task of testing every individual child personally, were voiced by Matthew Arnold, poet and H.M.I. Under the old system, he said, the Inspector had time to test:

> *'... the whole life and power of a class, the fitness of its composition, its handling by the teacher ... Now he has no time for anything but putting every child in the school through examinations ... he does not question them; he does not ... go beyond the three matters, reading, writing and arithmetic.'* [51]

It is no wonder, then, that the reports for the local schools consist of brief comments on orderliness and discipline, followed by tables of incomprehensible examination results. They do not make interesting reading (though, as needlework was compulsory for girls there is some wry amusement in reading the conscientious attempts of male inspectors to evaluate the results). All one can say is that schools in Warton parish appear usually to have come up to requirement.

The most detailed account of lessons comes from Mr. Orlando Pearce, head master of the Yealand British School from 1867 to 1869. In the school logbook he gives an account of the phonetic method he was using to teach reading - moving the child on from ar to ark and so by steps to hark, mark etc. He told one of his monitors to use *'concrete numbers'*, presumably actual objects, in arithmetic as a help to the more backward children. In March 1867 there was an eclipse of the sun and he made an opportunity for the children to see it and explained to them how it was brought about. Yet even he could not really move outside the narrow restrictions of the 1862 code. The week was a round of drilling in the basic rules of arithmetic, reading, spelling and grammar. Geography seems to have taken the form of learning the countries, capital cities and rivers of Europe. The children were given some lively poems to learn by heart, but the class seems to have always stayed with the same poem until every child knew it. Even *John Gilpin* must have lost some of its dash when studied for three months on end. No other headmaster left such detailed comments as Mr. Pearce, but it seems fair to say that until the 1890s teaching never moved far outside this limited circle of subjects. By the end of the century, however, there does seem to have been some widening of the curriculum to include drawing, singing and more science, at least in the form of nature study.

The lack of direct evidence from the logbooks that organised games, or indeed any form of physical exercise, were included in the curriculum is striking.

In 1881 it is noted that at Archbishop Hutton's school *'the time table* [was] *not regarded as Master frequently exercised the children before*

and after lessons - to get them warm.' That however was a special concession on a cold January day.[52] Gradually it seems to have been realized that children would benefit from exercise in school hours. Military Drill was introduced into the Code of Practice in 1871.[53] In 1867 there had already been an entry in the logbook of Yealands Friends' School which read *'About half an hour's drill. Good Effect'.*[54]. Carnforth National School was including musical and military drills in its curriculum by 1895.[55] Even Miss Pickford's young ladies went in for drill and gave drill exhibitions in the Co-operative Hall.[56]

Despite the silence of the logbooks Warton schools somehow contrived to participate in sports. Junior football teams existed (see Chapter 11) and sometimes seem to have been organized by school staff. When rugby was played at Carnforth National School in 1879 mention was made of the Headmaster, Mr. Clarke and of two pupil teachers, Taylor and Billington, taking part. It also seems reasonable to assume that games between Carnforth National School and Lancaster St. Thomas's in 1880 would be organized by the schools themselves.

Further Education

Primary education in the nineteenth century was still seen as an end in itself – to provide basic literacy and numeracy.[57] There was no built in system of scholarships and certainly no automatic right to secondary education.

There was the Lancaster Grammar School, but what with tuition fees and the cost of travel, of uniform, books and equipment, it could not have been available to the run of Warton boys (and of course not at all to girls). In 1888 the Grammar school set up scholarships to cover some of these expenses.[58] In 1890 the success of a late pupil of Archbishop

Hutton's, T. Hurst, in the Lancaster Grammar School was reported, along with that of another late pupil, G. Rathbone, in the College of Organists.[59] In 1895 a £20 exhibition for boys at Archbishop Hutton's to attend Lancaster Grammar School had been set up.[60] In 1898 Arthur Perfect of Archbishop Hutton's was described as a holder of '*an exhibition for £25*', when he came 11th in a civil service examination.

How far these £20 exhibitions would have opened the way to further education to most boys is another matter. In the case of the three boys mentioned there were special reasons why the parents might have been able and willing to keep their child on at school. Arthur Perfect was the only son of the headmaster of Archbishop Hutton's; T. Hurst was the grandson of a woman of private means. George Rathbone's family was both talented and probably reasonably well off since his father kept a music shop in Market Street in Carnforth. George made good use of his opportunity and in 1895 the children at Archbishop Hutton's were given a half-holiday in honour of his success in gaining a B.Mus. at Durham University.[61]

George Rathbone. B Mus.

Apprenticeship and Pupil Teachers

The apprenticeship system offered a way into technical education, but that too was not cheap. There was the premium to pay and then years of poorly paid or unpaid work. Some financial help was available in the parish from the Mansergh Charity.

There was also the particular form of apprenticeship, set up by the state in 1846, to enable children, both boys and girls, to train as teachers. From the age of 13 a promising pupil could become a pupil teacher and be formally apprenticed to the head teacher for training. The head's duty was to teach them and see that they passed the prescribed examination each year. In return he got the services of an increasingly competent teacher, and £5 a year from the state. At the end of the five-year apprenticeship the pupil-teacher could enter a competitive examination for a Queen's Scholarship and, if successful, gain a place for three years at a training college. The earliest pupil teacher of whom a record has been traced was Isaac Burrow who in 1871 was formally apprenticed as a pupil-teacher to Mr. George Spears, headmaster of the Friends' school. Isaac, one is sorry to note, did not win a Queen's Scholarship, though he did obtain a post as an assistant master (presumably unqualified) elsewhere.[62] In 1880 there is the first mention of a pupil-teacher at Archbishop Hutton's.[63] From 1888 the post of pupil-teacher in Archbishop Hutton's school was filled in succession by the daughters of Mr. Arthur Perfect, the head master - Eleanor Blanche, Ethelberta and Emily Gertrude. In 1900 the fourth daughter, Evelyn, was taken on as a monitor, presumably on her way to being a pupil teacher.

There was always, of course, the possibility of self-help and self-education. Both Archbishop Hutton's[64] and the Friends' School[65] at least tried to run night schools. There were an increasing number of organisations ready to offer opportunities to would-be learners. The motives of some of the organisers were, in the early days especially, a truly Victorian mix of philanthropy and condescension, as illustrated by a newspaper article on a proposal to open a Reading Room or a Library in Carnforth. Either project, it was held, would '*give young men* (the would-be-learner was assumed to be male) *an opportunity of devoting some of their leisure hours to the perusal of publications that would impart sound moral and religious instruction*'.[66]

It does seem that later in the century the rather oppressive attitude of moral improvement was giving way to a simpler interest in the possibility of learning about matters in which people just happened to be interested - an annual art and industry exhibition in Silverdale, a lecture on poultry in Warton, ambulance classes and so on. This was before the days of the more formal Workers' Education Association, which was only founded in 1903, but it was a very far cry from the dead lack of opportunities in the parish in the early nineteenth century.

Children at Work
Warton children were, certainly not suddenly, cut off from paid work by the 1870 Education Act. The Act itself was not designed to do so, for in the matter of school attendance it was very cautious. It only dealt with children up to the age of 13, and in practice any real

compulsion only applied to children of 10 and under and only up to eight if the work was part-time. In theory there were powers to keep older children in school, but there were so many loopholes that enforcing attendance must have been very difficult. Apart from anything else, it was perfectly legal for children over 10 to leave school if it could be shown they had reached a required educational standard, or even that they had made a certain required number of attendances in the previous five years.

Attempts do seem to have been made in the Warton townships to enforce attendance. A School Attendance Committee was set up as soon as this was made legally possible by an Act of 1876; an Act which also, for the first time, laid a legal obligation on parents to see that their children received education. Prosecutions were initiated, as when in 1880 notice was served on William Swallow of Carnforth, a gas inspector, *'requiring him ... to provide efficient instruction for his child.'*[67]

By 1898 demands for attendance were stricter. James Mashiter was brought before the court for failing to attend school. He was already 12 years old, old enough to leave school whatever his attainments, and the failure to attend was only partial; he was reported to have made 12 out of a possible 19 attendances. The case was settled when his father promised to see that he went to school.[68] Complete insistence on attendance continued to apply only to children of 10 and under until 1893 when the age was raised to 11. It was not till 1899 that the age was fixed at 12 and not till 1918 that it reached 14.

The effect of the regulations on child employment in Warton parish is hard to determine. It was hoped that a comparison of the 1851 and the 1891 censuses would illustrate what was happening, but the results proved very unclear. Both in 1851 and in 1891 the enumerators were particularly erratic in filling in the occupations of the young. Some of these had an employment entered, some were called *'scholar'*, but for a large number there was simply a blank. One does not know what to make of these last. Were the forms being carelessly filled in? Had the children left school but were still seeking employment? Were they simply picking up jobs where they could, waiting till they were old enough to be thought worth employing full-time? Entries in school logbooks make this last possible, for instance in 1869 there is an entry in a school logbook saying that Thomas Graham *returned to school again. He has been at service.*[69] In 1870 an entry reads *'Annie Barton has to remain at home and her sister Jane has come in her stead.'*[70] Which of the two was the scholar?

All that can be definitely said is that in the 1851 census only four children under 12 were said to be in employment: two domestic servants of 10 and 11 and two errand boys, brothers of 10 and nine. In the 1891 census there were no children under 12 entered as at work. Even if children who had reached 12 are included it makes little difference. Since, from other evidence it is known that some children of 12 and under did work, it seems that the census entries reflect what was thought proper rather than what actually happened. All the same it is difficult to believe there was wide scale full-time employment of children; possibly because of a lack of suitable jobs. Farm workers and ironworkers needed to have reached a certain level of strength, the railways did not employ children and child domestic servants may well have been found more trouble than they were worth.

[1] Lancaster Rural District Council, Medical Officer of Health's Annual Reports, 1890–1919. Environmental Health Department, Morecambe Town Hall.

[2] Victoria & Albert Museum of Childhood, www.vam.ac.uk/moc/collection/childcare.

[3] *Lancaster Guardian*, September 5th, 1891.

[4] Parliamentary. Papers, *Report on the Employment of Children*, vol. xii (1868) p.155.

[5] Yealand Preparative Meeting, *Log Book of Yealand British School*, (Yealand Friends' Society, 1866), November 2nd.

[6] Yealand Preparative Meeting, *Yealand British School*, March 1867.

[7] Yealand Preparative Meeting, *Yealand British School*, September 15th, 1868.

[8] Yealand Preparative Meeting, *Yealand British School*, February 15th, 1875.

[9] Yealand Preparative Meeting, *Yealand British School*, September 1st, 1868.

[10] Yealand Preparative Meeting, *Yealand British School*, September 14th, 1876.

[11] Yealand Preparative Meeting, *Yealand British School*, April 23rd, 1869.

[12] *Lancaster Guardian*, July 2nd, 1881.

[13] *Lancaster Guardian*, February 6th, 1897.

[14] *Lancaster Guardian*, June 11th, 1887.

[15] *Lancaster Guardian*, April 14th, 1894.

[16] *Lancaster Guardian*, January 21st, 1888.

[17] Yealand Preparative Meeting, *Yealand British School*, December 3rd, 1866.

[18] Guy Woolnough, & Joan Clarke, "The death of the boy Heslop," *The Mourholme Magazine of Local History*, no.1 (1991), p.9-12.

[19] *Lancaster Guardian*, October 2nd, 1875.

[20] *Lancaster Guardian* September 27th, 1879.

[21] *Lancaster Guardian* May 14th, 1881.

[22] *Lancaster Guardian*, January 15th, 1898.

[23] *Lancaster Guardian*, April 16th, 1898.

[24] *Lancaster Guardian*, August 31st, 1861.

[25] *Lancaster Guardian*, April 5th 1873.

[26] Parliamentary Papers, *Schools Inquiry Session* "Report on Grammar Schools in N. Lancashire", vol. xxvii (1867/8), p.427.

[27] J. Stuart Maclure, *Education documents England and Wales 1816 – 1968* (Methuen Educational Ltd, 1968), p.98.

[28] Papers concerning Archbishop Hutton's School, Lancashire Record Office, PR3332 Acc. 5192, location 2/708/5.

[29] Yealand Preparative Meeting, *Yealand British School*.

[30] Parliamentary Papers, *Schools Inquiry Session*, vol. xxvii (1867/8), p.427.

[31] Mourholme Local History Society Book Group, *Warton 1800-1850: How a North Lancashire Parish Changed*, (Mourholme Local History Society, 2005) p. 202-203.

[32] Mourholme, *Warton 1800-1850*, p.203.

[33] Guy Woolnough, "Carnforth National School", *Mourholme Magazine of Local History*, no.3 (1990), p.18.

[34] Mannex, *Topography and Directory of North and South Lonsdale, Amounderness, Leyland* (1866) p.565.

[35] *Lancaster Guardian*, July 23rd, 1864.

[36] *Lancaster Guardian*, February 18th, 1865.

[37] Ruth Badley, *Emmanuel Congregational Church, Carnforth* (1980).

[38] *Lancaster Observer*, October 28th, 1880.

[39] *Lancaster Gazette*, May 20th, 1882.

[40] *Lancaster Guardian,* July 28th, 1883.

[41] P. Barrett & Co, *Topography and Directory of Preston, the Fylde Lancaster and District* (1886), p.242.

[42] Silverdale School, *Manager's minutes*, in private possession.

[43] Priest Hutton School Inspection, 1895. Lancashire Record Office, SMPH 1/3/2.

[44] *Lancaster Guardian,* March 7th, 1896.

[45] Bulmer, *Bulmer's Directory of Lancaster & District,* (1918).

[46] Mannex and Company, *Topography and Directory of North and South Lonsdale. Amounderness, Leyland,* (1866), p.568.

[47] W.J. Cook, *Lancaster, Morecambe and District* (1901), p.288.

[48] *Lancaster Guardian,* July 29th, 1882.

[49] *Lancaster Guardian,* September 11th, 1886.

[50] *Lancaster Gazette,* July 25th, 1885.

[51] Matthew Arnold, "General Report for the year 1863," *Reports on Elementary Schools,* (H.M.S.O. reprinted 1910), pp.99-101.

[52] School Log Book, Archbishop Hutton's School, Warton, January 21st 1881, Lancashire Record Office, PR3332 acc.5192.

[53] H.C. Barnard, *Short History of English Education; from 1760 to 1944* (University of London Press, 1955), p164.

[54] Yealand Preparative Meeting, *Yealand British School,* March 15th, 1867.

[55] *Lancaster Guardian,* June 27th, 1896.

[56] *Lancaster Guardian,* June 27th, 1896; March 11th, 1899.

[57] John Stuart Maclure, *Educational Documents: England & Wales 1816-1968* (Methuen Education Ltd. 1968), p.150.

[58] J.L. Spencer, ed., *The Royal Grammar School, Lancaster: Quincentenary Commemorative Volume* (Edinburgh: Neill & Sons, 1969), pp.10 -16.

[59] *Lancaster Guardian,* August 9th, 1890.

[60] *Lancaster Guardian,* January 12th, 1895.

[61] School Log Book, Archbishop Hutton's School, October 11th, 1895.

[62] Yealand Preparative Meeting, *Yealand British School,* November 6th, 1876.

[63] School Log Book, Archbishop Hutton's School, July 20th, 1880.

[64] School Log Book, Archbishop Hutton's School, January 10th, 1879.

[65] Yealand Preparative Meeting, *Yealand British School,* November 2nd, 1868.

[66] *Lancaster Guardian,* September 19th, 1863.

[67] *Lancaster Guardian,* December 25th, 1880.

[68] *Lancaster Guardian,* November 19th, 1898.

[69] Yealand Preparative Meeting, *Yealand British School,* December 6th, 1869.

[70] Yealand Preparative Meeting, *Yealand British School,* October 20th, 1879.

Chapter Ten

WOMAN'S PLACE, IN THE HOME?

In 1865 John Ruskin, in his published lecture, *Sesame and Lilies,* laid out his opinion of the differing places in the world of men and women:

> '*The man, in his rough work in the open world, must encounter all peril and trial ... must be always hardened. But he guards woman from all this, within his house, as ruled by her ...* [she] *need enter no danger, no temptation...*'[1]

He voiced a truly Victorian ideal, but it was a very middle class ideal because most families had not the income to keep girls at home in idleness. In the 1851 census of Warton parish 38% of all women and girls who were over 12 years of age were in employment, but this includes the married who were the least likely to undertake work outside the home. It was the unmarried and, to a lesser extent, widows who went out to work. Of all unmarried women over 12 years of age, 65% had an occupation recorded.

Those women who had no occupation recorded fall roughly into three groups. There were some still at school. There were the girls entered simply as '*farmer's daughter*'. They have not been included among those counted as at work, but such girls, though they may not have earned a wage, would have been, like the farmer's sons, contributing to the family income by working on the farm, especially in the dairy and the poultry yard. In the third group were the daughters and other female relatives of the gentry, or near gentry. The occupation column against their names is either left blank, or contains some statement implying financial independence such as '*annuitant*', '*own means*', '*railway share holder*'. It seems likely that, apart from the wealthier, most girls in Warton parish would be expected to earn their own keep.

Jobs for Women in 1851
Domestic Service

Work for women in Warton parish at that time overwhelmingly meant domestic service. Of all the unmarried women for whom an occupation was recorded in the 1851 census 84% were in service. No  individual account of life as a domestic servant in Warton has survived, or has been found, but from accounts of service elsewhere it is clear that employers could sometimes be harsh or unfeeling, and that girls, knowing how much their families counted on their earnings, might endure much misery.[2] The girls were the more vulnerable because domestic servants seldom were local girls, but came from a distance, sometimes a considerable distance, and so were far from the support of their family.   The usual explanation given for this is that employers feared that too much gossip about them would be relayed in the village by local girls. It is probably too simplistic an answer, but there is no disputing the fact that employing domestic servants from a distance was a very widespread practice.

How the girls from a distance heard of jobs in Warton parish is not clear. The local newspapers very seldom carried advertisements of vacancies. There were Register Offices for servants in both Carnforth and Lancaster. However, the news of vacant places presumably also spread by word of mouth from girl to girl (in the census returns it can be seen that, where a number of servants were employed, they often came from the same part of the country). It was probable also that the very ladies who felt disinclined to employ a local girl would see it as their charitable duty to enquire around among friends elsewhere for a good place for a village girl. It has been said too that local tradesmen, in going their rounds, learnt where a servant was needed and acted as informal employment agencies.[3] It could be, but no local evidence has been found.

MISS KERR'S REGISTRY FOR SERVANTS

(LATE WILLIAMS AND DUFF).

17, LOWER BELGRAVE STREET, LONDON, S.W.

(Registered Agency).

SERVANTS' TERMS.

BOOKING FEE *(available for 6 months)*	1/-
ENGAGING FEE, *below £11 Wages*	1/-
,, ,, *from £14 to £30 Wages* ...	... 2d. in the £.
,, ,, *over £30 Wages*	... 3d. in the £.

Special Fees are charged for Jobs.

All Letters to be addressed to MISS KERR.

Payment by Cheque or Postal Order payable to MISS KERR.

The above advert shows an agency in London

One thing is clear from the census returns and that is that any preconceived picture of an upstairs, downstairs life for most servants needs modifying. Only about 20% of households in Warton parish employed a resident domestic servant at all, and of these 55% employed only one servant and only about 5% employed three or more. The pattern was much the same in all the townships, except in Yealand Conyers where as many as 45% of households employed a resident servant and of these 33% employed three or more, culminating in Leighton Hall where there were 11 resident domestic staff, all of them, except the kitchen maid, coming from outside the parish. Perhaps the kitchen maid's chances of even seeing her employers was too small for there to be much fear of her spreading gossip. In such big households there would have been, presumably, some sort of downstairs companionship (and a chance for a servant to rise through the servant hierarchy). In the single servant families, the general domestic might indeed become a much valued member of the household, but there was no obvious path of advancement for her, and however much she was seen as part of the family she would, in essence, remain a unit in someone else's family unless and until she left work and married.

Dress Making

The next most frequent occupation for women in the parish was dressmaking, though it came a very long way after domestic service, for there were only 16 women in the whole parish earning a living with their

209

needle. In the bigger towns ready-made clothes were beginning to take over - not yet factory-made, but made in workshops, often behind the front shop where they were sold. The whole trade tended to have a bad 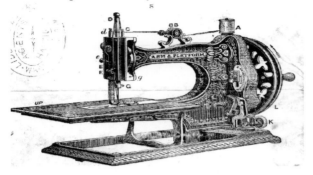 name for overworking and underpaying; so much so that Mayhew, in his investigation of *London Labour and London's Poor* said he was forced to accept the claim that '*the young girls were mostly compelled to resort to prostitution to eke out their subsistence.*'[4] It has even been suggested that dressmaker in the census returns was often a euphemism for prostitute. It seems unlikely that this was so in Warton parish. Almost all the needlewomen were living at home with their relatives and it is more probable that they were simply maintaining themselves by mending and making for neighbours who could afford their services - a suggestion rather supported by the finding that eight of the 16 lived in rich Conyers.

Professional and Clerical

The title of this section is not very applicable to 1851. Apart from teaching there was, to all intents and purposes, no professional work for women in the parish. There was one '*cottager nurse*', Mary Mason, a widow of 84 living in Carnforth, but there was small likelihood at this date that a woman of her age would have trained other than on the job. Seven women were employed in some form of teaching, but there is nothing to show if any held a formal qualification. Three women could be said to have clerical jobs: Miss Lydia Richardson, the postmistress in Carnforth who was assisted by her widowed mother, and Mrs. Sarah Story, postmistress in Yealand Conyers. No formal training was needed, but obviously the work implied a certain degree of both literacy and numeracy.

Other Occupations

There were four washerwomen in the parish and four charwomen. It was work that seemed to fall to widows and women with absent husbands. Catering offered some openings; two women kept lodging houses, three widows were listed as innkeepers. Two unmarried women worked as staff in inns, one as a '*waiter*' and one as a '*barmaid*'; both were related to the innkeeper. There were six women who kept shops; a baker's shop in Warton is the only establishment that was possibly more than a shop in a corner of the home. The baker was an elderly, unmarried woman, living alone, but keeping two servants. A 15 year old girl in Warton township claimed to be an '*earthern ware dealer*'. So were her father and two of her brothers. And that is really all, except for the four women who were farmers. They were all widows and, it seems, their husbands had left them the farm, even though there were grown sons at home.

Jobs for Women in 1891

It may have been the conscription of so many men into the army that enabled women to show just how many jobs, up till then considered only suitable for men, women could undertake perfectly competently. In fact women had been branching out into new work for decades before then. Domestic service remained the most common occupation, but not as overwhelmingly so as earlier in the century. Women were finding work in offices, in the central and local government services and in shops, fields of work up till then almost exclusively male - a trend probably helped by the fact that women were regularly paid less than men for the same job.[5] What follows is an attempt to show how far the women of Warton parish responded to this change.

Table 10.1

Census year	1851	1891
All women	38.6%	25.4%
Single women only	65.1%	53.9%

Percentage of women (aged over 12 years) in employment in Warton Parish

As can be seen from Table 10.1 (data taken from the 1851 and 1891 censuses), the percentage of women following an occupation outside the home fell between 1851 and 1891. Warton was not unusual in this. It was the pattern everywhere. It has been suggested that the rise in the real wages of men and the fall in the cost of living were making it less necessary for women to supplement the family income.[6] If this were so it would fit in with what is known about wages and cost of living in Warton parish (see the section on Market Prices in chapter one).

Domestic Service

Table 10.2

	1851	1891
Domestic service	84.0%	61.7%
Dressmaking	7.0%	16.0%
Clerical/professional	4.5%	8.4%
Catering	0.5%	1.0%

Percentage of employed women in certain occupations in Warton Parish

As table 10.2 (again taken from the 1851 and 1891 censuses) shows, domestic service remained much the commonest employment for women. Nationally an increasing difficulty of getting and keeping servants was the cause of many complaints among would-be employers; though the absolute number of female domestic servants was still rising in 1900, so was the population. More families were, for one reason and another, managing without a servant. In 1881 there are said to have been 218 female servants for every 1,000 families; by 1911 the figure had fallen to 170.[7] The same trend can be found in Warton parish; in 1891 only about 12% of all households employed a resident servant against 20% in 1851 - the change is not large, but it is there. It was probably more to do with the increasing number of households not aspiring to servants rather than to any difficulty in obtaining servants. In Carnforth, with its predominance of small terrace housing for a working population, 90.8% of households did not employ a resident servant. At the other end of the scale the percentage of households employing three or more servants remained much the same.

Dress Making

In 1891 there were 60 women in the parish working in the dressmaking trade (three married, the rest single); a rise in proportion to the rise in the population.

There was however a noticeable change in where they were to be found. In 1851 most of the townships had one or two dressmakers. In 1891 the dressmakers were now largely concentrated in Warton and

Carnforth (15 in Warton and 38 in Carnforth). The explanation seems to be that the area was catching up with the urban fashion of making ready-made dresses in workshops, though it is difficult to find where these workshops were. Directories of the period list plenty of establishments that might have employed seamstresses - places describing themselves as drapers, out-fitters, clothiers or merchant tailors. However, there is no mention of workshops, not even Stephenson Brothers, the drapers in Market Street, who are known to have had a workroom. They loaned it

to the new Congregational church for their Sunday services (see chapter seven).

By 1904 there must have been at least one workshop in Carnforth with powered machines. In June of that year Annie Barnham of Carnforth had '*a large portion of her hair torn off by the shafting of the sewing machines*' at James D. Ram and Co. of Oxford Road, makers of children's garments.[8]

Professional and Clerical

In the 1891 census 30 women were given as engaged in teaching, a four fold rise since 1851 and greater than the under 3% rise in the population. There were also signs suggesting an advance in professionalism, though the census is hardly the best place to judge this. The nine girls recorded as '*pupil teachers*' would certainly have been working towards achieving professional teaching qualification (see Chapter 9). The two entered as '*elementary school teachers*' would probably, but not necessarily, have been certificated, for the Board of Education was pushing to keep the untrained out of their schools. In 1875 it had been estimated that 57% of women teachers (and 70% of men) were trained and qualified.[9]

It seems unlikely that the three women working as governesses were trained. They were living in households where the children were so small they must have been more in need of nursery care than of teaching. Two of the teachers, it might be noticed, were married. The almost universal rule that women teachers were to be deprived of their job if they married did not come in until after the 1914-18 War. Mrs. Maria Unsworth was the head teacher of Warton Infant School for many years, though she had a husband working as a railway goods agent and three small children. Mrs. Ann Howitt of Priest Hutton, although she had a husband and a nine-year old son, was working as an assistant schoolmistress. In practice more married women were teaching than the census shows. The wives of elementary school headmasters were not credited with an occupation in the census returns, though it is known from elsewhere that they were employed on the staff. When a new headmaster was needed at Silverdale the advertisement said that '*his wife would be required to give instruction to the girls in the afternoon*'.[10] There was no mention of a separate salary however. Mrs. Perfect was entered in the census simply as the wife of the headmaster of Archbishop Hutton's school, but she is known from the school logbooks to have been acting for many years as an assistant teacher. The fact that she was not entered as an employed woman in the census certainly seems to suggest that she was not receiving a separate salary of her own.

Nursing, too, was moving towards the professional, though it was not until 1919 when the General Nursing Council was created that it became possible to control who called themselves sick nurses.[11] As a result there are problems with the census returns. In 1891 there were four '*nurses*' in the parish (not counting the young girls entered as '*nurse*' but also as '*domestic servant*' who would have been nursery maids). Two were '*monthly nurses*', looking after women lying in after childbirth. Their professional status is unknown. There was one who was described as a '*sick nurse*', Jane Carradus, a single woman of 47 living on her own in Priest Hutton. Nothing more is known about her. That leaves only one nurse who can be assumed to have had some sort of professional training: Kate Weeton, aged 24, entered as a '*hospital nurse*', was living in the home of the wealthy Boddingtons of Cove House in Silverdale. It is true there may have been other women from the parish working as hospital nurses, but they would not appear in the local census. Nurses were most strictly required to live in at the hospital.

There was, unsurprisingly, no woman doctor in the parish. It was still unusual work for a woman and it was not always considered quite proper. In a late Victorian novel a gentleman learns that the heroine is walking the wards as a medical student and exclaims '... *when I think of all that girl must know, it makes me sick - sick!*.[12] Not that everyone agreed with the horrified gentleman. In 1877 the *Lancaster Guardian* carried an article proclaiming that they were glad to learn that the University of London had agreed to admit women to higher medical degrees.[13] There was a woman dentist, Agnes Sartis, lodging in Carnforth along with her *'husband and agent'*. She might be counted as something of an exotic, coming as she did from the U.S.A.

The move of women into clerical work seems to have had little effect locally. In the 1891 census there were three women working in village post offices, and one *'telegraph clerk'*, Elizabeth Sandham of Yealand Conyers. She too may have been working in the village post office, for Conyers now offered a telegraph service. Otherwise no woman claimed to be earning her living as a clerk.

Other Occupations

Nor were women becoming shop assistants on any large scale; a few girls were listed as assistants to relatives who kept shops, but otherwise those listed as shop assistants were all male. A few more women were moving into the catering trade. They were inn-keepers, as in the past (in 1891 the Red Lion and the Black Bull in Warton, the West View Hotel in Millhead, the Silverdale Hotel and the Temperance Hotel in Carnforth all had women as innkeepers).

SHOVEL INN 1890
Carnforth Station Trust Collection

There were also, by the end of the century, a few women working in pubs other than in those owned by a member of the family. The Station Hotel in Carnforth was in the charge of a manageress, an unmarried woman of 25 years born in Cheshire. She had a resident staff of 11, seven of them women, though not locally born for they all came from Liverpool or Ireland.

215

Nine other women kept private lodging houses, seven of them in Silverdale with its growing tourist trade. And, of course, women still did charring and washing. There is also one woman calling herself a '*minder*'. The census does not say whom she minded, probably small children.

The other big occupation in the north of England at this time was work in the textile mills. It is known that there was a small flax-mill in Holme, just over the Westmorland border. In 1911 Mrs. Rawlinson Ford of Yealand Manor recorded that the older village women she spoke to had told her that '*Many of the women worked for the Holme Mill*'.[14] It is not easy to know what to make of this in view of the total absence of such work from the census returns. It may be of significance that the word '*for*' is used rather than the customary 'at'.

Work for Those who Left the Parish

Women might have been finding wider opportunities by moving away, but the evidence suggests otherwise. The information from the 1881 census (used for reasons outlined before (see Chapter 5)) had drawbacks. The following table illustrates some of the problems:

Table 10.3

No.	Relationship	No.	Relationship
90	Daughter	2	Grand-daughter
34	Wife	1	Lodger
19	Servant	1	Mother
6	Head	1	Mother-in-Law
4	Step-daughter	1	Niece
3	Boarder	1	Visitor

Women from Carnforth living in other townships in Lancashire; relationship to head of household

Of the 163 women recorded, 34 were wives. They seldom had an occupation entered and it is not known what work they had found before marriage. The 19 women entered as domestic servants may well have left to seek work for themselves, but the high proportion of daughters (90 out of the 163) most probably means that they moved when the head of the household moved and then found what work they could. These findings for Carnforth need to be kept in mind when judging the findings for the whole parish, which show domestic service as still the commonest employment. Only about a score of women found work in a textile mill. There are no really high-flyers - unless one counts the head of a boarding school and one matron of a Girls' Friendly Society Lodge. One woman from Carnforth found work as a bank clerk - the sort of work she might have done in her own community if Carnforth had been a little more advanced in appreciating the work women were capable of.

The Home
Housing

It seems likely that, one way or another, women must have spent much of their lives coping with housework, either in their own homes or in other people's homes as domestic servants, so that it becomes important to know something about these homes as places to work.

Since so few wives went out to work, or not on a regular basis at any rate, it is to be supposed that the husband's income sufficed (more or less) to pay the rent. Whether the modern housewife, harassed by trying to combine a job and the care of children in order to have a house at all, would think much of the house provided is another matter. At least it seems that the construction of the houses was not too bad.

The parish contained (and still contains) a number of very fine larger houses. The one illustrated is Capernwray Hall. Even its smaller

houses were likely to have been of relatively sound construction compared with other parts of the country, for it lay in an area where stone was freely available. They were however likely to have been both damp and chilly. Many have survived but today, double glazed and damp-proofed, give little idea of what they were.

A government inspector, Dr. Mivart, who came to Lancaster Rural District in 1901 to look into the state of sanitation, wrote that:

'dwellings appear to be of substantial construction. Older houses ... almost universally, are built of local stone ... In less satisfactory older dwellings ... the walls have been somewhat roughly put together and faced with mortar, the fall of which allows ready passage of moisture'.

He added that the use of brick in the construction of smaller dwellings was increasing. He was less happy about the sanitation, saying that:

'... stress may especially be laid upon want of ventilation in bedrooms, or upon the juxta-position of cesspits or filthy cowsheds to thin party walls of dwellings. Striking instances of this last-named fault were met with...at Galgate, Warton, and Bolton-le-Sands'.[15]

In rural areas there was little incentive to build. Local Authorities had no duty to build for the rural poor. Speculative builders might put up dwellings in towns as they did in Carnforth, but the wages of agricultural workers were too low to make building for them an attractive proposition. If landowners and farmers built, it was tied or rented cottages they favoured for the use only of those working on their land. Any worker who complained of the state of the house could be got rid of at the next hiring.

After the parliamentary reform of 1884, which gave a vote to many agricultural workers, government began to take a little more notice. A Royal Commission was set up in 1885 on *Housing of the Working Classes,* which included a survey of rural housing. The commissioners found that there were vigorous protests in rural areas about the use of tied cottages, about insecurity of tenure in general and such practices as evicting a tenant with one week's notice.[16] Poor rural housing continued almost unabated, and a strong body of opinion was growing that the bad housing conditions in the countryside were a major influence causing out-migration, the Flight from the Countryside as it was called, that was worrying people so.[17]

One thing is certain; the houses, good or bad, must often have been very cramped. In 1851 the average house occupancy in the parish was 5.1 and in 1891 4.9. For comparison, at the time of the 1991 census, there were on average 2.39 persons per house in Warton Ward and 2.51 in Carnforth Ward.[18] The high occupancy in the nineteenth century did not count as legal overcrowding according to the standards of the day, though in 1902 Dr. Mivart was a little doubtful about Millhead, (or Dudley as he called it, following local usage), '... *noticeable overcrowding of persons has occurred, and still existed at the time of my visit, in the village of Dudley'*.[19]

The Chores

In his report the conscientious Dr Mivart also noted that:

'The cleanliness of cottage interiors appeared to me noteworthy, and I was impressed by the fact that the occupiers of some of the most dilapidated and inconvenient dwellings were obviously trying to do their best with them'.[20]

Had the housework needed for this admirable result become any easier over the decades between 1850 and 1900? The answer seems to be a qualified yes. Facilities were still few; even in parts of the parish where there was running water there might be only one tap down in the kitchen and that was for cold water only (see chapter three). Except in the area served by the Carnforth Gas Company, hot water meant that a coal fire had to be lighted and maintained (involving the lugging about of heavy fuel).

One helpful invention had come in at the mid-century, an improvement so obvious that it is difficult to think of it as an invention at all. In 1868 Dr. Hunter, a government inspector, visiting the area to investigate the state of rural housing, commented that '*A sinkstone is a great advantage*'.[21] So it must have been. A sink-stone, or slop-stone, was merely a shallow stone sink with a drain hole at one end that allowed the water to run away into the ground outside. Without this simple invention housewives had not only to carry water to fill the washtubs, but also to carry the dirty water out again to empty it. It is true that, only a couple of years later than Dr. Hunter's report, the large house, Woodlands, in Silverdale had amenities which included '*a bathroom ... and other necessary conveniences*',[22] but that simply meant that there were servants to carry the water needed, or pump it up each day.

Coal fires created dust and dirt and so added more work; carpets to be hung up and beaten, floors to be cleaned by going down on hands and knees and scrubbing them. Clothes and bed linen were heavy to wash and difficult to dry. Getting the dirt out meant boiling the wash in a copper or pounding it in a tub with the heavy poss-stick. The notion of labour saving was coming in, but at a fairly primitive level. One tends to forget that even the mangle that now seems so old-fashioned came in as a labour saving device. Its primary job was not drying the clothes (usually achieved by wringing by hand). The mangle was for pressing the linen. This partially dried the washing, which, after passing between the heavy rollers, came out at least pressed flat enough to cut down on ironing - a skilled, heavy and hot job when there were only flat irons that had to be heated over an open fire. Mangles were unwieldy and took up precious space. It sometimes seemed better to carry the heavy, half-dried linen to

someone in the village who took in mangling for pay. There may have been a professional mangler in Yealand Conyers. The memory has survived that at the beginning of the twentieth century there was a monster mangle in a house there, with its rollers weighted by stones.[23]

The nineteenth century even produced washing machines, though the word machine perhaps gives the wrong idea. They had to be worked by hand - heavy work, one suspects, though an advertisement for '*The Thorough Washer*' (patented in 1871) shows the machine with a young woman standing elegantly by, with not a hair out of place.[24]

Lighting too was improving even without the advantage of gas. In 1859 a shop in Lancaster offered '*Patent Paraffin Oil Lamps*' which were promised to supply a '*light equal to gas*'.[25] The so called paraffin was colza oil, but a few years later a shop was offering '*American Rock Oil*'.[26] Both probably gave enough light to enable the use of another invention even at night - '*Wheeler & Wilson's Marvellous Sewing Machines*'.[27]

Altogether there was an increasing range of inventions that must have helped lighten housework. The local newspaper carried advertisements for ready-made soaps and cleaning agents as well as devices for easing chores - bottles of blacking, furniture polish, firelighters and knife polish. Sunlight Soap was even advertising, in large letters, that its use meant '*Less Labour*'[28] - the death knell of the Victorian work ethic perhaps? It can be entertaining going through advertisements, finding what was and what was not available, but unfortunately the advertisements seldom mention a price, so that it is impossible to estimate from them how far down the financial scale the goods would have been affordable.

Cooking

In 1865 the same Dr. Hunter who had approved of sink-stones wrote that in the northern counties *'where coal is cheap there should be,*

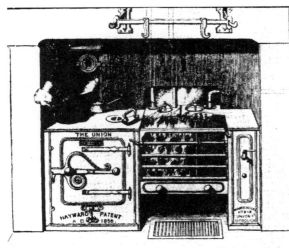

and usually is, an iron oven', but went on to lament that the landlords too often left it to the tenant to install it which meant that cooking was still being done wastefully on an open fire. He thought it *'a stupid and cruel arrangement'*.[29] Only a few years later the houses in Millhead had coal-fired ovens fitted as standard.[30]

Households in the north were still considered to enjoy a better diet than those in the south, just as they had done earlier in the century.[31] In 1893 it was reported by a Royal Commission that:

> *'It is certainly not surprising when a comparison is made between the dietary of the men in the North with that of the Eastern counties to feel that the latter cannot compare with the former in physique and intellect.'*[32]

(Was the writer a Northerner himself?*)*.

Yet even in the north new fast foods were finding their way in. In 1887 Alexander Satterthwaite, a Lancaster grocer, sent a catalogue to a Mr. Wright of Yealand Conyers.[33] It lists a surprising amount of ready-made food. A hypothetical Mrs. Wright could have served a dinner entirely out of tins, (and

222

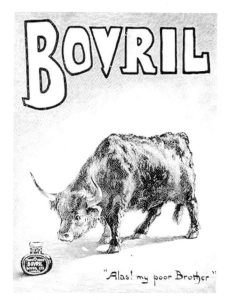

"Alas! my poor Brother"

she could also purchase an *'opening knife'* to get into the tins). Mr. Satterthwaite offered her 10 varieties of soup, nine of fish and 10 of meat (including roast mutton and stewed kidneys) that could have been served with a choice of tinned asparagus or tinned peas. For dessert there were tinned fruits in five varieties. If Mrs. Wright still preferred home cookery there were aids to quick cooking - baking powder, beef extract, gravy browning, ready-made sauces, blancmange powder, custard powder, mushroom powder, pudding powder. Once again it is difficult to know who could have afforded such food - nothing as vulgar as a price is entered in the catalogue.

By the very end of the century the ultimate nineteenth century fast food had reached Carnforth; in 1898 the idea of a fish and chip shop at the market in Carnforth was being mooted.[34] In fact fried fish could already be purchased before that. In 1889, according to a local directory, there was a fried fish dealer, James Higson, established in Market Street.[35] (It seems this was a new venture, for in 1886 Higson was calling himself *'tripe dresser and neat's foot oil manufacturer'*.)[36]

Child Bearing and Child Rearing

Despite all these improvements it seems likely that a good many women must have been chronically tired by the combined strain of heavy housework and the rearing of a large family. The census returns frequently show a pattern of regular childbirth at two-year intervals or less, often continuing until the mother was well into her forties. Put in statistical terms, the birth rate, (that is the number of children born per 1,000 of the population), in the Lancaster Rural District in the last decades of the nineteenth century was 28.1, much what it was everywhere.[37] Today the national rate is under 11.

Knowledge of more efficient methods of birth control was spreading, but was very hedged about by disapproval, and certainly not advertised or easily available to the majority of women. There was little she could do for herself to limit family size (though the prevalence of breast feeding may at least have helped keep the interval between births at two years rather than less). It does seem, however, that some women were so anxious to escape the round of childbirth and child rearing that there was a market for abortifacients. The sales promotion is discreet, but what else can one make of the two following advertisements?

APIOL & STEEL PILLS for Ladies.

A REMEDY FOR ALL IRREGULARITIES.

SUPERSEDING BITTER APPLE, PIL COCHIA, PENNYROYAL, etc.

Price 4/6 post free.

Obtainable only from MARTIN, Chemist, Southampton.

> *'To women irregularities and obstructions etc., removed by a new and entirely certain method...no pill ... no useless injections ...'*

and

> *'To married ladies ... remedy for restoring regularity ... acts almost immediately and does not interfere with household duties'.*[38]

They happened to have appeared in the same newspaper on the same day in 1895, but their like appeared week in week out. Unfortunately the methods advertised to the public at the time would have been either useless, or dangerous, or both.

Women in Public Life

By the end of the century it was becoming possible for a woman to enter public life, but there is little evidence from the parish to show that women did so. There had, in fact, never been anything laid down to prevent women householders voting in the old vestry and town meetings, just as male householders could; though there was a catch for married women. Until the Married Women's Property Act of 1870 it might have been difficult for a married woman to claim ownership of a house since by law all her property belonged, absolutely, to her husband to do with as he chose.[39] However, it was probably more the ingrained habit of centuries rather than any legal bar that kept women out of parish politics.

It was simply not something that women did. However in 1895 a woman, Mrs. Margaret Burrow, felt sufficiently sure of herself at a Warton township meeting to second the proposal that James Dickenson, a postal clerk, should be on the new Parish Council.

When School Boards were set up under the 1870 Education Act, women were allowed to vote for, and to serve as, board members. It so happened that there never was a school board in Warton parish (see Chapter 9), so the matter was not put to the test. Women had been allowed to vote for Poor Law Guardians from the time of the Poor Law Amendment Act in 1834, and after 1875 were allowed to stand for office themselves. It seems there was no rush to take up the option locally. In 1891 Freelance, a local newspaper correspondent, pointed out that while the Chester Board of Guardians had appointed '*a lady member*' their example had not been followed.

> '*Why not have several ladies nominated as candidates for election. One or two ladies on the Workhouse Committee would be a great acquisition and would do good service in gaining attention to the needs of the old people in the home*'.[40]

A letter appearing the next month gives a picture of how even a sympathetic man might view such female ventures. He wrote to support the appointment of women to the Board of Guardians and pointed out that there were more women than ever voluntarily engaged in '*philanthropic ways*' and he thought other committees, too, would benefit on '*little matters of detail*' if they obtained the help of women.[41] The implication, one fears, is that on larger matters of policy these admirable women were not likely to have anything to contribute. By 1895 three women had been elected to the Lancaster Board of Guardians, one of them, a Miss Edith Willis, was from Carnforth. On her election she became a member of the School Attendance Committee.[42] Miss Willis was active in public life in various ways. She was a faithful member of the Carnforth Women's Liberal Association, attending meetings regularly and, by mid-1895, was President.[43] In 1897 she was also President of the Women's Guild.[44] She seems to have been an enterprising young woman, being only 28 when she became a guardian.

Edith Currer Willis was the youngest child of Thomas Willis, a surgeon and Member of the Royal College of Surgeons of London. Both her father and her mother, Jane, were from Beverley in Yorkshire, but Edith and her siblings were born in Burnley.[45] By 1891 Edith Willis was living at 46 New Street, Carnforth, with her sister Elizabeth and her brother-in-law Dr. John Joseph Butler. In 1894 she was living with Elizabeth and John at Ormonde House, 2 New Street, Carnforth, where Dr. Butler carried out his profession as physician and surgeon.[46] Edith Willis continued as a guardian into the twentieth century and carried on living at Ormonde House until at least 1918.[47]

Under the 1888 County Council Act women could vote for members of the new County Councils, and in 1895 it was laid down that women could not only vote in Parish Council elections, but also serve on the council themselves. No examples from Warton parish have yet been found before the turn of the century.

As everyone knows women did not achieve the parliamentary vote until after the First World War, but there is plenty of evidence that the women of the parish were very active in all the political movements. A Women's Liberal Association had been founded in Carnforth in 1892 and in 1894 the chairman (a man, one is a little sorry to see) was able to say that since the Association was founded the women had kept their cause *'well to the front'*.[48] When, at the time of the 1895 election, the Liberal candidate, Baron Halkett, set himself to go through *'every village and hamlet in this scattered community'*, he was accompanied by the ladies of the Association.[49] No reports have yet been found from before the end of the nineteenth century of campaigning by women for the vote, but it must have been going on, for Mr. R.F. Cavendish, the successful Unionist candidate for North Lonsdale in the 1895 election, presented in 1897 a petition *'from Carnforth'* to the House of Commons in favour of the Parliamentary Franchise (Extension to Women) Bill.[50] Plainly more research is needed.

Good Works

It has often been noted that one way women moved into public life was through charitable work. No man could object to that. To strive for political power might be deplorable, but to practise charity was sweet and womanly and to be encouraged. Men had perhaps not foreseen on what a large and professional scale women would take advantage of this to find a rôle beyond the purely domestic; district visiting, workhouse visiting, the Charity Organisation Society - all became women's work.

For District Visitors alone it has been estimated that by the beginning of the First World War the number had reached nearly 200,000, an impressive number of workers at a time when there were only 168,000 established civil servants, male and female, in Britain.[51]

Victorian ideal of a lady bountiful

Warton parish seems to have joined in Good Works in its own small way. Of course there had always been charitable women (and men) who were good neighbours and helped in time of trouble. There had also been the Lady Bountiful who was able to give on a larger scale. Mrs. Boddington of Silverdale gave '*Christmas parcels*' to 120 children at a Juvenile Treat. (Unfortunately the parcels were delayed in the post. However the vicarage sent 12 Christmas puddings.)[52] In 1891 a spinster lady in Carnforth gave an Old Folks Treat in the form of a '*meat tea*' to 60 old people.[53]

These examples could be multiplied, but attempts to find out about more formal charitable work by women in the parish have proved tantalising. The newspapers more frequently reported on social occasions than on the background committee work. As far as fund raising events and treats went it was obvious (and scarcely surprising?) that it was the women who presided over the tea tables. When the vicar of Warton '*waited upon*' the children at a Sunday school tea it was newsworthy (and even so he was helped by his wife and other ladies).[54] Whether women served on the working committees is harder to find. One would guess that the larger the organisation the less likely were women to be in charge. The British Women's Temperance Society, surely a suitable organisation for women to run, only had one woman on the committee in 1899. When a soup kitchen was opened in Lancaster in 1891 there were no women on the organising committee.[55] When it came down to smaller organisations like the Warton Band of Hope the committee was made up half of men and half of women.[56]

Conclusion

The lives of women in the nineteenth century may have been hard and their treatment often unjust. The battle for equal civic rights - for the right to follow their bent in work and education, to have the same right to their own property as men, the same legal right to sue for divorce - was being fought for all through the century. It was not till the mid-century that a husband's legal right to beat his wife was taken from him, and not till the Married Women's Property Act in 1872 that the husband lost his absolute right to treat all his wife's property as his own. There is very little to be found in local sources of this battle.

If, nevertheless, one tries to argue that women in Warton parish must have been discontented, then one is going well beyond the evidence. No woman in nineteenth century Warton parish left any account of her feelings. There is, however, an account from the early twentieth century. The diary of Helen Escolme of Yealand Conyers covers the years between 1911 and 1913, but it is probably a fair enough picture of what life at the end of the nineteenth century would have had to offer a lively young farmer's daughter. Helen did not go out to work (except occasionally to help at a neighbour's house) and apparently did not wish to. She had plenty of work to do on her father's farm and seems indeed to have been largely in charge of the poultry side of the business. She was able to develop her musical talent playing the organ in Borwick Church and entering singing competitions with the choir. She had a wide circle of friends in the neighbourhood, flirted with the boys, had long sympathetic talks with the girls, and went to dances and other festivities, which often did not end until the early hours of the morning. No-one seems to have worried about her walking or cycling home even alone in the dark, though, to be honest, she was not often left to do so. There was usually a cheerful group to go with her or, more and more frequently, the young man she later married.[57]

[1] John Ruskin, *Sesame and Lilies* (Lecture II, 1864) sect. 68.

[2] Pamela Horne, *The Rise and Fall of the Victorian Servant,* (Alan Sutton Publishers Ltd., 1990), Chapter 7.

[3] Judith Flanders, *The Victorian House* (Harper Perennial, 2004), p.97.

[4] J.M. Golby ed., *Culture & Society in Britain 1850-1890* (Oxford University Press, 1986), p.7.

[5] Norman McCord, *British History 1815 - 1906* (Oxford University Press, 1991), p.452.

[6] McCord, *British History,* p.452.

[7] McCord, *British History,* p.453.

[8] *Lancaster Guardian*, August 6th, 1904.

[9] Lee Holcombe, *Victorian Ladies at Work: Middle Class Working Women in England and Wales 1850-1950* (David and Charles, 1973), p.37.

[10] *Lancaster Gazette*, January 1st, 1858.

[11] Holcombe, *Victorian Ladies at Work*, p.102.

[12] Graham Travers, *Mona Maclean: Medical Student* (William Blackmore and Sons, 1894), p.50.

[13] *Lancaster Guardian,* March 10th, 1877.

[14] Helena C. Ford, *Sketches of Yealand* (Kendal: Atkinson & Pollitt, 1931, reprinted from *The Lancaster Guardian*, 1911), p.16.

[15] F. St. George Mivart, *Report to the Local Government Board on the General Sanitary Circumstances and Administration of the Lancaster Rural District* (H.M.S.O., 1902), no. 172.

[16] Gordon Mingay "The Rural Slum", in Martin Gaskell, ed., *Slums* (Leicester University Press, 1990), p.119.

[17] Mingay "The Rural Slum", p.125

[18] Lancaster City Council, *Census of City Population 1991: A Census Handbook for Lancaster District* (1993).

[19] Mivart, *Report to the Local Government Board on the General Sanitary Circumstances...*

[20] Mivart, *Report to the Local Government Board on the General Sanitary Circumstances...*

[21] Parliamentary Papers, *Inquiry into the State of Dwellings of Rural Labourers* (vol. xxvi, 1865)

[22] *Lancaster Guardian,* "sale notice", April 23rd, 1870.

[23] Robin Greaves, *Personal Communication.*

[24] Judith Flanders, *The Victorian House* (Harper Perennial, 2004), p.126.

[25] *Lancaster Guardian,* November 12th, 1859.

[26] *Lancaster Gazette,* January 17th, 1863.

[27] *Lancaster Gazette,* September 19th, 1863.

[28] *Lancaster Guardian,* Supplement, January 16th, 1891.

[29] Parliamentary Papers, *Inquiry into the State of Dwellings of Rural Labourers* (vol. xxvi, 1865), pp.141-142.

[30] Jean Chatterly & John Findlater, "Millhead: the Initial Colonisation," *The Mourholme Magazine of Local History,* no.1 (1993), p.13.

[31] Mourholme Local History Society Book Group, *Warton 1800-1850; How a North Lancashire Parish Changed* (Mourholme Local History Society, 2005), pp.191-192.

[32] Parliamentary Papers, *Report of Royal Commission on Labour,* "Summary Report by Mr. Arthur Miles" (vol. xxxv, 1893/4), p.6.

[33] Alexander Satterthwaite, grocer, Wright's account, Yealand, Lancaster Reference Library, MS 1.

[34] *Lancaster Guardian,* September 10th, 1898.

[35] Well's *Lancaster and District Directory* (Wells & Co., 1889), p.166.

[36] P. Barrett & Co., *Topography and Directory of Preston, the Fylde, Lancaster and Districts* (1886), p.790.

[37] Environmental Health Department, *Annual Reports of Medical Officer of Health, Lancaster Rural District* (Morecambe Town Hall, 1889-1919).

[38] *Lancaster Guardian,* October 12th, 1895.

[39] Sidney Webb & Beatrice Webb, *Development of English Local Government 1689-1835,* vol.iv (Oxford University Press, 1963).

[40] *Lancaster Guardian,* March 28th, 1891.

[41] *Lancaster Guardian,* April 4th, 1891.

[42] Lists of Guardians and Paid Officers 1840 - 1904. List of Guardians and Paid Officers &c. for the Year 1895 – 96, p.3. Lancashire Record Office, PUL 6/1.
Lancaster Poor Law Union. Guardians' Minute Book 1893 – 1896. 5th January 1895, pp.247-249. Lancashire Record Office PUL/1/24.

[43] *Lancaster Guardian,* June 15th, 1895.

[44] *Lancaster Guardian,* October 9th 1897.

[45] Censuses of England and Wales, 1871, Burnley, St James, District 1, RG10/446, f.9, p11. 1881, Burnley, Habergham Eaves, Holy Trinity, District 36, RG11/4153, f.11. pp.15, 16.

[46] *Lancaster Guardian*, 8th December 1894.
Census of England and Wales, 1901, District 7, Carnforth, Christchurch, RG13/3995, f.11, p.14

[47] *Kelly's Directory of Lancashire (exclusive of the cities of Manchester and Liverpool)* (London: Kelly's Directories Ltd., 1918).

[48] *Lancaster Guardian*, March 17th, 1894.

[49] *Lancaster Guardian*, July 27th, 1895.

[50] *Lancaster Guardian*, May 15th, 1897.

[51] Frank Prochaska, *Christianity and Social Service in Modern Britain, The Disinherited Spirit* (Oxford University Press, 2006), pp.65, 66.

[52] *Lancaster Guardian*, January 3rd, 1891.

[53] *Lancaster Guardian*, February 7th, 1891.

[54] *Lancaster Guardian*, January 7th, 1882.

[55] *Lancaster Guardian*, January 10th, 1891.

[56] *Lancaster Guardian*, February 14th, 1891.

[57] Robin Greaves, "The Diary of Helen Escolme," *The Mourholme Magazine of Local History* (1990-1996).

Chapter Eleven

LEISURE TIME

At the beginning of the nineteenth century leisure was something that belonged to the leisured classes. A leisured working man was merely unemployed or idle.[1] Of course working people did take time off, but that was because they chose to forgo pay in favour of play. There were certain times when such breaks from work were more or less accepted; times associated particularly with the church calendar and the agricultural seasons - church feasts or wakes, Plough Monday, the hiring fairs. By the end of the century the notion of a right to time off, even perhaps paid time off, was becoming established. Bank Holidays, weekly half days and legally limited working hours replaced the more erratic country traditions. By the end of the century a whole new leisure industry was growing up - cheap train travel, sea-side resorts, all sorts of professional entertainments like circuses, travelling theatres, concert companies, the music halls.

Warton parish was inevitably on the edge of all this; it was too small to support its own professional companies or attract the more expensive. People still had to make much of their amusement in the old way. All the same there was change, and by the end of the century there was so varied a programme of leisure activities that the account has had to be condensed into a brief compendium - an ABC of Sport and Leisure. However before going on to that there are one or two points to be considered.

Music and Song

Music and song have played their part in village life for centuries - though, when one stops to think about this, it seems it is rather that one assumes that it must have been so, than that one has any particular local evidence that it was so.

No record of the performance of traditional songs or dances has been found. That a musical tradition must have been kept up in Warton parish is implied, however, by the finding of how very much, in the nineteenth century, music was seen as essential to any gathering. It is known, for instance, that if a local firm gave its workmen an annual supper singing was part of the entertainment. We even have the words of one comic song plainly written, or at least adapted, to the locality. *The Rattling Old Gray Mare* was performed at a works supper in 1871 at the Carnforth Inn. The singer, in his character of a *'jolly steane* [stone] *loader'* assures his audience:

> *'I've one to bear me company,*
> *Of work she does her share,*
> *It's not my wife, upon my life,*
> *But a rattling old bay mare'.*

Then back comes the chorus:

> *'Round goes the World,*
> *Troubles I defy,*
> *Carting steanes to the Iron Works,*
> *My rattling mare and I'.*[2]

A Brass Band was a necessary part of any parade or ceremony - sometimes a visiting band, but more often local bands were to the fore. By 1870 there was a Carnforth Iron Works Band (conductor Mr. B. Evans) and a quite separate Carnforth Brass Band, both of which failed to survive, but were revived in 1882. The Iron Works band was only called upon from time to time, (possibly because the conductor insisted it was a private band and not liable to be called upon by the public to play either outdoors or in),[3] but Carnforth Brass Band was very active, heading many processions and giving outdoor concerts. Neither brass band had uniforms at first, but it is known that Carnforth Brass Band acquired new dark blue uniforms, supplied by Stephenson Bros., the Carnforth drapers. They wore them for the first time at the Carnforth Athletic Festival in July 1886.[4] Whether the band had any civic status or support is not known. It seems likely that the bandsmen were self-taught volunteers. It is recorded that when a collection was made for charity after one performance, part of the takings went to the band.[5] Of course when the Salvation Army Band started to play in the 1890s that was entirely a volunteer effort. The Salvation Army Band outlasted its rivals by many years. In the 1860s fife and drum bands were popular, possibly because the instruments were not too taxing for such groups as the

Carnforth Church of England School and the Band of Hope in Carnforth and in Warton.

Carnforth had its own dance band too. In 1880 the Cornish, Cock and Carr Quadrille-Band played at the Furness Railway Employees' Ball.[6] A little later Cornish & Cock, under the title of the Carnforth String Band, played at the Carnforth & District Horticultural Show. By the 1890s Cornish's name had gone, and it was just Cock's Quadrille Band which played at the Co-op. balls.

Concerts (at all levels from the frivolous to serious oratorios) were a more and more frequent part of the local scene and there was a very lively amateur musical life. Singing was plainly popular and there were an increasing number of singing classes available. In 1877 a Mr. Thomas Johnson was conducting a singing class in Carnforth and in 1879 a Glee Class was formed under the conductorship of Mr. C.

Spencer of Barrow. In 1880 Mr. G.H. Rathbone (of whom much more later) started a Tonic Sol-fa Class. This method of presenting a musical score had been perfected by Mr. Curwen, a clergyman, who hoped to improve the hymn singing in his church. In 1851 he published a teaching primer. The system caught on widely. It meant that whole choirs of those who had never had the chance of a musical education, and could not read staff notation, could sight-read new music. Warton schools were beginning to teach singing (see Chapter 9) but there is no evidence that they were offering any other musical training.

Musically speaking Warton owed much to Mr. Rathbone who ran a music shop in Carnforth. He was a man of enthusiasm. He was organist and choir leader at St.

234

Oswald's. He took over the charge of the Carnforth Glee Class. In 1883 the Warton & District Choral Society (to become the Carnforth & District Choral Society in 1885) was formed through his initiatives.[7] In 1891 Mr. Rathbone was running a Tonic Sol-fa Class in Silverdale and conducting a string band there.[8] He was also whipping the Silverdale Choral Society into shape for a performance of Mendelssohn's oratorio, *St. Paul.*[9] The Silverdale Choral Society was among those who entered the musical competitions at the festival set up by Miss Mary Wakefield in Kendal in 1885. Miss Wakefield herself conducted some rehearsals of the Silverdale choir and tendered advice - not an uncommon proceeding for this enthusiastic amateur musician.

Where Did the Musical Meet and Who Sponsored Them?

There is no doubt that the various religious denominations and the temperance societies were of great importance in encouraging music (and indeed many other forms of entertainment and sport). Among other reasons it had been borne in on them that you cannot preach abstinence or anything else to an audience unless you have gathered one first, and that one way of doing this was to offer wholesome entertainment. The other point of importance in forwarding the growth of entertainment was the growth, over the century, of places where people could meet. In summary it could be said that at the beginning of the century any group that wanted to meet anywhere under cover from the elements had a choice of a pub

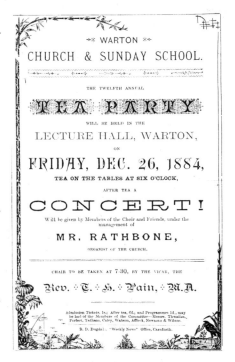

(pleasant, but not acceptable to all groups), the very limited accommodation at Archbishop Hutton's school and, for parish meetings, the church vestry. Sometimes a farmer might hire out his barn. All these, apart from the pubs, would have been unheated. Even when Mr. Ford of Yealand Manor presented Carnforth workers with a Wooden Hut where they could meet '*in inclement weather*' heating was a problem.[10] The Silverdale band had to abandon practising there because it was so cold and in December 1869 the Carnforth Band of Hope had to suffer from '*the numerous chill airs from the chinks in the wooden building*' when the fire had to be extinguished because of a defect in the stove pipe.[11] By the end of the century, meeting places had multiplied in number and comfort. They have all been mentioned in their place in previous chapters, but as a reminder there were new school rooms, (Warton Infant School had been purposely designed in 1865 to double as a lecture room), there were the political club houses; temperance hotels (offering the comfort of a pub without the taint of alcohol); from 1879 the Station Hotel Assembly Rooms at Carnforth gave extra accommodation; there was the Town Hall (i.e. the Wooden Hut); and lastly Carnforth Co-operative Hall, which was able to cater for 500, and eclipsed them all when it was opened in 1888.

So now for the compendium of sport and leisure.

ABC of Sport and Leisure
Angling

As long as there have been rivers and lakes, so will there have been anglers. Long before 1653, when Izaak Walton wrote *The Compleat Angler* there would have been anglers on the river Keer, but it was not until 1865 that a River Keer Angling Association held its first A.G.M. at the Black Bull Hotel in Warton. Nothing more has been found of this club, indeed there is very little mention of the sport at all in the newspapers; it is only known that in 1889 a meeting was called in the Station Building in Carnforth to form a new fishing association. In 1895 the Lune Fishery Board announced that it was unable to afford a permanent watcher on the River Keer. The article added that the Keer angling season that year had commenced in March with trout in good supply after a rainy period in late summer.

Association Football

Football has been played for many, centuries. It is known that a form of football was played in the main street in Warton township by schoolboys in the seventeenth century,[12] but it may come as a surprise to readers that soccer, as a fully organised sport, did not establish itself until the last decades of the nineteenth century.

An early cup game

The Football Association was founded in 1862. The F.A. Cup was inaugurated in 1871 and not until 1888 was the Football League founded. Against this background it is easier to understand why for so long soccer played second fiddle to the handling code in the townships of Warton parish. Not until October 1879 was there any mention of a soccer match being played in the parish, and that was under the auspices of Carnforth Rugby Club. Then, after a long gap, there was a report, in January 1891, of a match between Carnforth Post Office and Lancaster Post Office; the Lancaster team emerging victorious 3-0.

In the 1891/92 season the Carnforth Rugby Club switched experimentally to the Association Code and in October of 1891 a Carnforth team travelled to Burton-in-Kendal, only to lose 5-1. At least eight more matches are known to have been played that season, but there were heavy defeats by Lancaster Rangers and others, and that was the end of organised local soccer for a number of years.

Athletics

Athletic contests are as old as ancient Greece and older. In the nineteenth century athletics as an organised recreation came to the fore again, culminating in the first modern Olympics in 1896.

The first known athletic event in the parish was in August 1879, when the Carnforth Working Men's Institute held a gala on the cricket field, a feature of which was foot racing. This was to become an annual event. In 1896 it was noted that the sports held in Millhead brought competitors from far and wide and attracted a crowd of 1,500.[13] Queen Victoria's Golden Jubilee in 1887 inspired Warton township to include athletic sports in its celebrations and these too became an annual feature with, in 1889, a fell-race, wrestling, brass pitching (what form this took was not further specified) and a hound trail.[14]

Silverdale is known to have held a sports day as early as 1878, as there was a report of trouble when intoxicants were sold without the permission of the Committee,[15] but the event must have lapsed as its annual sports had to be revived in 1895. Such sports days might be organised by Temperance Societies who tended to see sport as promoting abstinence and wholesome living. Not that this motive was always to the fore. In 1896 J.T. Addison, of the Shovel Inn Carnforth, promoted sports in a field close to his pub and when Bobby Carlisle undertook to complete a 50 mile run his course took him back and forth 16 times between the Shovel Inn at Carnforth and the Black Bull at Warton.[16] It seems likely that the prospect of slaking his thirst at the end of each leg was not displeasing!

Children had their own sports days, usually organised as treats by the various denominational Sunday Schools. Carnforth's National School entered the field of athletics in February 1883 with a hare and hounds race over eight or nine miles.[17] Whether participation was voluntary or compulsory has not been revealed.

Billiards

When Shakespeare made Cleopatra say '... *Let us to billiards. Come, Charmian*',[18] it was evidence that the game, in some form, was in existence, if not in ancient Egypt, then at least in Shakespeare's England. In the nineteenth century the well-to-do had billiard rooms in their houses for themselves and their guests, but it was with the founding of working men's and other clubs that the game gained general popularity.

The first mention found of a club team in Warton parish came in 1885 when it was reported that a Carnforth Working Men's Institute team defeated their counterparts from Ulverston, but lost the return fixture.[19] By 1890 the Carnforth & District Conservative Club had formed a team of 12 players.[20] The Liberal Club formed its team at about the same time. Billiards continued to be popular for many years into the twentieth century, but its appeal began to wane as snooker gained popularity.

Circuses

Circuses, in the modern not the Roman meaning, had been growing in popularity since the 1760s, when Mr. Phillip Astley, a riding-master, opened his circus in London. Travelling circuses followed and in 1869 were certainly visiting Warton parish, for there is an entry for that year in the logbook of the Yealand Friends' School, which reads *'Most of older children away to a circus in Carnforth.'*[21]

The next mention of a circus comes in 1881 when the Royal Windsor Menagerie visited Carnforth.[22] Other circuses also came. Swallow's raised their big top in Mr. Miller's field. This field, now the

site of Christ Church School, seems to have been a useful facility. He loaned it out not only to the circus, but at various times to the Cricket Club, the Carnforth Floral and Horticultural Show and the Rugby Club. Ginnett's in 1895 thrilled Carnforth townsfolk with a procession of the animals through the town.

Cricket

In the reign of Henry VIII, some time in the 1540s, a certain John Denwicke, a scholar at the Free School in Guilford with *'several of his fellowes did runne and play there at creckett.'*[23] In 1744 the first laws of cricket were formulated and by the middle of the eighteenth century the Hambledon Club in Hampshire had become the major influence in the game, to be succeeded later by the Marylebone Cricket Club.

The Preston Cricket Club (1821) claims to be one of the earliest in the world; Kendal Cricket Club dates from 1836 and the Lancaster Cricket Club from 1841. The Lancashire County Club was formed in 1864.

The first known report of a Carnforth Cricket Club was on July 31st, 1869; Cartmel were the visitors in a drawn two-innings match on a ground said to be in excellent order. Few matches for this club were recorded, though it is known that in 1871 the club decided to use Mr. Miller's field rather than their old site at Warton Lane End.[24] In May 1872 it was announced that

> '... the old Carnforth Cricket Club has been broken up and the property sold by public auction ... Of the causes which have led to this dissolution the less said the better, they have their origins in the weaknesses of humanity.'[25]

A Carnforth and Railway Cricket Club arose from the ashes and played its first match in 1873. An unimpressive performance seems to have stifled enthusiasm and no more was heard of cricket in Carnforth until 1877. In that year a few Carnforth Cricket Club matches were reported (the Railway part of the title having disappeared) and by 1879 cricket was in full swing with 11 wins out of 17 fixtures. In the following season a score of 200 was recorded against Long Preston, an exceptionally high score in an era of low scoring on under-prepared wickets. It is possible that the club was having difficulty in securing a ground, for at a meeting in March 1882 it was decided that the club should continue, but that henceforth matches would be played on the ground alongside the River Keer as they had done several years previously.

For some years thereafter Carnforth played generally undistinguished cricket against local teams, including regular fixtures against Lancaster Royal Grammar School. In 1885 there were a couple of 2nd XI fixtures, but it may be significant they were on dates when the 1st XI was apparently unoccupied. It was not until 1893 that the club applied for, and was granted, admission to the Lancaster & District League for the following season. The club's first venture into league cricket in 1894 was successful, with Carnforth finishing in second place. In 1895 a move was made to Mr. Aldren's old field (the present venue), but that season's results were depressing and, whether for that reason or not, it was decided to withdraw from league cricket. Performance in the next years was variable. The 1899 season ended with a visit in early

September to the Isle of Man for three games against Manx opponents. Sadly the first game was washed out completely and in the other two more rain interfered after Douglas Asylum and Douglas Town had raised formidable totals, so that no Carnforth batsman had the opportunity to show his mettle. Nevertheless, the secretary, Robert Hodgson, was presented with a silver mounted pipe and a pouch for organising the trip[26] (which, one must think, would have been of benefit only to those with plenty of money and leisure time). In later years the captain of the club was the well-known Dr. E.S. Jackson of Carnforth (of whom much has already been said). Indicative of the difference in styles of bowling between then and now is the illuminating comment from Lux, a correspondent for the *Lancaster Guardian*, '*Dr. Jackson was again successful with those curious under-handers of his.*'[27]

Carnforth Cricket Club in the 1890s
Standing: W. Wrightson, Simpson, S. Buttle, Driver, Wilkinson, ---, .---
Seated: ---, Palmer?, Dr. E.S. Jackson, McKenzie, J. Dickinson
Front: G. Hartley, T. Dickinson

Other Carnforth teams were raised and turned out from time to time. Carnforth's General Post Office is known to have put a team into the field in 1885.[28] In 1891 they were beaten handsomely by Dr.

Jackson's team in what must have been a festival atmosphere with Carnforth Brass Band in attendance, and tea for about 150 people provided by the Carnforth grocer J. Hartley & Co. Hartley's also had their own team at times. Latecomers on the scene were Carnforth Congregational Church and the Carnforth Wesley Guild, both clubs being formed in 1898.

The smaller townships had more difficulty in keeping a team in the field. The origins of cricket at Silverdale are unknown, but a club must have existed prior to 1885 when a meeting was convened to re-form it.[29] Nothing further was reported until 1889 when a victory against Milnthorpe 2nd XI was recorded, after which cricket again died out. In August of 1893 the newly appointed vicar, the Rev. W. Sleigh, called a meeting and cricket was revived in such good measure that four matches were played before the season was out. Then followed a chequered period, seemingly because of the difficulty of finding a suitable permanent venue; almost every year a different field had to be found. In 1896 and 1897 no cricket at all was reported. The indomitable Mr. Sleigh made one more effort in 1898, captaining a team himself, but the next year there were no reports of cricket at Silverdale.

At Yealand Conyers there were no reports of cricket until 1882, when two impressive victories were recorded, but apart from a crushing defeat at Carnforth in 1885 nothing more is known until 1889. Thereafter Yealand played with only limited success to the end of the century. Warton township, though the biggest village after Carnforth and Silverdale, had to wait till 1907 before the formation of its cricket club.

There is almost no record of organised cricket for juniors. Two games did, however, reach the pages of the *Lancaster Guardian*, the first in 1891 when Burton Boys were too strong for the lads of Yealand, and the other in 1898 when Silverdale Juniors gained a narrow victory over Heversham.

Cycling

Penny Farthing

An item of Carnforth news in 1869 was that James Samuel of Hall Street had made a good quality velocipede[30] - a word that had come to be used for the new machine, propelled by pedals, that was also called a bicycle. It had only been in 1860 that the first commercially produced bicycle, the bone-shaker appeared – appropriately so named for it was not until 1868 that the ride was softened by covering the wheels with solid rubber tyres. Shortly after that the Ordinary Bicycle (better known as the Penny Farthing) came on the scene, so it is difficult to know whether James Samuel was keeping up with the latest advances, or not, since further details of his velocipede were not given. By 1896 the Carnforth Cycling Co. was established in Scotland Road. It was said to be equipped with up-to-date plant for the various processes of manufacture, and to have about eight in employment. The leading speciality of the firm was called the *Storm Light Cycle*.[31]

Carnforth Cycle Co.,

Manufacturers of the Celebrated

"Storm Light" Cycles.

We build Machines from £5 10s. to £16 0 0.
RIDING TAUGHT FREE TO PURCHASERS.

Call & see our £10 10s. Machines.

REPAIRS
PUNCTUALLY AND EFFICIENTLY EXECUTED.

PLATING & ENAMELLING a Speciality.

FIRST CLASS LADIES' & GENT'S MACHINES on HIRE, 2/6 per day, 10/6 per week.
[150H]

The other result of the increasing popularity of bicycling as a sport and leisure activity was the burgeoning everwhere of cycling clubs. In 1878 a national club, the Bicycle Touring Club (soon to become the Cyclists' Touring Club) was formed. Only a year later a Vale of Lune Cycling Club was formed. That club was disbanded in 1882, but in 1887 a new local club, the Lancaster Cycling Club was founded. Meanwhile a Carnforth & District Cycling club had been set up in June 1886. It organised rides around the locality; at the club dinner in the autumn, it was stated that by the end of the season 359 miles had been covered.[32] Information is then lacking until 1890, about the time when pneumatic tyres came in. More and longer rides were being reported. For example there was one in which the cyclists took the train to

Grange-over-Sands before cycling to Lakeside, taking the ferry to Bowness, then cycling on to Kendal where deterioration in the weather persuaded them to complete the journey back to Carnforth by train.[33] There were usually perhaps ten or a dozen cyclists participating and these small numbers probably contributed to the club's apparent demise sometime after 1890. A new Carnforth & District Cycling Club was formed in 1895. In 1896 rides were arranged for Tuesdays, Thursdays and Saturdays. In 1897 the Carnforth Cycling Club announced an amalgamation with what it called the old Cycling Club, suggesting that the original club had not after all completely faded out. In 1897 the Ladies' Branch (with its own committee) was set up.[34]

Advantage was taken on one ride of the opportunity to purchase some equipment from the old Milnthorpe club.[35] Most cycling clubs tried to provide such practical services for their members. Later Carnforth club also started an insurance fund to cover the cost of cycle repairs. The rides and these useful services formed what one might call the serious business of the club, but there was a lighter side. Cycle races were introduced at the Carnforth Athletic Sports with a fancy-dress cycle parade at the conclusion. The parade made its way from Carnforth to Warton, preceded by Carnforth Brass Band in a wagonette.[36] As part of the Queen's Diamond Jubilee celebrations another evening cycle parade was arranged. The ladies' bicycles were decorated with flowers and the gentlemen were dressed in fancy costumes. Another fancy dress cycle parade was arranged for the gala at Millhead, but perhaps the novelty had worn off as only 26 cyclists turned out for the occasion. Indeed, support for the Club rides was often poor that summer, sometimes with only three members turning out, even though the membership was nearly 80 (54 gentlemen and 24 ladies).

Bycycle made for two

In 1898 still another cycling club was formed, the Carnforth Wesley Guild Cycling Club. Its first run was to Lancaster, where the members listened to the Rev. T. Waugh preaching,[37] but many other rides soon followed - to Beetham, Grange, Kirkby Lonsdale, Lancaster (where they were forbidden to wheel their bicycles through the Williamson Park), Morecambe (where they visited the Winter Gardens), Kendal and Galgate.[38] Events which would no doubt arouse local interest were the passage through Carnforth of the tandem cyclists Mills and Edge en route from Land's End to John o' Groats in 1895 and a year later the passage of a solo cyclist from Carlisle attempting the same feat.

Golf

Golf, or at least a form of it, was being played in Scotland by the fifteenth century; a popular sport played originally on the links or common land by the seashore. In 1848 the gutta percha ball, or gutty, was invented and rapidly replaced the stone-hard stuffed leather feathery. The game was slow to find its way farther south and few, if any, clubs existed in England before the 1870s.

Neither Lancaster nor Morecambe could boast a golf club prior to the twentieth century. Silverdale can therefore claim to have been reasonably early on the local scene, for at the boundary riding in 1895 playing golf was among the festive activities, though it is not known where it was played. What is more certain is that in October 1896 the first golf was played on the Marsh Links of the new Silverdale Golf Club, which had 25 members.[39] In August 1897 F. Shortland Ball was the winner of a Silverdale golf competition. The ball he used would be of the gutty type, as the rubber-cored ball, which succeeded it, was not invented until 1899. The 1896 Golf Club is not to be confused with the present-day Silverdale Golf Club, which was not founded until 1906.

Handball

Only one reference has been found to handball as a local sport, and that was in 1896 when it formed part of the Carnforth Wesleyan Sunday School treat. It was presumably some form of the game in which a ball is struck to and fro using the palm of the hand. Fives is a formal derivative, but it had been a traditional form of amusement at village festivities. Why the Wesleyans revived it is not known, nor under what rules they played.

Horse Racing

Races had been run on Warton sands since at least the seventeenth century. The last of these were held in 1852 by which time they had descended into a rough and tumble jollification in which serious racing played no part.[40] The only other occasion when horse racing is known to have taken place in the parish was in September 1895 when the Silverdale Boundary Riding was followed by various sports including horse racing. The advent of the railways, however, meant that racing enthusiasts (of sufficient means) could still attend races elsewhere as there were plenty of excursions to races laid on.

Horticultural and Floral Societies

Horticulture for the amateur was the in thing in the nineteenth century. The *Lancaster Guardian* carried a detailed column of seasonal hints for gardeners in every issue.

In 1848 Burton-in-Kendal had already staged a successful Floral & Horticultural show. Carnforth Horticultural and Floral Society put on its first annual show in the National School Room in August 1875. At first the society flourished. In 1883 the show was extended to two days.[41] Perhaps that was a mistake, as the next known mention of the show was in January 1891 saying that the Carnforth & District Floral and Horticultural Exhibition which had been discontinued many years before was to be revived. The effort was backed by some big local names (such as Mr. Barton, manager of the Iron Works and Mr. Sharpe, the wealthy lawyer who lived in Borwick) but their efforts were apparently unavailing since there are no more reports of the Society or the Show.

The Horticultural Society in Silverdale (originally known as the Silverdale, Lindeth and Arnside Floral & Horticultural Society) was on a sounder footing. Its first annual exhibition was in 1882 and the exhibitions were continued annually thereafter. Eventually the society came to an agreement with the Art & Industrial Society to have their exhibitions on the same day.

Hunting

References in the newspapers to any local hunting tended throughout the century to be very short on detail, but there is enough to

246

show that, as might be expected, hunting took place. Among the animals chased were otters and on one occasion at least, deer. A few reports of fox hunting earlier in the century have been found (Mr. Gillow of Leighton Hall was a fox hunter) but no references to fox hunting have been found after the 1840s. Harriers are frequently mentioned. The Holker Hall Harriers met from time to time in Carnforth. In 1860 there was mention of a party from Holker Hall (that included the Marquis of

Hartington, Mr. R.T. Gillow of Leighton Hall and Mr. Bolden of Hyning Hall), meeting near Warton. They started three hares and killed one after chasing it all round from Warton by both Kellets and back to Warton. The rather less aristocratic Lancashire Harriers had also sometimes gathered at Carnforth, but the last recorded time was in 1850. From 1880 the Vale of Lune Harriers met regularly, usually three or four times a year, at Yealand Hall or Tewitfield, but so little was recorded in the newspaper entries that it has been impossible to draw from them any account of what took place or who attended.

Pigeon Shooting

It is known that pigeon shooting contests had taken place in the parish earlier in the century - that is contests that involved shooting at live birds specially released from traps. The sport continued. In 1873, for instance Mr. Holder of the Carnforth Inn organised a pigeon shoot,[42] and the Silverdale Hotel was the venue for a pigeon shoot in 1889. In the latter year Charles Fernyhough, a local man, won the pigeon shooting Handicap Sweepstake and Plate at the Border Shooting Club at Kelso.[43] In 1893 there was a shoot at the   Longlands Inn at Tewitfield and in the same year pigeon shooting was one of the events at the Tewitfield annual sports.[44]

Poultry and Pigeon Fancying

As the nineteenth century progressed, interest turned more from pigeon shooting to pigeon exhibiting and racing. Poultry shows also multiplied.

The North Lancs. Poultry Association was founded in 1880 and held a Poultry, Pigeon and Cage Bird show in two rooms of the Queen's

Hotel in Carnforth. There were no fewer than 471 exhibitors and the accommodation was not unexpectedly described as '*cramped*'.[45] No more is known of that particular association, but a Silverdale Poultry Society is known to have been in existence by 1893. The Silverdale Poultry Show (which included pigeons and, on at least one occasion, dogs) was an annual event until the turn of the century.

For those whose ambitions stretched beyond local competitions, there were prizes to be won in more exalted circles: John Till of Warton won prizes at the Oxford Poultry Show in 1879 and his Houdans took second prize at the Staffordshire Great Chicken Show of 1880.[46] Dr. E.S. Jackson gained two first prizes for Wyandottes at the London Dairy and Poultry show in 1896, at which show Miss Barton of Warton won prizes for her Langshans and T. Dobson of Carnforth for his Plymouth Rocks.

Plymouth Rock

The more knowledgeable pigeon-fanciers travelled to distant shows as judges. William Slater of Bigland House, Silverdale, and P. Proud of Silverdale were appointed judges of poultry and pigeons at the Newchurch-in-Rossendale Agricultural Show of 1897. Slater, who had won several prizes with his own Plymouth Rocks, had previously been a Club Judge for the breed at the Crystal Palace in 1895. Poultry breeding became so popular that it was one of the subjects chosen for the series of Technical Instruction lectures held in Carnforth, Warton and Silverdale in the late 1890s.

The Carnforth & District Homing Society was founded in the mid-1890s.[47] The distance for each race was progressively increased; the first race was usually from Stafford (100 miles) and the last of five from Ventnor in the Isle of Wight (258 miles) and at least once from

Jersey (342 miles). As the season progressed and the distance increased the number of birds competing could drop from well over a 100 to not many more than 50. Dr. E.S. Jackson, on giving up the presidency in 1897 (to his wife, who was also a pigeon fancier), marked the occasion by presenting a challenge cup to the society.[48]

Fancy Pigeons

Quoits

Quoit Pit

Quoits, the pitching of iron rings over stakes, had long been a popular pub game everywhere. The rules for the Northern Game were formalised in 1881 by the Association of Amateur Quoits Clubs for the North of England. Reporting was patchy, but it is known that there were quoiting matches in the parish - held in pubs - the Shovel Inn and the Travellers' Rest in Carnforth and the Black Bull and the Shovel in Warton.

Rugby Football

Tradition has it that the game of Rugby originated in 1823 when William Webb Ellis, in a game of footer, picked up the ball and ran with it. Development thereafter was everywhere slow, and it was not until 1877 that a Carnforth club came into being.[49] The first match played by the club was against Holker and was played out on Church Field. In those early days the clubs provided their own umpires, a source of potential unrest, and the Carnforth team was involved in several unsavoury incidents, which led to accusations against the Carnforth team of such faults as slovenly play and a tendency to be quarrelsome. On the other hand there must have been no lack of enthusiasm as an internal match in 1880 lasted for two hours and forty minutes![50]

By 1882 Carnforth could field a 2nd XV, despite a newspaper claim that the club was not strong enough. Nevertheless over the next few seasons tolerably good results were achieved by both XVs. In 1886 Carnforth Grasshoppers team beat Warton Harriers, but it is uncertain whether the Grasshoppers were a senior or a junior team and the name does not appear again in connection with Carnforth. Carnforth's early club colours (possibly from its first opening in 1877) had been blue and white, but in 1887 a change was made to scarlet, black and amber. It was simultaneously decided that the Queen's Hotel should be the clubhouse instead of the Station Hotel as previously.[51]

In 1889 a team called Carnforth Excelsior took the field. As Warton A and Lancaster Rangers A were among its opponents it might be assumed that it was the Carnforth A XV, yet when Carnforth (without the Excelsior) lost heavily at Dalton in 1890 it was said that Carnforth was a newly formed club and that some of the players had appeared for Carnforth Excelsior in the previous season. Perhaps some crisis had arisen at Carnforth through the recent formation of a Warton Club, which may have drawn off some of their players.

In 1891 changes were made affecting the rules governing the system of points scoring, but this did not immediately affect the

Carnforth team, which had, for the 1891/92 season, temporarily adopted the Association code. By 1892/93 the oval ball was back and incidentally, thanks to Dr. Jackson's generosity, the club had new blue jerseys.[52]

The season of 1893/94 was a good one; the verdict of one newspaper writer was that the Carnforth XV was a strong one and played a fairly good game, even if a bit lacking in finish.[53] The team reached the final of the Infirmary Cup only to be beaten by Morecambe. 1894/95 was a poor season for the Carnforth Club. They lost even to a Carnforth Iron Works team, a defeat attributed to the suspension of several players (for what reason is not known). The following season a bitter pill for The Blues was defeat at the hands of Warton.

In 1896/97 the Carnforth and Warton clubs amalgamated and the A team, which had been disbanded some time previously, was resurrected. Even so there was difficulty in raising the team, with as many as nine reserves having to be summoned to play at Morecambe.

In 1895 twenty-two northern clubs split off from the Rugby Football Association to form a Northern Rugby Union (later to become the Rugby League). The split was largely over professionalism; the custom followed by the more working-class northern clubs of compensating their players for time lost from work offended the more gentlemanly tradition in southern clubs. In the light of this split it is interesting that in the 1895/96 season Carnforth refused to play extra time against Morecambe A because some of the players had to leave to go to their work.[54] In the 1897/98 season the amalgamated Warton/Carnforth team played in the Furness & District League, though friendlies against traditional local rivals continued as before and it seems that some of the matches (perhaps all) were played under Northern Union rules. At the next A.G.M. it was decided to continue thus in the1898/99 season. They also apparently decided not to continue in the Furness & District League. It has to be noted that though in the earlier years Carnforth played against the first XVs of Kendal, Barrow and

Ulverston and even teams from Manchester and from Rochdale, they gradually came to be regarded as fit only to play against the A teams of the bigger clubs.

Of those who played for Carnforth mention may be made of A.E. Barton, the Iron Works manager's son Albert, or Bertie, who captained the team in the 1880s and was selected for a North Lancs XV in 1886. A. Whinnerah (possibly related to the successful Warton Hall farming family, but not so far individually identified) and J.P. Graham were similarly honoured in 1888. Graham (who also represented Cumberland with distinction) was the most notable of several Carnforth cricketers to play for the Rugby team.

Where in Carnforth was rugby played? Probably at first in the ever useful Mr. Miller's Field which has already been mentioned in connection with other sports. In the 1884/85 season Carnforth played on Mr. Aldren's field (thought to be the present Carnforth cricket field) and in 1893 it was noted that they were to play on '*the cricket field*'.[55] In 1895 a new ground in Kellet Lane was chosen as the venue; just which one is not certain, but it was said of one match that season that Carnforth played uphill in the first half and it seems that this unorthodox venue was used for the remainder of the century.

The smaller townships made their own attempts to set up rugby teams. The first mention of rugby in Warton township was in February 1886 when a team called Carnforth Grasshoppers, possibly a junior team, played against Warton Harriers. In August of the following year a meeting was held with the object of forming Warton Rugby Club.[56] The meeting was successful in its object, though the first recorded game was not until December 17th when Warton lost away to Kendal A. The following week it suffered the same result at a match played in Warton against Morecambe A. On the last day of 1887 Warton secured their first victory against Lancaster A. Over the next few seasons Warton fulfilled many fixtures, but after a heavy defeat at Ulverston the newspaper commented that of course they were outclassed, and added that to give details of such a one-sided game would be a mere waste of space.

Like Carnforth they were not free from disputes; for example their match against Lancaster Christ Church in 1891 had to be abandoned when Christ Church objected to decisions of the referee. Very little is known about the following seasons and, as has been said, after the 1895/6 season Warton and Carnforth clubs amalgamated. Exactly where Warton played is not known, but in 1891 the club thanked Mr. and Mrs. Bainbridge for the use of one of their fields. The Bainbridges were a mother and son living at the time of the 1891 census on their '*own means*' at The Cedars in Main Street, Warton. In 1893 the *Lancaster Guardian* reported that Silverdale football teams had their opening games on the Marsh and thoroughly enjoyed themselves.[57] It is assumed that the game was rugby rather than association football, but whichever it was it does not seem to have inspired Silverdale to play on a regular basis.

There is a good deal more mention of junior rugby than of junior cricket. Some schools had their own teams. In 1879 a game was played at Carnforth National School (no further details are known). A year later Carnforth National School played two matches against St. Thomas' School, Lancaster, winning the first and losing the second. Almost a year later, in February 1881, Carnforth Juniors lost to Kendal Hornets Juniors and in March 1883 another junior team under the name Carnforth Grapplers didn't grapple hard enough as they lost to Over Kellet Rovers. Whatever junior rugby was played thereafter did not reach the pages of local newspapers until the epic battle of 1895. In November the Carnforth Rugby Club had organised a junior league for teams from Carnforth, Dudley, Warton, Yealand, Bolton-le-Sands and Kellet. In the event only four teams entered the league, three of them from Carnforth and one from Warton. It seems that the teams played against each other several times until only two teams were left, both from Carnforth; the Hunter Street Hornets and the North Road Wanderers. There had been trouble in a previous match between the two when, with Hunter Street Hornets leading by two tries to nil, North Road Wanderers refused to turn out for the second half. North Road again declined to play against Hunter Street in the final, so under the direction of the referee, Latherton, Hunter Street were proclaimed champions. The following week the Hunter Street champions overcame the Rest of League. Then followed a procession, headed by Carnforth Brass Band to the Public Hall for the presentation ceremony, at which the losing teams were said to show some dissatisfaction. Among the winning team was a boy whose name was spelled Latheron. Was he really a Latherton and related to the referee and was this why North Road Wanderers had refused to play?[58] Could it also be that a photograph of the winning team still exists somewhere? Arthur J. Blaney, ironmonger of New Street who died on 28th April 1896 aged 35, had taken an interest in the Junior Football League and had been photographed with the Hunter Street Hornets on 20th April.

Swimming

No mention of teaching children to swim has been found. The assumption must be that there would be some swimming in the canal or the River Keer or, in the case of Silverdale residents and visitors, in the waters of Morecambe Bay. The only organised event to come to notice was the Carnforth  Swimming Gala, which took place at the Winter Gardens, Morecambe, on the 29th August 1885.[59]

Tennis

 The opening game of Carnforth Tennis Club, played out on the cricket field, was reported in August 1880. No further reference has been found which is a little surprising. Tennis was becoming, in general, increasingly popular in the latter part of the nineteenth century. Perhaps it was mostly confined to the lawns of the larger private houses.

Wrestling

    There are few references to wrestling in the newspapers, though it is known that there was a wrestling match at the Shovel Inn at Warton in 1855,[60] and that in 1860 T. Rawlinson of Warton was a wrestler of some note. The Mountain Range Lodge of the Mechanics' Friendly Society included wrestling in their gala held in Carnforth in 1879.[61] At the Lancaster Annual Athletic Festival of 1884 no fewer than six Carnforth wrestlers competed, which suggests that wrestling was a fairly popular sport despite the lack of press coverage. It is presumed that wrestling would be Cumberland and Westmorland style.

---

[1] Judith Flanders, *Consuming Passions; leisure and pleasure in Victorian Britain* (Harper Press, 2006), p.206.

[2] *Lancaster Guardian*, January 28th, 1871.

[3] *Lancaster Guardian*, December 31st, 1870.

[4] *Lancaster Guardian*, August 7th, 1886.

[5] *Lancaster Guardian*, September 5th, 1896.

[6] *Lancaster Guardian*, January 31st, 1880.

[7] *Lancaster Guardian*, November 10th, 1883.

[8] *Lancaster Guardian*, June 20th; 1891; September 26th, 1891.

[9] *Lancaster Guardian*, July 25th, 1891.

[10] *Lancaster Guardian*, December 22nd, 1866.

[11] *Lancaster Guardian*, December 4th, 1869.

[12] J. Rawlinson Ford & J.A. Fuller-Maitland, eds., *John Lucas's History of Warton Parish (compiled 1710-1740)* (Kendal: Titus Wilson, 1931), p.35.

[13] *Lancaster Guardian*, August 22nd, 1896.

[14] *Lancaster Guardian*, June 15th, 1889.

[15] *Lancaster Guardian*, June 22nd, 1878.

[16] *Lancaster Guardian*, September 12th, 1896.

[17] *Lancaster Guardian*, February 10th, 1883.

[18] William Shakespeare, *Antony and Cleopatra* (1606), Act 2, Scene 5.

[19] *Lancaster Guardian*, February 28th, 1885; March 7th, 1885.

[20] *Lancaster Guardian*, April 26th, 1890.

[21] Yealand Preparative Meeting, *Log Book of Yealand British School*, (Yealand Friends' Society, 1869), April 23rd.

[22] *Lancaster Guardian*, August 6th, 1881.

[23] Guildford Borough Records, *Guild Merchant Book of Guildford* (1598).

[24] *Lancaster Guardian*, May 6th, 1871.

[25] *Lancaster Guardian*, May 11th, 1872.

[26] *Lancaster Guardian*, September 9th, 1899.

[27] *Lancaster Guardian*, May 20th, 1899

[28] *Lancaster Guardian*, August 15th, 1885; August 22nd, 1885.

[29] *Lancaster Guardian*, March 21st, 1885.

[30] *Lancaster Guardian*, August 7th, 1869.

[31] *The Illustrated Guide to the Holiday Resorts on the Furness Railway* (1900).

[32] *Lancaster Guardian*, November 6th, 1886.

[33] *Lancaster Guardian*, May 17th, 1890.

[34] *Lancaster Guardian*, May 22nd, 1897.

[35] *Lancaster Guardian*, July 25th, 1896.

[36] *Lancaster Guardian*, August 22nd, 1896.

[37] *Lancaster Guardian*, May 7th, 1898.

[38] *Lancaster Guardian*, June 18th, 1898.

[39] *Lancaster Guardian*, October 10th, 1896.

[40] Mourholme Local History Society Book Group, *Warton 1800-1850: How a Lancashire Parish Changed* (Mourholme Local History Society, 2005), pp.216-217.

[41] *Lancaster Guardian*, September 1st, 1883.

[42] *Lancaster Guardian*, January 4th, 1873.

[43] *Lancaster Guardian*, March 2nd, 1889.

[44] *Lancaster Guardian*, June 3rd, 1893.

[45] *Lancaster Guardian*, November 13th, 1880.

[46] *Lancaster Guardian*, September 25th, 1880.

[47] *Lancaster Guardian*, June 1st, 1895.

[48] *Lancaster Guardian*, March 13th, 1897.

[49] *Lancaster Guardian,* September 15th, 1877.
[50] *Lancaster Guardian,* October 9th, 1880.
[51] *Lancaster Guardian,* August 20th, 1887.
[52] *Lancaster Guardian,* June 26th, 1892.
[53] *Lancaster Guardian,* November 18th, 1893.
[54] *Lancaster Guardian,* March 7th, 1896.
[55] *Lancaster Guardian,* September 2nd, 1893.
[56] *Lancaster Guardian,* August 20th, 1887.
[57] *Lancaster Guardian,* November 11th, 1893.
[58] *Lancaster Guardian,* April 18th, 1896.
[59] *Lancaster Guardian,* September 5th, 1885.
[60] *Lancaster Guardian,* September 22nd, 1855.
[61] *Lancaster Guardian,* August 30th, 1879.

Manuscript and Other Unpublished Sources Consulted

Archbishop Hutton's School, Warton School Log Book. Lancashire Record Office, PR3332 acc.5192.

Archbishop Hutton's School, Warton, papers. Lancashire Record Office, PR3332 Acc. 5192, location 2/708/5.

Censuses of England and Wales 1841 -1901.

County Medical Officer of Health, Annual Reports, Lancashire Record Office, PHR.

Erving, James, of Carnforth: notebook with memoranda on international news and local and family events in Carnforth and Rochdale 1838-73, Lancashire Record Office, DP494/1 acc 5192.

Greaves, Robin, Personal Communication.

Guildford Borough Records, *Guild Merchant Book of Guildford* (1598) Inspector of Nuisances' Reports, 1889-1894, Lancashire Record Office, RDLa/12/2.

Jackson Dr. W. & Jackson, Dr. E.S. Prescription Note Book, begun in 1869. Now in the possession of Dr. John Findlater.

Lancaster Friends Monthly Meeting Minute Book, 13 January 1864 – 13 August 1879. Lancashire Record Office, FRL 2/1/1/20.

Lancaster Friends Monthly Meeting, Minute Book, 12 May 1852 – 9 December 1863. Lancashire Record Office, FRL 2/1/1/19.

Lancaster Rural District, Medical Officer of Health, Annual Reports, 1889-1919. Environmental Health Department, Morecambe Town Hall.

Lancaster Rural Sanitary Authority. Medical Officer's Annual Reports, 1876. Photocopy kindly given to the archives of the Mourholme Local History Society, by Dr. John Dyer.

Laybourn, K. *A Comparative Study of Holme and Burneside*. M.A. Thesis, University of Lancaster, 1969.

Priest Hutton School Inspection, 1895. Lancashire Record Office, SMPH 1/3/2.

Rectoria de Warton, a terrier. Trinity College, Cambridge, (a photocopy is held by the Mourholme Local History Society).

Reynolds, James, letter concerning pew in Warton Church, 17th December 1969. Warton Parish Church archives.

Rural Sanitary Authority, Minute Book, May 16th, 1876 p.122. Lancashire Record Office, SAL/1.

Sanitary Inspectors' Reports 1906-1911, 27th October, 1906, Lancashire Record Office, RDLa/12/7.

Satterthwaite, Alexander, grocer, Wright's account, Yealand, 1887 - 1889. Lancaster Reference Library, MS 1.

Silverdale School, Manager's minutes, in private possession.

Surveyor and Inspector of Nuisances Reports, 1898-1902, Lancashire Record Office, RDLa/12/13.

Surveyor and Inspector of Nuisances Reports, 1899-1901, 20th October, 1900, Lancashire Record Office, RDLa/12/11.

Warton Parish, Churchwardens' Accounts, Lancashire Record Office, PR 572.

Watson Mr. J.F. Death of, Warton, 18th November 1903. Obituaries 1882 – 1905. Lancaster Reference Library, G191 NEW.

Wesleyan Methodist Circuit Plans, Lancaster Record Office, Mla, 1/1/5.

Willan, Leo. & Dawson, E.B. Note book referring to Willan and Dawson, with notes and figures relating to estate management 1846-58. Lancaster Reference Library, MS 2905.

Yealand Preparative Meeting, Log Book of Yealand British School. Yealand Friends' Society, 1866.

Yealand Preparative Meeting, Minute Book, 1844. Lancashire Record Office, FRL 8/1/1/.

Printed Sources Consulted

Andrews, Michael. "The Origins of the Furness Railway," part 1, *Railway and Canal Historical Society Journal* (October 1965)

Andrews, Michael. "The Origins of the Furness Railway," part 2, *Railway and Canal Historical Society Journal* (January 1966).

Anonymous. "James Ward – Pioneer of Tarmacadam," *Keer to Kent, Journal of the Arnside/Silverdale AONB Landscape Trust*, no 40, (Autumn/Winter 1999): p15.

Arnold, Matthew. "General Report for the year 1863," *Reports on Elementary Schools*, H.M.S.O. reprinted 1910.

Ashmead, Robert & Peter, David. "Warton Crag Mines," *The Mourholme Magazine of Local History*, no.1 (1983): pp.5-9

Ashmead, Robert & Peter, David. "Warton Crag Mines," *The Mourholme Magazine of Local History* no.2 (1983): pp.5-8

Badley, Ruth. *Emmanuel Congregational Church, Carnforth 1880-1980.* 1980.

Barnard, H.C. *Short History of English Education; from 1760 to 1944.* University of London Press, 1955.

Barnwell P.S. & Giles, C. *English Farmsteads.* Royal Commission on the Historical Monuments of England, xiv, 1997.

Barrett P. & Co. *Topography and Directory of Preston, the Fylde Lancaster and District.* 1886.

Beaulah, Kenneth & van Lemmon, Hans. *Church Tiles of the Nineteenth Century.* Shire Publications Ltd., 1987.

Best, Geoffrey. *Mid-Victorian Britain 1851-1875.* Fontana, 1979, first published 1971.

Best, Geoffrey. *Mid-Victorian Britain 1851-1870*. Fontana/Collins, 1982, first published 1971.

Bulmer. *Bulmer's Directory of Lancaster & District*. 1918.

Cartwright, Philip. *History of Anaesthesia in Lancaster*. n.d.

Chadwick, Edwin. *Report on the Sanitary Conditions of the Labouring Population of Great Britain*. originally published 1842, reprinted, Flinn, M. W. ed. Edinburgh University Press, 1965.

Chatterley, Jean. "Millhead, Mr. Edward D. Barton", part 6a; *The Mourholme Magazine of Local History*, no.1 (1995): pp.19-28.

Chatterly, Jean, & Findlater, John. "Millhead: the Initial Colonisation," *The Mourholme Magazine of Local History*, no.1 (1993): pp.12-24.

Clapham, J.H. *An Economic History of Modern Britain 1873-1946*, 3 vols. Cambridge University Press, 1930-1938.

Clarke, B. & J. "Dr Walling and Dr Matthews, Two Yealand Conyers Doctors," *Mourholme Magazine of Local History*, (No.2 1990): pp.7-12 & 17-18.

Clarke, Joan. "Pedder Potts and Mr. Barton," *The Mourholme Magazine of Local History*, no.2 (1996): pp.16-23.

Cook, W.J. *Lancaster, Morecambe and District Directory*. 1896.

Cook, W.J.. *Lancaster and Morecambe District Directory*. 1901.

Craigie, W. *The New English Dictionary*, vol. 10. Oxford University Press, 1926.

Dobson, Bob. *Policing in Lancashire 1839 to 1980*. Landy Publishing, 1989.

Ensor, R.C.K. *England 1870-1914*. Clarendon Press, 1936.

Evans, Eric. *The Complete A-Z; Nineteenth and Twentieth Century British History*. Hodder & Stoughton, 1998.

Farrer, William, & Brownbill, J., eds. *Victoria History of the County of Lancaster*, vol.8. Constable, 1914.

Findlater, John. "Robin Hill: No. 24 Market Street, Carnforth," *Mourholme Magazine of Local History* (No. 2 1994): pp.14-20.

Flanders, Judith. *Consuming Passions; leisure and pleasure in Victorian Britain*. Harper Press, 2006.

Flanders, Judith. *The Victorian House*. Harper Perennial, 2004.

Fletcher, T.W. "Lancashire Livestock Farming During the Great Depression," *British Agricultural History Society Journal*, vol.9: no.1 (1961): pp.17-42.

Ford, C. *Sketches of Yealand*. Kendal: Atkinson & Pollitt, 1931, reprinted from The Lancaster Guardian, 1911.

Ford, J. Rawlinson & Fuller-Maitland, J.A., eds. *John Lucas's History of Warton Parish (compiled 1710-1740)*. Kendal: Titus Wilson, 1931.

Garnett, Emmeline. *John Marsden's Will, the Hornby Castle Dispute, 1780-1840*. Hambledon Press, 1998.

Garnett, F.W. *Westmorland Agriculture 1800 – 1900*. Kendal: Titus Wilson, 1912.

Gladstone, David, ed. *Before Beveridge; Welfare Before the Welfare State* (Choice in Welfare No 47). London: Institute of Economic Affairs, 1999.

Golby J.M., ed. *Culture & Society in Britain 1850-1890*. Oxford University Press, 1986.

Gooderson, Phillip J. *Lord Linoleum: Lord Ashton, Lancaster and the Rise of the British Oilcloth and Linoleum Industry*. Keele University Press, 1996.

Greaves, Robin. "The Diary of Helen Escolme," *The Mourholme Magazine of Local History* (1990-1996).

Harrison, Brian. *Drink and the Victorians*. Faber and Faber, 1971.

Hawkins, Chris & Reeve, George. *LMS Engine Sheds, Vol.4, The Smaller English Constituents*. Oxford: Wild Swan Publications, 1984.

Heywood, Kevin, "End of an Era for Middlebarrow Quarry," *Keer to Kent, Journal of the Arnside/Silverdale AONB Landscape Trust*, no 45, (Summer 2001): p.9.

Higgs, Edward. *Making Sense of the Census*. H.M.S.O., 1989.

Hilton, A. *The Catholic Revival in Yealand, 1782-1832*. Preston, 1952.

Hobsbawm, E.J. *Industry and Empire*. Penguin, 1968.

Hodgkinson, Ruth. *The Origins of the National Health Service*. Wellcome Historical Library, 1967.

Holcombe, Lee. *Victorian Ladies at Work: Middle Class Working Women in England and Wales 1850-1950*. David and Charles, 1973.

Horne, Pamela. *The Rise and Fall of the Victorian Servant*. Alan Sutton Publishers Ltd., 1990.

Kelly's Directory of Lancashire (exclusive of the cities of Manchester and Liverpool). London: Kelly's Directories Ltd., 1918.

Lamb, H.H. *Climate, History and the Modern World*. Routledge, 1995.

Lancaster City Council. *Census of City Population 1991: A Census Handbook for Lancaster District*. 1993.

Lancaster Gazette, 1842 – 1913.

Lancaster Guardian, 1846 – 1916.

Lancaster Observer, 1880.

Loudon, Irvine. *Medical Care and the General Practitioner 1750- 1850*. Clarendon Press, 1986.

Maclure, John Stuart. *Education Documents England and Wales 1816 –1968*. Methuen Educational Ltd, 1968.

Mannex and Co. *History, Topography and Directory of Westmorland and the Hundreds of Lonsdale and Amounderness in Lancashire*. Preston: Mannex & Co., 1851.

Mannex, P. *Topography and Directory of North and South Lonsdale, Amounderness, Leyland*. Mannex & Co., 1866.

Mannex P. & Co. *Topography and Directory of Lancaster and Sixteen Miles Round*. Mannex & Co., 1881.

Marshall, J.D. "Corrupt Electoral Practices at the Lancaster Election of 1868," *Transactions of the Lancashire and Cheshire Antiquarian Society* 63 (1955-6).

Marshall, J.D. ed. *The History of Lancashire County Council 1889-1974*. Martin Robertson, 1977.

McCord, Norman. *British History 1815 – 1906*. Oxford University Press, 1991.

Midwinter, E.C. *Social Administration in Lancashire 1830-1860: Poor Law, Public Health and Police*. Manchester: Manchester University Press, 1969.

Mingay, Gordon. "The Rural Slum", in Gaskell, Martin, ed. *Slums*. Leicester University Press, 1990.

Mivart, F. St. George. *Report to the Local Government Board on the General Sanitary Circumstances and Administration of the Lancaster Rural District*, no. 172. H.M.S.O., 1902.

Mourholme Local History Society Book Group. *How it Was: A North Lancashire Parish in the Seventeenth Century*. Mourholme Local History Society, 1998.

Mourholme Local History Society Book Group. *Warton 1800 – 1850: How a North Lancashire Parish Changed*. Mourholme Local History Society, 2005.

Needham, Eva. *Yes in Christ: Warton Methodist Church 1838-1938*. 1988.

O'Donoghue, J., Goulding, L. & Allen, G. *Economic Trends* 604 "Consumer price inflation since 1750". House of Commons Library: Office for National Statistics, March 2004.

Parliamentary Papers. *Inquiry into the State of Dwellings of Rural Labourers*, vol. xxvi. 1865.

Parliamentary Papers. *Report of Royal Commission on Labour*. Summary Report by Mr. Arthur Miles, vol. xxxv. 1893/4.

Parliamentary Papers. *Report on the Employment of Children*, vol. xii. 1868.

Parliamentary Papers. *Schools Inquiry Session: Report on Grammar Schools in N. Lancashire*, vol. xxvii. 1867/8.

Pevsner, Nikolaus. *Buildings of England: North Lancashire*. Penguin, 1969.

Press cuttings from Lancaster and Westmorland papers, formerly in the church archives and now in the possession of the Mourholme Local History Society, give detailed reports on the consistory court and parish meetings.

Price, James. *Sharp, Paley and Austin: a Lancaster Architectural Practice 1836-1942*. Lancaster: Centre for North-West Regional Studies, University of Lancaster, 1998.

Prochaska, Frank. *Christianity and Social Service in Modern Britain: The Disinherited Spirit*. Oxford University Press, 2006.

Prothero R.E., (Lord Ernle). *English Farming Past and Present*. Longman, Green & Co. 1912; 4th edition, 1927.

Roberts, John Easter. *The Changing Face of Carnforth*. Carnforth: J.E. Roberts, Mayoh Press, 1974.

Rose, Michael E. *The Relief of Poverty 1834-1914*. Prometheus, 1986.

Ruskin, John. *Sesame and Lilies*, Lecture ii (1864).

Russell, Marion. *How Carnforth Grew. A Simple Outline to 1900 A.D.*. Carnforth Bookshop, 1997.

Saul, S.B. *The Myth of the Great Depression 1873-1895, Studies in Economic and Social History*. Macmillan, 1968.

Seymour, Charles. *Electoral Reform in England and Wales*. David & Charles, 1915; reprinted 1970.

Shakespeare, William. *Antony and Cleopatra*. 1606.

Silverdale Methodist Church Council. *Silverdale Methodist Church, a Short History 1879-1979*.

Simmons, Jack & Biddle, Gordon, eds. *The Oxford Companion to British Railway History*. Oxford University Press, 1997.

Smith, Adam. *An Inquiry into the Nature and Causes of the Wealth of Nations,* book v. 1779.

Spencer, J.L., ed. *The Royal Grammar School, Lancaster: Quincentenary Commemorative Volume*. Edinburgh: Neill & Sons 1969.

Stobbs, Neil. "The Whinnerahs of Warton Hall Farm," *The Mourholme Magazine of Local History,* no.3 (2000/01): pp.18-23.

Stobbs, Neil. "Further Notes from the Whinnerah's Diary," *The Mourholme Magazine of Local History*, no.1 (2001/02): pp.21-35.

Stobbs, Neil. "Further Information about the Whinnerah's of Warton Hall Farm," *The Mourholme Magazine of Local History*, no.1 (2002/03): pp.26-29.

The Bible, The Authorized King James Version. First published 1611.

The Illustrated Guide to the Holiday Resorts on the Furness Railway. 1900.

Travers, Graham. *Mona Maclean: Medical Student.* William Blackmore and Sons, 1894.

Trevelyan, George Macaulay. *British History in the Nineteenth Century, 1782-1901.* Longman, Green and Co, 1922.

Victoria & Albert Museum of Childhood, www.vam.ac.uk/moc/collection/childcare

Walton, John K. *Lancashire; a Social History 1558-1939.* Manchester University Press, 1987.

Walton, John K. *The Second Reform Act* Methuen, 1987.

Watson. *History. Topography, General and Commercial Directory Lancaster & Morecambe.* Watson & Co., 1899.

Webb, Sidney, & Webb, Beatrice. *Development of English Local Government 1689-1835,* vol.iv. Oxford University Press, 1963.

Wells. *Lancaster & District Directory.* Wells & Co., 1889.

Winchester, Angus. *Yealand Quakers: The History of a Country Meeting.* Philoscopus Publications, 1993.

Wohl, Anthony S. *Endangered Lives; Public Health in Victorian Britain.* Methuen, 1983.

Woolnough, Guy, & Clarke, Joan. "The death of the boy Heslop," *The Mourholme Magazine of Local History,* no.1 (1991): pp.9-12.

Woolnough, Guy. "Carnforth National School," *Mourholme Magazine of Local History,* no.3 (1990): pp.8-12 & 17-20.

Index

Vant, (Councillor) 42, 109

Wacke, Joseph 54
Waithman, William 15, 149, 154
Wakefield, Mary 235
Walduck, H J 47, 59, 84, 128
Walker, Francis 122
Walker, Robert 76
Walmsley, J 75
Walton, John K 98
Ward, James 82
Warem, Bishop Dr 143
Warton and District Choral Society 235
Warton and Silverdale Mining Co Ltd 83
Warton Crag 29
Warton Grange 102
Warton Hall 13
Warton Harriers 250, 252
Warton Mining and Colour Co Ltd 84
Warton Road 49, 50, 73
Warton Rugby Club 252
Warton School 192, 193, 214, 236
Washing 220
Washington House 119
Water 178
Water closets 79
Watson, Captain 157
Watson, John Frederick 17
Waugh, Rev T 245
Weeks, J 77
Weeton, Kate 214
Wegber Quarries 36, 81, 82, 84
Wesleyan Methodists 136
West, Mary 38
West, (Mr) 87
West View 50, 64, 123
West View Hotel 50, 57, 126, 215
Whiles, Joseph 50
Whinnerah, A 252
Whinnerah diary 7, 9, 17
Whinnerah, E 13, 16
Whitehead, Dr 164
Whitsuntide Hirings 19, 70, 232
Whittaker, Sir Thomas 123
Wilcock, Thomas 10

William Street 50, 52, 55, 56, 57
Williamson, James (Lord Ashton) 155
Williamsons of Lancaster 84
Willis, Edith Currer 225, 226
Willis, Thomas 226
Wilson, Amelia 63
Wilson, (Mrs) 50
Wilson, W 100
Winter, (Dr) 168
Women's Liberal Association 102, 226
Wood, Christopher 22
Wooden Hut 120, 235, 236
Woodlands 151, 220
Woods, Richard 125
Woodward, Captain John 132
Worcester, Chapter 137, 139, 146
Workhouse 116, 117, 119, 130-131
Workhouse Visiting Society 115
Working Men's Institute 101
Workmen's Compensation Act 41
Wren, Joseph 30
Wrestling 255
Wright, William 151, 152
Wrightson, S 105, 194

Yates, Captain 150
Yealand British School 186, 192, 195, 198
Yealand Friends' School 17, 70, 186, 188, 192, 195, 196, 199, 201, 239
Yealand Hall 247
Yealand Manor 235
Yorke, (Mr) 38
Young Offenders 129-130